LOST TREASURES

THE WORLD'S GREAT RICHES REDISCOVERED

THIS IS A CARLTON BOOK

Design copyright © 2010 Carlton Books Limited
Text copyright © 2000, 2010 Dr Jane McIntosh
First published under the title *Treasure Seekers* in 2000.

This updated edition published in 2010 by
Carlton Books Limited
20 Mortimer Street
London W1T 3JW

A CIP catalogue for this book is available from the British Library.

ISBN 978-1-84732-299-9

Senior Executive Editor: Lisa Dyer
Managing Art Director: Lucy Coley
Designer: Katie Baxendale
Picture research: Ben White
Production: Kate Pimm
Map illustrator: William Smuts

Printed in China

Previous page: The beauty of the gold in this Minoan pendant is
enhanced by the exquisite workmanship. It dates from between the
sixteenth and seventeenth century BC and was found in Mallia, Crete.

Opposite: These monstrous heads in the temples at Chavin
de Huantar, Peru, would have created a sense of awe and wonder
among worshippers more than 2,000 years ago.

Overleaf: Pirate treasure – coins and a ring – salvaged from Black Sam
Bellamy's pirate ship, the *Whydah*, that was wrecked in 1717.

LOST TREASURES

THE WORLD'S GREAT RICHES REDISCOVERED
DR JANE MCINTOSH

CONTENTS

INTRODUCTION

The thought of treasure and seeking it out stirs the blood and fills most of us with the spirit of adventure. But what is treasure? If you asked people today, most would probably say it is gold, silver and precious stones. When we look at peoples of the past or at other cultures in the modern world we find that these same materials have been treasured by many societies. Why? And why have some cultures placed their highest value on other materials, such as jade, textiles, obsidian or even feathers?

WHAT IS TREASURE?

Treasured materials have many features in common. They are almost without exception attractive – who is not thrilled, for example, by the sparkle of gems or the brilliance of gold? Treasures stir powerful aesthetic feelings. For many cultures the feelings go beyond this: the magnificence of precious materials inspires feelings of awe and reverence, so that, for example, the Incas regarded gold as the sweat of the sun and silver as the tears of the moon, both sun and moon being gods. Many cultures have attributed supernatural powers to such materials, regarding them as protective or healing or even life-giving – the ancient Chinese, for example, believed that jade conveyed immortality.

Another element that most treasures have in common is rarity. The first treasures that we know of were rare and curious objects picked up as long ago as 120,000 years by Neanderthal people in their travels and treasured by their finders: things such as fossils. Objects produced as little as 50 years ago and available then for a modest price become modern treasures because so few of them remain – and this has always been true: the Romans, for example, collected Greek antiquities and the Aztecs those of the earlier Toltecs, though in these and other cases there were also other considerations, such as reverence for the skill of the earlier craftsmen and respect for ancestral cultures. In the same way heirlooms mean more to people than other pieces of equal absolute value: they are invested with sentimental value as well as intrinsic worth.

Thus rarity adds an extra dimension to the aesthetic value of materials. Quartz may shine with the brilliance of diamonds, or iron pyrites glitter like gold, but we accord little value to common quartz and pyrites compared with the highly prized diamonds and gold. Rarity, especially when combined with the great distance over which a material has to travel between source and ultimate owner, has always enhanced the prestige of certain materials. In the ancient Near East, for example, one of the most highly valued materials was lapis lazuli, a beautiful stone of the most brilliant blue, which for many centuries could only be obtained from a remote source at Badakshan in Afghanistan. However, the people of the Indus valley civilization, who gained a monopoly over its supply, prized lapis lazuli only for its commercial value in trade with the Near East. They themselves were much more interested in harder

gemstones, such as jasper and agate, which would hold a high polish.

This leads to a further ingredient in what constitutes treasures: their properties. Materials are valued for qualities that set them apart and make them strange, mysterious or seemingly supernaturally efficient. Exceptional hardness is one such quality, found in jade, for example. Incorruptibility is another. Gold does not tarnish or corrode but emerges from the ground as pristine as when it was buried, even after thousands of years. Obsidian,

Above: *This Spanish map from 1524 shows the Aztec capital, Tenochtitlan. Set in Lake Texcoco, it was dominated by the temple pyramids at its centre and linked to the mainland by four causeways.*

Left: *A glass bottle from the treasures that were hidden at Begram, Afghanistan, in 241AD. It would have been highly valued for the skill involved in its manufacture, which was at the cutting edge of technology at the time.*

the natural glass formed by volcanoes, can be chipped like flint to make tools, but the edge so formed is much sharper – it is, in fact, the sharpest edge that can be produced by human hands, far sharper than metal, and it is used today in brain surgery. In the past, in areas as far apart as the Near East and Mesoamerica, obsidian was traded over enormous distances by early farming communities.

These values are inherent in the materials themselves. But treasured value also comes from the skill, craftsmanship and labour of the creator. A piece of jewellery from a high-street store may contain gold and gems of no less original value than those used in a piece created by Fabergé, but the price attached to the latter item is infinitely higher. The Incas and other South American cultures placed a very high value on finely woven textiles of alpaca wool, and reserved those of vicuña wool for the emperor himself. The elongated carnelian beads made by the Indus people 4,000 years ago were both superlative works of skill and extremely time-consuming to make: a necklace represented as much as a year's work for an ancient craftsmen.

Most treasures have several or all of these features. Wonderful carved items of obsidian were highly valued by the Maya, for example. These combine the aesthetic qualities of the glass-like obsidian, often in beautiful dark shades of green or blue; rarity, since obsidian was only available in a few localities; and the skilled craftsmanship that could work this fragile material into elaborate shapes, often

creating three or four human faces in profile around the edge of a piece.

QUEST FOR TREASURES

Two emotions motivate the majority of those seeking treasures. One is the desire to get rich quick: the same feeling that drives people to bet on sporting events or buy lottery tickets, week after hopeless week. This is generally not greed: more the fulfilment of dreams. Who does not wish to be rich? The mere thought of it allows us to indulge in happy speculation about what we might do, without any real expectation of achieving those dreams. Treasure-hunters sometimes do strike lucky, just as some people do win the lottery, but often the time, effort and money invested are greater than the material rewards.

So why do it? Probably because of another emotion: excitement. Treasure-hunting is an adventure, a searching for clues and following of trails, along paths often richly littered with the earlier adventures of others. There is mystery, the search for something known or suspected but lost. There is the mystique of the treasure, most often based on the stories that go with its original acquisition or deposition – for example, the history of those whose burials were filled with valuables, such as the young Egyptian king Tutankhamun or the cruel Chinese emperor Shi Huangdi, buried with his terracotta army; the plight of those caught up in natural disasters from which they sought

vainly to escape, such as the victims of the eruption of Vesuvius at Pompeii or those unfortunate people who went down with the *Titanic*; the mysteries of treasure hidden when danger threatened and never recovered because of the death of the owner – pirate gold, for example.

Mysteries and murders inevitably seem to be associated with treasure believed to have been hidden by pirates. Stolen after years of careful planning or taken on the spur of the moment when an opportunity seemed too good to pass up, treasure acquired illegally has to be hidden and the pirate's tracks covered before it can be recovered and enjoyed. Often death overtakes the thief before he can return and the secret details are passed on, shrouded in ever-greater obscurity.

Even the hint of treasure can inflame the imagination. Take the Money Pit, for example: a mysterious shaft discovered over 200 years ago and carefully booby-trapped by its makers. There is no information that this hole in the ground actually contains treasure, but people have spent millions trying to penetrate its secrets. Why? Because they reason that there would have been no point in creating such an elaborate arrangement if it didn't conceal and guard treasure.

But before the adventure comes the preparation. There is more to treasure-hunting than going out with hope or a metal detector. Careful planning is essential: finding out what to look for and where, obtaining appropriate licences and permissions and researching the laws on different kinds of treasure – both looking for it and dealing with it if you strike lucky. Some people become so obsessed by their hobby of treasure-hunting that they end up devoting their lives to it. For others it is an absorbing pastime. But for all there is the heady thrill of the quest.

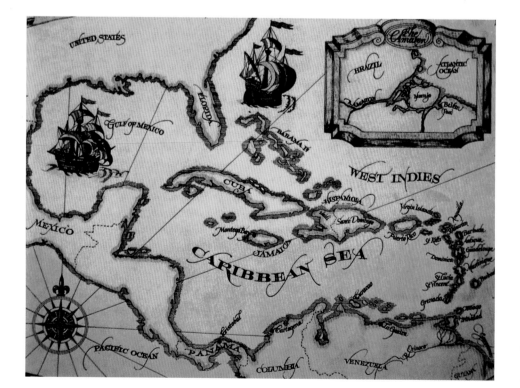

Left: *An old map can sometimes be the starting point of a quest for lost or hidden treasures. The Caribbean is the site of many wrecks, including Spanish treasure ships and pirate hoards.*

Right: *Magnificent ornaments of turquoise and gold were buried with the Moche Lord of Sipan (Peru). Such beautiful materials have been valued by people around the world and throughout history.*

Far right: *Obsidian is a form of natural glass that is created by volcanoes. Many cultures have prized it for its rarity and for the sharpness of the cutting edges that can be created from it.*

FINLAND

ESTONIA

LATVIA

HUANIA

BELARUS

UKRAINE

MOLDOVIA

57
59

ROMANIA   58

Black Sea

56
53   51   55
     52

BULGARIA

ONIA   54
                    50

46
49

47 48

EUROPE

Above: *Many ships of the ill-fated Spanish Armada, pictured here in battle with the English, were wrecked as they attempted to sail home around Britain's shores. Some have been found and excavated, but others broke up as they sank and were lost forever.*

CHIEFTAINS' GOLD FROM THE DAWN OF EUROPE'S AGE OF BRONZE

Farming communities spread across Europe during the seventh and sixth millennia BC. By the fifth millennium those in south-eastern Europe lived in substantial settlements, often fortified with a palisade, and traded extensively with their neighbours.

GOLD FOR THE ANCESTORS

Although there was undoubtedly conflict and competition between these communities, often this was expressed more through the accumulation and display of prestige materials than by military activity. The early farmers had made simple pottery; the skills involved and particularly the technology needed to fire fine pots at high temperatures developed gradually. Now these skills were to find a new outlet. The

farmers had occasionally come across pure copper and gold occurring naturally in the places where they sought stone for making tools and this strange type of "stone", which when hit changed shape instead of breaking, was made into small ornaments by cold hammering. But in the fifth millennium it was discovered that heating metal made it possible to shape it more easily, and soon kilns were being used to smelt copper ores, and gold and copper were

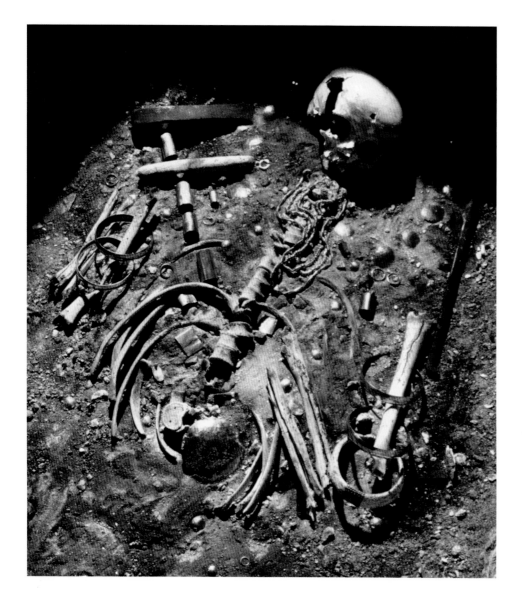

melted and cast into simple shapes. Metal objects were now added to the repertoire of prestigious display goods such as dentalium and spondylus seashells, fine flint axes and blades, and beautiful graphite-decorated pottery, and they were in some ways more impressive. Gold in particular is likely to have had a deep significance for these people, as for many societies throughout history.

In 1972 spectacular proof of this significance was found when construction work beside a lake at Varna in Bulgaria exposed part of a Copper Age cemetery of 300–350 graves, dated around 4560–4450 BC. The people buried there had lived beside the lake in houses raised on piles to keep them dry. Men, women and children were buried in carefully-dug rectangular pits. Most of the men were laid out on their backs with their limbs extended, while women were generally laid on their right side with their knees drawn up and their heads bent forward. Almost everyone was furnished with pottery and some tools and ornaments, of stone or sometimes copper; around a fifth of the graves also contained goldwork.

One man, probably aged between 40 and 50, was buried with an astonishing array of gold objects in addition to offerings of pottery, shell and bone ornaments, and copper tools. In his right hand he held a stone hammer-axe with a shaft of beaten gold: probably a badge of office. Heavy gold bracelets adorned both arms and all over his body were small gold discs and beads that must originally have decorated his clothing. A large gold disc was at his waist and beneath this the excavators found a gold tube: probably a penis sheath. Large gold discs covered each knee. In all, the man had 990 gold objects, weighing more than 1.5 kilograms (3¼ pounds).

More than 40 graves were empty of human remains – too many to be the graves of people whose bodies were lost. In each, the grave goods were carefully

Above: *This necklace of minute gold beads was found with thousands of other gold objects in votive pits at Dabene in Bulgaria. Many cultures in prehistoric Europe buried offerings to the gods.*

Opposite: *One of the richly furnished burials at Varna. This individual was interred with a number of gold discs and bracelets and several massive stone axes.*

arranged in the positions they would have occupied had there been a body in the grave: pots and stone and copper tools around the "head", jewellery on the "body". Curiously, these cenotaphs contained more goldwork than the majority of burials. In three graves lay clay masks where the face would have been and these were decorated in gold. Three of the empty graves contained large quantities of gold objects, weighing about

1–1.5 kilograms (2¼–3¼ pounds) in each case. Among them were sheet-gold plaques in the shape of cattle, which had once been attached to clothing. Puzzling over the meaning of these cenotaphs, some archaeologists have concluded that they were intended as the symbolic burials of long-dead ancestors. In this case the richly furnished male burial was probably a spiritual rather than worldly leader: a priest or magician rather than a chief.

GOLD FOR THE GODS?

A chance encounter led archaeologists to another Bulgarian treasure. While excavating a Roman site in 2004 they met a peasant woman wearing a necklace that looked like ancient goldwork. Her husband had found it while ploughing their fields, she said, and she took the archaeologists to the spot, in the village of Dabene. They soon organized excavations there, which continued until 2007.

The field was covered with little mounds. Under them the archaeologists found neither a settlement nor burials but holes containing pottery, bronze and silver vessels, and more than 20,000 gold objects. It appears that these were buried around 2000 BC as offerings to the gods – a practice that was widespread and long-lived in Europe. The vessels were placed in the holes and the jewellery scattered on top before the earth was piled back over.

Most of the gold objects were beads, spacer-beads and rings from necklaces, but there were also tiny amulets, earrings, hairpins and other pieces of jewellery, a plaque and a cup. These objects exhibit remarkable craftsmanship and technical skill. Some of the ornaments are less than 2 millimetres (0.07 inch) across. A long gold tube was created to make one spiral ornament. The most extraordinary find of all was a dagger made of gold alloyed with a small amount of platinum, still as sharp and bright as the day when it was buried.

CHIEFTAINS' GOLD

By 2500 BC copper- and goldworking was widespread in Europe, often associated with a new fashion in pottery, the cord-decorated beaker that was probably used for drinking beer or mead – a new prestige activity. A grave discovered in 2002 grave at Amesbury near Stonehenge reveals the range of international movement in the later third millennium. The "Amesbury Archer" was richly endowed, with around 100 objects, including a pair of gold basket-shaped earrings or hair ornaments, a tanged dagger made of Spanish copper, a shale belt-ring, 15 barbed and tanged flint arrowheads, two archer's wristguards, several beakers, boars' tusks and a small anvil for metalworking. Oxygen-isotope analysis of his teeth indicated that he had spent a significant part of his life in the Alps. A younger man buried nearby had spent his entire life in southern England: shared physical features suggest they were father and son, so the older man had presumably settled in England before his son's birth.

By 2000 BC bronze was in widespread use – tin was added to the copper to make it harder and therefore more suitable for making tools. As tin is a rare material, occurring only in certain areas, its new importance provided a tremendous stimulus to international trade. Chiefs were now emerging, whose role included boosting their community's social standing in the region by ensuring a good supply of traded prestige goods, to be displayed upon their own person. When a chief died, the community could continue to demonstrate its wealth and status by burying him with these luxury objects – taking them out of circulation.

One such burial, the Bush Barrow, was discovered in 1808 by Sir Richard Colt Hoare and William Cunnington, enthusiastic barrow diggers whose workmen excavated more than 400 barrows in Wiltshire. The Bush Barrow was one of many Bronze Age funerary mounds constructed in the vicinity of Stonehenge, already an ancient monument by that period and one whose sanctity may have enhanced the importance of burials placed in its neighbourhood. Although the Bush Barrow is the most richly furnished grave in the Wessex area, there were other contemporary barrow burials containing goldwork and it seems this region was particularly prosperous at the time.

The individual buried in the Bush Barrow was a tall, robust man. On his chest was placed a lozenge of gold finely decorated with geometric patterns. A much smaller lozenge and a similarly decorated belt-hook in gold lay on his right side along with three bronze daggers and a stone

Left: *The dagger buried with the "Amesbury Archer" reflects the wideranging trade links already operating more than 4,000 years ago.*

Right: *Beautifully crafted barbed and tanged stone arrowheads are among the prestigious grave goods found in many Copper-Age elite burials.*

Above: *A lunula (left) and the Gleninsheen gorget (right), two examples of the magnificent products of Bronze-Age British goldworking.*

Below: *A skilfully decorated lozenge and a belt-hook, both made of sheet gold, were among the remarkable objects found in the Bush Barrow.*

macehead originally mounted on a wooden shaft ornamented with zigzag bands of bone. The wooden hilt of one of the daggers had been decorated with a zigzag design made of thousands of minute gold studs far smaller than a pin – the workmen shovelled out quantities of these with the soil before the excavators, armed with a magnifying glass, could recognize the studs for what they were. Enough remained for them to work out the design.

INTERNATIONAL METAL TRADERS

The people of the Stonehenge region were well placed to participate in the international trade in raw materials such as metal ores, however the source of these lay elsewhere. Tin was to be found in Cornwall along with gold, but the greatest producer of gold was Ireland, which was also rich in copper ores. Trade between the two areas is attested by the discovery in Cornwall of a number of Irish lunulae, which were traded for Cornish tin to alloy with Irish copper, producing the bronze now being used in substantial quantities to make axes, halberds and daggers. Lunulae were the most characteristic products of the Irish goldsmiths. These huge, crescent-shaped metal collars, generally made of gold, were popular exports to various parts of northern Europe during the Early Bronze Age. Sheet-gold earrings and gold discs to wear on

clothing were also produced at this time.

Ireland continued as a major centre for goldwork throughout the Bronze Age. From around 1200 BC many hoards were deposited, presumably hidden by their owners in times of danger. These included gold earrings, bracelets and necklaces of twisted gold ribbons or bars – elegant pieces known as torcs. Other gold objects were decorated by punch and repoussé techniques. Of these the most splendid are the gorgets, like the one found by chance in a rock cleft at Gleninsheen, County Clare, in 1932. This is a massive collar decorated with rounded bands hammered up in relief from behind (i.e. repoussé). Between the bands are fine rope patterns. Each end of the gorget is completed by a massive gold disc decorated with repoussé dots and circles, sewn on with gold wire.

The most spectacular hoard of Irish goldwork was discovered in 1854 by men constructing the West Clare railway. A stone was untidily jutting out of the side of the railway cutting at Mooghaun North, perhaps part of a stone setting. Workmen pulled it out and were greeted by a torrent of gold objects – at least 138 in number. The men dived on them and many were sneaked off and sold. A few were retrieved, including a spectacular gold collar, and can now be seen in the National Museum of Ireland and the British Museum.

A PREHISTORIC CALENDAR

A secret rendezvous, a looted treasure and a police sting operation – the modern story of the Nebra sky-disc reads like the plot of a detective novel. In 1999 an extraordinary object, a bronze disc inlaid with gold, appeared briefly on the market. A prospective sale fell through when it transpired that it had been illegally removed from a German site and it disappeared from public view. It changed hands several times on the black market but reappeared in 2001 when its new owners publicized the piece, hoping to increase its perceived value. Harald Meller of the State Museum for Prehistory in Halle was able to set up a meeting in Switzerland, supposedly "safe" territory, pretending to strike a deal to buy it, but he had arranged for the police to swoop on the black marketeers when they showed him the disc.

Other Bronze Age objects recovered by the authorities, including two swords with gold-inlaid hilts, showed that the cache of bronzes dated from around 1600 BC. The finders were traced and under legal pressure revealed that the cache had come from a hill in Saxony-Anhalt, the Mittelberg, on which there are Bronze Age earthworks. Archaeologists who then excavated this site found a tiny piece of gold, exactly matching a hole in the golden circle, confirming that the object had genuinely been dug up rather than faked. Further confirmation came from scientific analyses: the size of the corrosion crystals showed that it was very old; and the copper from which it was made could be matched to the Austrian Alps and the gold to the Carpathian region, sources known to have been mined in the Bronze Age.

The bronze disc, a unique object, was inlaid with two matching narrow strips of gold (one is now missing) near the edge on either side, and between them a crescent, a circle and 32 dots, representing the crescent moon, the sun or the full moon and the stars. Another strip at the bottom edge may depict a boat with oars, perhaps associated with the sun's hidden journey through the night. Each of the gold strips occupies 82 degrees of the circumference, the angular distance between the places on the horizon where the sun sets at the summer and winter solstices at the latitude of Mittelberg. The peak of Brocken in the Harz mountains, visible from the hilltop, provided a fixed point on the horizon that the Bronze Age astronomers could use for sighting. Stars on the disc included the constellation of the Pleiades, which appears in the sky in March, around the beginning of the agricultural year. It has been suggested that the disc also contains other information for calendric calculations. Such astronomical knowledge was crucial to farming communities in order to determine the timing of key activities, such as sowing their crops. A number of European prehistoric monuments, including Stonehenge, were also designed to provide astronomical information, but the Nebra sky-disc is the first-known portable device for this purpose as well as an object of beauty.

Below: *The sky-disc has its own dedicated visitor centre near Nebra in Germany. The disc is quite large, measuring around 31 centimetres (1 foot) across.*

TREASURES OF THE MINOANS AND MYCENAEANS

EXILED FROM TROY

Heinrich Schliemann's fascination with the legendary world of Homeric Greece and his determination to rediscover its truth had led him in 1870 to excavate Hisarlik in Turkey, revealing its identity as Troy (see page 108). But, when in 1873 he smuggled a hoard of precious Trojan goldwork out of Turkey, he made himself persona non grata with the authorities and was therefore forced to turn his attentions elsewhere.

Where better to go than the Greek city of Mycenae, home of the high king Agamemnon, who had led the Greek heroes to Troy? Returning here in triumph, his overweening pride angering the gods, the conquering king was ingloriously struck down by his treacherous wife Clytemnestra and her lover Aegisthus. The Greek geographer Pausanias, travelling in Greece in the second century AD, stated that Agamemnon and his family had been royally buried within the city walls, while Clytemnestra and her lover were ignominiously interred outside.

Schliemann applied for permission to dig at Mycenae and was most indignant when permission was made conditional on him resolving his dispute with Turkey. The Greek authorities had learned a lesson from this altercation: granting Schliemann his permit in 1876, they hedged it round with many strict requirements to ensure that there was no repeat of the Trojan pillage. Schliemann was to open no more than one trench at a time, his activities were to be supervised and authorized by a government representative, the experienced archaeologist Panagiotes Stamatakes, and without exception all the finds were to remain the property of Greece and in Greek hands.

Below: *The magnificent gold death mask attributed by Schliemann to Agamemnon. The five gold masks and other gold finery from the shaft graves found within Mycenae's citadel mark them out as royal graves.*

PROUD MYCENAE

Mycenae still stood, a glorious and romantic ruin atop its steep mountain. A massive wall, traditionally built by the giant Cyclops of huge dressed stone blocks carefully fitted together, surrounded the citadel and was pierced by the magnificent Lion Gate, with its lintel carved with two lionesses rampant flanking a pillar. Other expeditions had worked here in previous decades and the walls and gateway had been partially cleared. It was generally held that Pausanias's reference to the royal tombs located them within the outer wall of the town. Schliemann took a different view, looking for them inside the citadel.

In August 1876 Schliemann and his wife began work at Mycenae. From the start they were in conflict with the unfortunate government representative, who did his best to hold them to the terms of the permit. His interference to stop several trenches being dug at once and to prevent the work going destructively fast brought down upon him the wrath and insults of both Schliemanns. However, their ill humour was dispelled by the magnificence of the finds that came to light.

Immediately inside the gate the ground opened out on the right into an esplanade. Here Schliemann began excavating in October, revealing sculptured slabs that seemed likely to mark graves. Digging down deeper, in November the workmen uncovered a tomb. Lying within this were three bodies, adorned with gold diadems and other jewellery and accompanied by gold and silver vessels. Four more tombs were uncovered nearby, each with a number of burials richly furnished with jewellery and goldwork. Among these items was a magnificent silver bull's head with gold horns and a gold floral medallion on its forehead.

THE MASK OF AGAMEMNON

Five of the bodies wore magnificent death masks. Made of beaten gold, they portrayed the rulers whose faces they had covered: a smiling, wide-eyed, almost imbecilic young man, a round-faced elderly man, two sad-faced men with beetling eyebrows and a magnificent and noble bearded man in his prime. Looking at the latter, Schliemann had no doubt that he was gazing on the face of Agamemnon, although the earlier storms that had greeted his enthusiastic identification of the Trojan remains with Trojan heroes made him reluctant to say so publicly.

Along with the bodies Schliemann had uncovered a quite staggering amount of treasure. "Agamemnon" and several of the other men were wearing gold breastplates. An infant was entirely encased in sheet gold, from face to feet. Hundreds of gold leaves were scattered in the tombs, some forming part of diadems attached to gold bands around the forehead. A gold rhyton (drinking vessel) in the shape of a lion's head, innumerable golden discs, massive gold cups, miniature battle-axes of gold, fine gold bracelets and other jewellery – the finds far outstripped the treasures Schliemann had carried off from Troy. Among the most beautiful objects after the mask of Agamemnon are two engraved gold signet rings, one showing a chariot drawn by two mettlesome horses, the other a battle between four warriors; these are works of extraordinary craftsmanship. Similarly impressive are two beautiful daggers of bronze decorated in gold and silver on a black metallic background. One showed leopards hunting wild ducks along a river, the other a battle between lions and men carrying huge shields.

Schliemann had achieved another coup. Some might still doubt that Hisarlik was really Troy, but Mycenae's identity was never in dispute. Why doubt, then, that these magnificently furnished graves were those of Agamemnon and his royal line? Schliemann was exceedingly annoyed that he did not manage to keep any of the splendid objects he had uncovered, but the glory and fame that he craved were now his. Although we now know that the occupants of these shaft graves died at least 300 years before the time of the Homeric heroes, Schliemann's achievement is in no way reduced. He had

again revealed a new chapter of the Greek pre-Classical heroic past – the stuff of legend, but real.

LAND OF THE MINOTAUR

His dispute with the Turkish authorities resolved, Schliemann returned to dig at Troy, but he also excavated at two more Greek sites, Orchomenos and Tiryns, at the latter uncovering the remains of a palace whose walls were adorned with magnificent frescoes. He now yearned to add Crete to his investigations and therefore began negotiations to dig at Knossos, where previous work by local investigators had already revealed substantial buildings, but he ran into difficulties. The owner of the fields in which Knossos lay knew something of Schliemann's wealth and demanded the exorbitant price of 100,000 francs for the land. Schliemann beat him down to 40,000 francs, but withdrew his offer when he found that the land was not as valuable as it had been represented to be: there were only 889 olive trees instead of the stated 2,500. Business sense and hatred of being cheated triumphed over his antiquarian interests. Perhaps he would have renewed his attempt had not Troy engrossed him and death overtaken him in 1890. It was left to an Englishman, Arthur Evans, to follow the story into Crete. Four years after Schliemann's death, he purchased the disputed olive grove and soon began excavations at Knossos.

A greater contrast with Schliemann is perhaps not possible. Arthur Evans came from a wealthy family and a long scholarly tradition and held the post of Keeper of the Ashmolean Museum in Oxford. His excavations at Knossos were orderly

investigations, but, like Schliemann, he was impatient to obtain results and, similarly to the German, he uncovered a new and unexpected chapter of the past: the world of the legendary king Minos.

BRONZE AGE CIVILIZATIONS

On the evidence of the frescoes that Evans uncovered at Knossos, this world was one in which young men and women performed unbelievable feats of daring acrobatics on the horns and backs of massive bulls, watched by ranks of politely interested noble spectators. Massive plaster double axes crowned the walls and a stately staircase led up to the private apartments where the queen took her bath in a beautifully ornamented terracotta tub. Below ground was a maze of rooms and passages, an actual counterpart to the Labyrinth of legend in which the Athenian Theseus was supposed to have slain the Minotaur. Huge pottery vessels lined the storerooms, filled originally with the agricultural riches of the island:

Below: *A bronze dagger from Mycenae, inlaid in gold and silver, depicts a scene with warriors holding typical Mycenaean figure-of-eight shields, hunting lions.*

Opposite: *This magnificent gold cup, of Minoan workmanship from a tholos (beehive-shaped) tomb at Vapheio near Sparta, depicts the capture of wild bulls with ropes and nets.*

Opposite below: *The Minoans were acute observers of the natural world and often portrayed it in their artwork, such as this superbly crafted pendant from Mallia.*

---

grain, olive oil and wine. The Minoans had been a race of seafarers as well, their pottery covered with images of the sea, particularly octopuses. Theirs had been the first civilization to emerge in the Aegean, still flourishing at the time of Mycenae's warrior kings, but by 1450 BC in decline, no match for the later Mycenaeans who came from the mainland citadels to take control of Crete. In the centuries before the Trojan War, which occurred around 1200 BC, the Mycenaeans traded widely throughout the eastern Mediterranean, Odysseus's terrifying adventures with Scylla and Charybdis coming straight out of Mycenaean experience of the perilous Strait of Messina.

These civilized Aegean palace dwellers were masters of craftsmanship. Many of their masterpieces have been turned up in the years since Evans and Schliemann. At Vapheio, near Sparta, a tomb yielded two fabulous gold cups, their sides depicting the capture of ferocious wild bulls, either for sacrifice or for the sport of bull-leaping. Huge nets are stretched in which a bull has become entangled. A tame cow lures another bull, who is swiftly secured. But it is a risky business: one man has been tossed and trampled, while another is being gored.

In some pieces, the workmanship is breathtaking. The Aegean craftsmen had mastered the difficult art of granulation, building up decoration from tiny beads of gold. One such piece is a pendant formed of two wasps holding a flower head or honeycomb, crowned with a cage containing a gold bead. This was found in French excavations at Mallia, an early palace on the north Cretan coast.

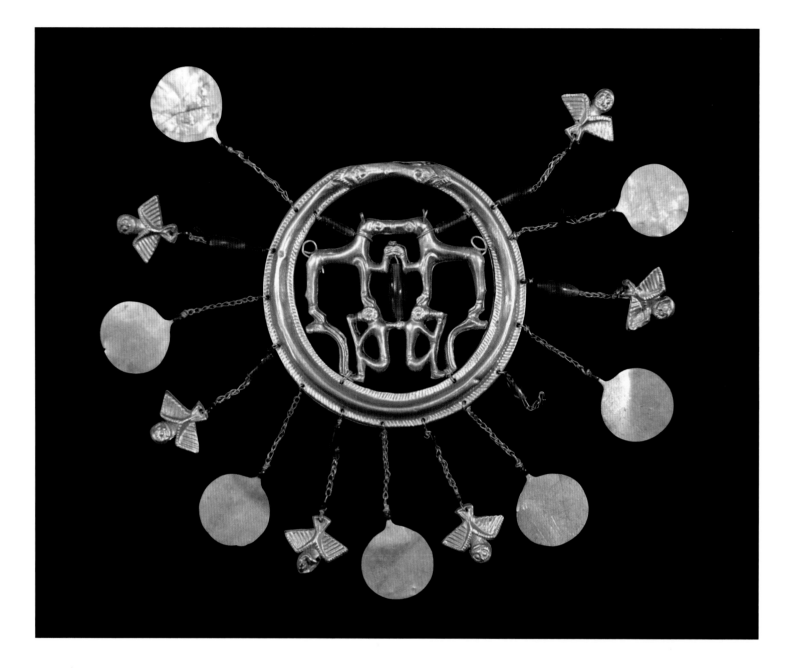

STOLEN TREASURES?

The Mallia wasp pendant came from a great royal burial enclosure known as "Chrysolakkos" ("Gold Hole") – a huge rectangle of small burial chambers. This had been plundered at some time prior to the French excavations. In 1891, a hoard of gold jewellery was offered for sale to the British Museum. It included headbands, necklaces, pendants, rings and earrings made of embossed sheet gold, decorated with filigree and often with precious stones or lapis lazuli. One particularly fine pendant depicts a figure in a Minoan tunic grasping a pair of waterbirds by their necks. There was also a beautiful gold cup with spiral decoration.

The material was allegedly found by sponge divers in a Mycenean tomb on the island of Aegina but the majority of pieces in the hoard are Minoan in design and workmanship. Until recently it was thought that at least some of the treasure had been plundered from the Chrysolakkos tomb on Crete. The British Museum certainly did not ask awkward questions but bought the objects, something they would not do today.

Recently, however, it has become more plausible that the material was looted from rich tombs on the island of Aegina itself. Evidence of such burials came with the discovery in 1981 of a rich shaft grave associated with the fortified town of Kolonna, an important trading centre in the Minoan (Middle Helladic) period. The warrior buried here was wearing a gold diadem and was furnished with a boar's-tusk helmet, a spear, obsidian arrowheads and a sword and dagger decorated with gold, as well as fine Minoan and Cycladic pottery and a bronze razor.

Above: *This elaborate Minoan earring of gold and carnelian was allegedly found in a Mycenaean tomb on the island of Aegina during the nineteenth century. The central design is a pattern of dogs and monkeys.*

GOLDEN OFFERINGS FROM KING PHILIP'S TOMB

END OF A GLORIOUS ERA

Philip II of Macedon (382–336 BC) tends to be overshadowed by his famous son, Alexander the Great, whose achievement in conquering most of the world known in his day still seems more the stuff of legend than sober truth. But Philip himself was a remarkable man who brought his backward, barbarous kingdom to the position of master of the civilized Greek world.

When the tiny Greek city states drove back the might of the vast Persian Empire in 490 and 480 BC, there began a period of tremendous confidence and self-esteem in the Greek world and particularly in the city of Athens, which had been sacked by the Persians. Under Pericles, Athens rebuilt its shattered monuments in great splendour, creating masterpieces of architecture and sculpture of which the Parthenon is justly the most famous. The other arts, such as music, drama and poetry, similarly flowered, and this was a time when the finest minds of the age were bent on understanding everything in the world around them. Philosophy, medicine, natural science, mathematics and political science were all endlessly and earnestly discussed in the streets and groves of Athens.

This glorious world did not endure for long. Athens and Sparta, which could both claim to have led the Greeks to victory in the Persian Wars, soon came to blows in a power struggle that was perhaps inevitable. Athens turned the Delian League, which it led, into an Athenian Empire, and the Spartans felt the threat to their own power, an unease exacerbated by their suspicion of Athenian democracy, the antithesis of their own oligarchic tradition. In the wars that followed both cities were badly mauled. Plague eventually brought Athens to its knees, but victorious Sparta had had its wings severely clipped. Thebes, hitherto a minor player on the Greek stage, stepped into the partial power vacuum and in the early fourth century BC these three city states began to tear each other and their neighbours to shreds, with Persia dipping its fingers into the muddied waters from time to time. Things came to a head with the battle of Mantinea in 362 BC, which left all the participants severely weakened.

Below: *The golden larnax containing the cremated remains of a member of the Macedonian royal family, probably King Philip II, is elaborately decorated with floral designs and the royal sunburst motif.*

WARRIOR KING

Enter Philip II. He was the youngest son of the king of Macedon, an ancient kingdom in the north which was almost outside the Greek world, and in his youth had been sent to Thebes as a hostage. Here Philip encountered the charismatic Epaminondas, Thebes's principal general, a brilliant soldier and strategist from whom he learned much. In 359 BC his remaining brother was killed in battle and Philip, aged 23, became king of Macedon. Swiftly crushing both his rivals for the throne and the hostile tribes on his borders, he set about turning his little kingdom into a state capable of playing its part in the contemporary world.

In the second year of his reign Philip led his superbly trained army against the city of Amphipolis, an Athenian colony that controlled gold and silver mines in Thrace. Taking the city by the siegecraft for which he was later to be renowned, Philip gained a huge guaranteed annual income with which to fund his wars. The Athenians were not amused: they had lost control of the city some years before and had been making efforts to regain it. They failed to take effective action against Philip, but instead harboured a permanent grudge against him.

MOPPING UP GREECE

Philip now began to take an active interest in the continuing Greek conflicts, allying himself with Thebes against Phocis. By 349 BC he was master of Thessaly and Thrace and completed his control of the north in 347 by taking over the Chalcidice peninsula. Its chief city, Olynthus, had appealed to Athens for help, but Philip was a diplomatist as well as a warrior. He bribed a number of Athenians to act on his behalf, and moves in the Athenian assembly to declare war on him were repeatedly voted down by his adherents. Meanwhile, Phocis had lost the war against Thebes and Macedon, and Philip stepped into its place in central Greek political life. Events in the next few years galvanized Athens into open war against Philip, and Thebes also turned hostile. But at the battle of Chaeronea, in 338, he decisively defeated both of them, becoming effectively master of Greece.

Next Philip turned his attentions to the Persian Empire, whose sack of Athens in 480 was still an unavenged wound to the Greeks. His preparations for war against the Persians were well advanced when, in 336, domestic problems caught up with him, and it was left to his son Alexander to conquer Persia.

DOMESTIC TROUBLES

In 357 BC Philip had married Olympias, a princess from the neighbouring kingdom of Epirus, who became his principal queen.

Two important consequences came of this marriage – it secured Philip important allies and it brought Alexander into the world – but at a personal level it was not a success. A classic domestic tragedy developed, Olympias using Alexander and his sister in her battle against her husband and ruining their relationship with their father. Despite their antipathy, however, Alexander and Philip fought side by side for Macedon and Alexander was his father's acknowledged heir.

Things took a desperate turn for the worse when, in 337, Philip married a seventh wife, a young woman called Cleopatra, the only one of his wives who was a member of the native Macedonian aristocracy. At the marriage feast Alexander, who felt his position as heir was threatened, quarrelled violently with his father and he and his mother withdrew to her native Epirus. Although Philip later became reconciled with Alexander, his marriage to Olympias had entirely broken down and young Cleopatra became his new principal queen. The following year she bore him a child, underlining the precariousness of Alexander's position. Philip tried to ease the situation by marrying his daughter to her uncle, Olympias's brother, who was king of Epirus, but at the wedding a disaffected Macedonian nobleman assassinated Philip. Although this nobleman held the dagger, the mind and will behind it could well have been that

of Olympias. Alexander ascended the throne and Philip was cremated and entombed with all pomp and honour.

SEARCHING FOR THE ROYAL TOMBS

The kings of Macedon had recently moved to a new capital at Pella, but the old capital, Aigae, continued to be the royal burial ground and a major centre. In 274 BC it was captured by Pyrrhus, King of Epirus, and was left under the guard of a band of Gaulish mercenaries who took the opportunity to pillage the royal tombs. The destruction they left was later tidied and a huge mound erected to cover the royal graves. In the centuries that followed, Macedon lost its elevated place on the stage of history and the location of Aigae was forgotten.

In 1952 Professor Manolis Andronikos of Thessaloniki University began investigating the town of Vergina as the possible location of Aigae. A huge mound dominated the site, and when Andronikos in his 1976 excavations found many traces of destruction in the surrounding cemetery, he dared to believe that the mound was Aigae's Great Tumulus. In 1977 things began to move fast. Beneath the southern portion of the mound he came upon the façade of a massive subterranean chamber tomb. The professor's team began to clear this, expecting to find a hole showing that robbers had broken in.

But to his amazement, as they cleared the massive doors he realized that these were still intact: the tomb had not been pillaged. He now had to revise his plans. Instead of using a robber's entrance hole, he had to imitate their methods and make one himself, by removing the keystone of the arch at the back of the 10-metre (33-feet) long tomb.

Andronikos found it hard to contain his excitement as he peered into the tomb through the hole left by the removed keystone. What would he see? One of the younger members of the team climbed down a rope into the tomb and positioned a ladder for the professor and the others. To their surprise the interior walls of the tomb were quite plain, covered with a rough layer of stucco, in contrast to the splendid painted exterior of the façade. But the finds were extraordinary. With all speed, but taking the utmost care, Andronikos and his team recorded, photographed, lifted and packed the material from the tomb and transported it back to Thessaloniki. It was only then that they could relax and begin to appreciate the splendour of the things they had found.

ROYAL GOLD

They did not yet know to whom the tomb had belonged, though it was evidently a Macedonian royal grave. Clearly the occupant had been a warrior, for it contained many pieces of armour and weapons: an iron

helmet, three pairs of bronze greaves (leg guards), a sword with gold and ivory on its handle, an iron breastplate and the remains of a leather shield, both decorated with gold plaques, and many spears. There were also vessels of fine pottery and of silver, with small heads of gods and heroes placed to hide the join between handle and body. And a decorated circle of gold found near the helmet must have been a royal diadem or crown.

Five tiny ivory portrait heads were also found, and of these two could instantly be recognized as Philip and Alexander, known from other representations. The others were presumably also members of the family – among them Olympias perhaps.

Pride of place within the tomb went to a sarcophagus of fine marble in which Andronikos expected to find a funerary urn of fine pottery or bronze. Instead it contained an amazing collection of funerary materials. First came a magnificent box (a larnax) made of more than 10 kilograms (22 pounds) of gold. In the centre of its lid was the starburst symbol of the Macedonian royal house. Inside the larnax the excavators found a magnificent gold wreath of oak leaves and acorns. Under this the bones of the king were carefully arranged – charred from the funerary pyre but still intact, and washed clean of ash – wrapped in what had been a purple cloth but was now a mere coloured stain.

OTHER OCCUPANTS

Between the tomb chamber and the façade was an antechamber, which Andronikos and his team entered by removing a block from the party wall. Unlike the tomb chamber itself, the stucco in the antechamber was carefully laid on and smoothly finished, with fine mouldings and hooks from which cloths had originally been hung. Within this chamber there was a further marble sarcophagus containing another golden larnax – smaller than the first but with the same starburst on the lid. Inside the larnax was a similar bundle of bones, but this time the gold and purple cloth in which they were wrapped had survived.

Pieces of gold, ivory and glass were the only surviving remains of gilded furniture. A golden wreath of myrtle leaves had fallen beside the sarcophagus. One of the most

Opposite: *Delicately made wreaths of oak and myrtle leaves, flowers and berries modelled in gold were worn by the two individuals buried in the royal tomb at Vergina. One was slightly damaged by the cremation pyre.*

Above: *A beautiful golden diadem was found beside the gold and purple cloth within the smaller larnax. The floral design combines plant stalks, leaves and flowers in an intricate pattern.*

those of Alexander's feeble-minded brother, Philip Arridaeus, and his ambitious wife, Eurydice. Both were killed when the faction that they supported in the succession wars after Alexander's death was defeated by the faction supported by Olympias. If this identification is correct, Philip II, Cleopatra and their infant son may instead be the man, woman and baby found in a looted cist in the Great Tumulus.

Another tomb, smaller but similar, was also found within the Great Tumulus. This housed the pathetic remains of Alexander IV, the posthumous son of Alexander the Great by his Bactrian wife, Roxana. The unfortunate child was used as a political pawn by Alexander's generals, who fought for the position of regent. When in 311 Cassander was successful in gaining control of Alexander and Macedon, his rivals began to argue that the king no longer needed a regent but was old enough to rule in his own right. Cassander's brutal response in 309 was to poison the 13-year-old Alexander and retain the throne in his own name.

Alexander's bones were interred in a silver jug and a wreath of golden oak leaves was hung on it. A magnificent wooden couch inlaid with gold and ivory was placed in the tomb, along with other silver vessels, a pair of gilt bronze greaves and other fine objects.

MACEDONIAN ANCESTORS

Philip's capital, Pella, has recently yielded some of the secrets of earlier times: excavations begun in 2000 and still continuing are slowly uncovering the vast Archontiko cemetery which dates from the seventh to third centuries BC. Already more than 900 burials have been investigated, out of a possible total of 20,000, and many of them have golden treasures including masks of beaten gold. The warrior burials are fully equipped with armour such as breastplates and helmets, bronze shields, and weapons such as swords, daggers and spears, many of these decorated with gold. Beside them lie their wives, also lavishly adorned with goldwork. As well as fine pottery, gold and silver vessels and bronze tools, many graves contain metal models of everyday objects such as wagons and furniture.

Above: *The tradition of golden death masks among the Bronze Age kings at Mycenae found echoes 1,000 years later in a delicate gold mask from the Archaic burial ground at Sindos in Macedonia, found with a bronze helmet.*

---

magnificent objects in this chamber was the golden cover from a quiver and bow case decorated with scenes from the fall of Troy. A pair of gilded greaves stood beside it.

WHOSE TOMB?

The finds from the tomb showed clearly that one of its occupants was a king of Macedon and a warrior. Could it be Philip II? The material that could be dated belonged to the appropriate period: the late fourth century BC. Ivory portrait heads were also a clue in this direction. Andronikos believed the tomb was Philip's, but could this be proved?

Physical details of the bones now seem to have clinched this identification. Those in the tomb chamber belonged to a man aged between 35 and 55, narrowing the identification down to two candidates: Philip II, who was 46 when he was murdered, or his son Philip Arrhidaeus, who was murdered in 317, aged about 40. Alexander was only 33 when he died, and he was buried in a splendid tomb in Egypt, as yet undiscovered. All other male members of the royal family in the appropriate period died much younger.

The skull was studied by a team at Manchester University who specialize in reconstructing faces from skeletal remains. They were able to establish that

the individual had suffered an eye wound inflicted from above – exactly matching the ancient information that Philip had lost his right eye from an arrow fired at the siege of Methone. A slight asymmetry of this individual's jaw also matched one of the portraits thought to be of Philip.

An additional twist to the story is given by the second body in the tomb. Usually if a tomb was to house two individuals, they were buried in the same chamber, so the burial in the antechamber looks very much like an afterthought. Forensic evidence indicates that the bones belonged to a young woman aged between 20 and 30. It is tempting to see this as the body of Cleopatra, Philip's last wife. Not long after Philip's murder Olympias did away with Cleopatra and her infant. This was much to Alexander's horror as Cleopatra's father was a leading Macedonian nobleman whom he could not afford to antagonize. Perhaps, as the forensic scientists suggest, Cleopatra was given an honourable burial in Philip's tomb as a way of appeasing her powerful kinsmen.

Not everyone is convinced that these are Philip and Cleopatra: some scholars argue, on grounds that seem reasonable though not conclusive, that the bones in this tomb are

SPLENDOURS OF THE BARBARIAN WORLD

IDLE WARRIORS

When the Greeks began to establish colonies on the northern shores of the Black Sea in the seventh century BC, they encountered barbarian societies of Scythians and Thracians among whom the elite were horse-riding warriors. These, the Greek ethnographer Herodotus claims, regarded idleness as noble and agricultural work as dishonourable. Warfare and plundering were the most noble way to live. Nevertheless, there was a substantial lower class of cultivators, whose produce the Greeks were keen to acquire in exchange for luxuries such as wine and the gold and silver vessels to drink it from. The Greeks also sought slaves, a common by-product of warfare.

The Persians also encouraged the Thracian taste for wine and luxury tableware, employing Thracian mercenaries in their war against the Scythians in the sixth century BC. The Thracians began making their own metal wares, using local silver and gold. Eventually, the Macedonians, southern neighbours of the Thracians, seized control of both the mines

and the region and Philip and Alexander employed Thracian mercenaries in their armies. After Alexander's death in 323 BC, foreign involvement in Thrace grew less but a love of wine and fine silver and gold vessels was firmly established.

NOBLE BURIALS

Most dead Thracians were cremated and their ashes buried in flat grave cemeteries, but the small number of aristocrats were accorded a more lavish burial in substantial barrows. About 20,000 of these still dominate the landscape in Thrace, but the vast majority have been opened and plundered in the past, though nowadays they are protected by law.

There are a few exceptions. The Mogilanska grave mound at Vratsa in Bulgaria was found to contain three undisturbed tombs. The principal one had two chambers. Within this were buried the prized possessions of a Thracian chief: his chariot and the two horses that drew it, and his riding horse, splendidly equipped with a silver bit and 200 silver harness decorations. A young female

attendant had been sacrificed with the horses, a spear through her ribs.

In the main chamber lay the nobleman himself, a man of about 30, accompanied by his weapons and armour: an iron sword, a quiver filled with bronze arrows and several daggers, a helmet and, curiously, a single greave. The latter was an extraordinary object. It was made of silver with a design inlaid in gold, in the form of a face striped with tattoos. There were also silver vessels. A young woman of about 18 was buried with the man. She too

Below left: *This gold rhyton in the form of a deer's head was one of four drinking vessels from the Thracian hoard found at Panagyurishte in Bulgaria – the others represent a goat, a bull and a ram.*

Below: *A silver-gilt plaque from a hoard found at Lenitsa in Bulgaria. It depicts a Thracian warrior clad in full body armour. Mounted warriors were the elite of Thracian society.*

was arrayed in her finery, a veil decorated with gold appliqués, gold earrings and a beautiful wreath of gold laurel leaves. A knife driven through her chest showed that she had also been sacrificed. Herodotus reported that when a Thracian nobleman was buried his many wives would compete to be selected as his favourite by friends of the deceased. The fortunate winner would then be sacrificed to accompany her lord, while the others would retire in shame.

TROUBLED TIMES

Herodotus claimed that the Thracians would have been a great and dominant nation if they had not always been fighting one another. When not at war among themselves they were often subject to invasions by others: not only their Macedonian neighbours but also bands of Celts, who passed through the region in the fourth century BC. In the face of these conflicts and troubles, many wealthy individuals hid their valuables in the ground – and not all returned to retrieve them.

One such hoard was rediscovered in 1949 at Panagyurishte in Bulgaria. It contained vessels made of more than 6 kilograms (13¼ pounds) of gold, manufactured by Greek craftsmen for export and mainly connected with wine-drinking. They included four amphorae with handles in the shape of centaurs, decorated with scenes from Greek mythology, and actually used as drinking vessels rather than as flagons. Four other drinking vessels were of the type known as a "rhyton", an L-shaped vessel with a wide conical top leading into a tapering base, in this case in the form of animal heads – a stag, a goat, a ram and a bull. The hoard also contained three relief jugs in the form of women, of which one was the goddess Athene, and a bowl decorated with 72 Negro heads.

A puzzling hoard was discovered in 1986 at Rogozen in Bulgaria. It consisted of 165 silver vessels, some gilded. Probably contained in two sacks when it was hidden, it weighed exactly 3,600 Persian sigloi (just under 20 kilograms/44 pounds). Why had this weight been assembled and why had it been hidden? We shall never know. Suggestions include its collection to pay tribute (but why was it never delivered?)

Left: *A single silver greave decorated in gold was found in the chieftain's tomb at Vratsa. The gold stripes on the face are tattoos, which Thracian noblemen wore to indicate their rank.*

and its concealment to avoid Celtic raiders (but why the measured amount?). The pieces in the hoard were a great mixture. Some were Greek imports, such as a bowl decorated with a scene from the adventures of Hercules. Others were locally made pieces but showed considerable Greek influences in both style and subject matter. Others again showed more distant influences, from as far afield as India (as a result of Alexander's expedition in which Thracian mercenaries participated) and Celtic western Europe.

THRACIAN KINGS

In the fifth and fourth centuries BC, the Greeks traded with the Thracian kingdom of the Odrysai, stretching from the Sea of Marmara to central Bulgaria and ruled from the fortified royal stronghold city of Seuthopolis, not far from modern Kazanluk. This was surrounded by cemeteries with numerous mounds: the area is known today as the "Valley of the Thracian Kings" because of the richness of the burials, which often include gold and silver vessels and jewellery. One such cemetery near Shipka has been under investigation since 1992. Several of the tombs beneath these mounds are decorated inside with richly coloured murals depicting Thracian aristocratic life.

In 2004, a royal grave was discovered in the Sveticata tumulus, with grave goods including Greek pottery made around 430–420 BC and two Greek amphorae, possibly some of the spoils from a Thracian military expedition into Macedonia in

432–429 BC. A gold ring bore a beautifully executed design of a rower. Abundant military equipment, including a bronze breastplate and chain mail, two swords and other weapons, accompanied the man buried here. Only his lower jaw and legs were present, but where his face should have been was an amazing death mask of solid gold. It was not an attractive face – fat-cheeked, glowering, mean-mouthed, cruel and heavy.

The following year excavations were concentrated on the Golyamata Kosmatka tumulus. Just outside the tomb's entrance was found a life-sized bronze head from a statue, depicting a bearded man, perhaps the tomb's occupant. An impressive stone façade opened into an entrance passage, originally lined with wood. At its end was a magnificent marble door, the entrance to the first chamber within which was a sacrificed horse. Through a corbelled empty second chamber lay the burial chamber itself. In this was an enormous sarcophagus carved from a single block of granite weighing 60 tonnes (66 tons). A gold wreath of oak leaves and acorns lay within the sarcophagus but of the king himself all that remained were three teeth. He was splendidly furnished with gold and silver jugs and drinking cups, amphorae of wine and a panoply of arms, including a bronze helmet decorated with gold and silver, greaves, a sword and 10 spears, as well as gold horse ornaments. Inscriptions on some of the silver vessels indicate that this was Seuthes III, an Odrysian Thracian king who had waged war against both Alexander and Lysimachus, Alexander's successor in Thrace.

Above: *Many of the silver vessels from the hoard found at Rogozen are either of Classical workmanship or inspired by Classical themes and designs, like this large gilded dish.*

Below left: *This gold burial mask was originally thought to belong to the Thracian king Seuthes III, but more recently it has been argued that it belonged to an earlier ruler, Sitalkes, who was king 431–424 BC.*

Below right: *Two of more than 70 fine objects from the tomb of Seuthes III in the Golyamata Kosmata mound; 20 of these were made of gold.*

CELTIC TREASURES

LOCAL LORDS MADE GOOD

Around 600 BC the Greeks founded a colony at Massilia (Marseilles) in Mediterranean France and this soon became the major base for Greek trade into central Europe. The Greeks were after raw materials such as metal ores, timber and furs. In exchange they offered a whole new way of life: the civilizing influence of wine-drinking. In order to facilitate this trade they gave lavish gifts to Celtic chiefs in areas that were strategically placed on the trade routes that led up the Rhône valley into central France and from there along the Seine and Rhine to the Atlantic coast and central Germany. These gifts were often purpose-made to suit barbarian taste, like the gigantic bronze krater (wine-mixing vessel) given to the potentate who ruled the hillfort of Mont Lassois, situated at the crucial transhipment point where the trade route left the Rhône to branch out westwards along the Seine. The krater, 1.64 metres (5 feet 5 inches) high, was buried in the grave of a woman known since her discovery as the "Vix princess",

along with a quantity of valuable grave goods, including a gold torc at her neck.

A number of rich burial mounds have been excavated in the vicinity of several German hillforts, containing locally made luxuries and many imported treasures, such as fine Greek pottery, Etruscan bronze jugs and even Chinese silk, finally deposited here after who knows what adventures. Many of the mounds have been looted, sometimes not long after the burial; one at Magdalenenberg in southern Germany was robbed within 50 years of its construction. In 1977, however, ploughing revealed a stone kerb round a low mound at Hochdorf, near the hillfort of Hohenasperg, and excavation of the mound uncovered a completely intact chieftain's burial within a substantial wooden chamber (now decayed away). A huge bronze cauldron decorated with figures of lions and filled with locally made mead was the main imported Greek luxury within the chamber. Encased in decorative ironwork, a wooden cart bore a large collection of bronze vessels. The chief himself lay on an elaborate bronze couch

amid a blaze of gold: gold-coated slippers on his feet, a belt decorated with gold around his waist, with a gold-hilted dagger in a golden sheath, enormous gold bracelets on one arm, elaborate gold pins fastening his clothing and a gold ring about his neck.

CELTIC ADVENTURERS AND GOLDWORKERS

By the fifth century BC the scene had changed. The Greeks were no longer trading through Massilia but through ports on the northern Adriatic coast, via the Etruscans, who controlled much of northern Italy. Celts from various parts of central and western Europe were now on the move, raiding adjacent lands or leaving home to seek their fortune as mercenaries. Many of these eventually returned with Mediterranean goods acquired as plunder or as wages, while others settled in the lands they visited, particularly northern Italy. Celtic traders also travelled widely, and it was presumably a Celt who deposited four magnificent gold torcs and three gold armbands under a stone at Erstfeld on a route leading through the Alps via the St Gotthard pass. We can only speculate what trouble caused him to hide his stock-in-trade – the work of a single goldsmith (perhaps himself) – and what misfortune befell him to prevent his return.

GILDED WARRIORS

Classical writers describe the Celts as a warrior society, and this view finds confirmation in their own oral traditions and in their rare burials, where weapons and armour feature prominently. Severed heads were stuck on posts at the entrance to their hillforts and displayed in special stone racks in sacred places such as the shrine at Roquepertuse in southern France. Although they went into battle with shields of wood and leather, and helmets of bronze or iron, and some ferocious bands fought naked, elite warriors also possessed elaborate parade armour of bronze decorated with enamel and sometimes gold. Chance has preserved a few such objects, masterpieces of Celtic craftsmanship. Among these are the magnificent gold-plated iron helmet discovered in pieces in the 1980s in a cave at Agris in France and the similar helmet of bronze and iron, covered by a repoussé gold band and inlaid with red enamel, which was found in 1861 in an old channel of the Seine at Amfreville.

Elite Celtic men and women also wore magnificent jewellery, particularly torcs of twisted bronze or gold with huge elaborate terminals. A collection of fabulous gold torcs was discovered by chance at Snettisham in Norfolk, England, in 1948, when a field was deep-ploughed. There were three hoards, each containing several torcs, and in one there was also a hollow gold collar. The most impressive item was a torc made of electrum – in this case two parts silver to three parts gold. Each of the eight strands of which it was twisted was made up of eight wires twisted together clockwise. The ends were soldered into massive, ring-shaped terminals with a decoration of swirling patterns and blocks of fine cross-hatching.

Above: *A selection of gold torcs, found at Snettisham in Norfolk, Ipswich in Suffolk and Needwood Forest in Staffordshire, England.*

Right: *This splendid iron helmet, plated with gold and inlaid with bronze strips and coral, was found in pieces in a cave at Agris in France. Fine armour like this was designed for ceremonial occasions, rather than use in battle.*

Opposite: *This gold armband and gold fibulae (elaborate safety-pins) were worn by the chieftan buried at Hochdorf, Germany.*

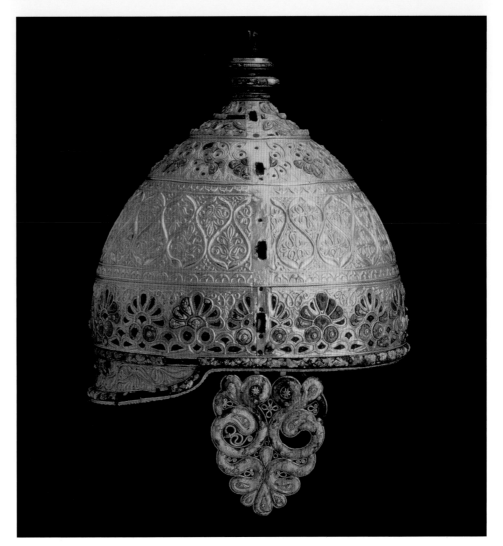

Two further torc hoards were found at the site in 1950 and in 1990 a bronze vessel was discovered containing nearly 600 pieces of metalwork, including more than 50 torcs. At this point the British Museum decided to investigate the field in detail and its excavations revealed another five hoards. A total of 12 hoards, including nearly 200 torcs, of silver, electrum, bronze and especially gold, have been uncovered, along with bracelets and coins, placed mainly as small hoards of a few items each, packed tightly in pits. Opinions are divided on the significance of these hoards. One suggestion is that this was a tribal "bank", a place of safe storage for valuables. Most probably the hoards were votive offerings, deposited in a sacred spot. Hoards elsewhere in Europe placed in similar unmarked locations contain the same limited range of objects – torcs, armrings and coins – which may have had a particular ritual significance.

THE WINCHESTER HOARD

In 2000 another such hoard was discovered in a field near Winchester, England, disturbed and slightly damaged by ploughing. Its first piece, a brooch with a gold chain, was found by a metal detectorist, Kevan Halls, who immediately reported it to local archaeologists and worked alongside them to investigate the site. They recovered two sets of jewellery, each comprising an unusual necklace torc, a pair of fibulae (safety-pin brooches used to fasten clothing) linked by a chain and a small plain bracelet, all made of gold of an exceptionally high purity. Both the metal composition and details of the workmanship, such as the use of granulation, suggest that the objects

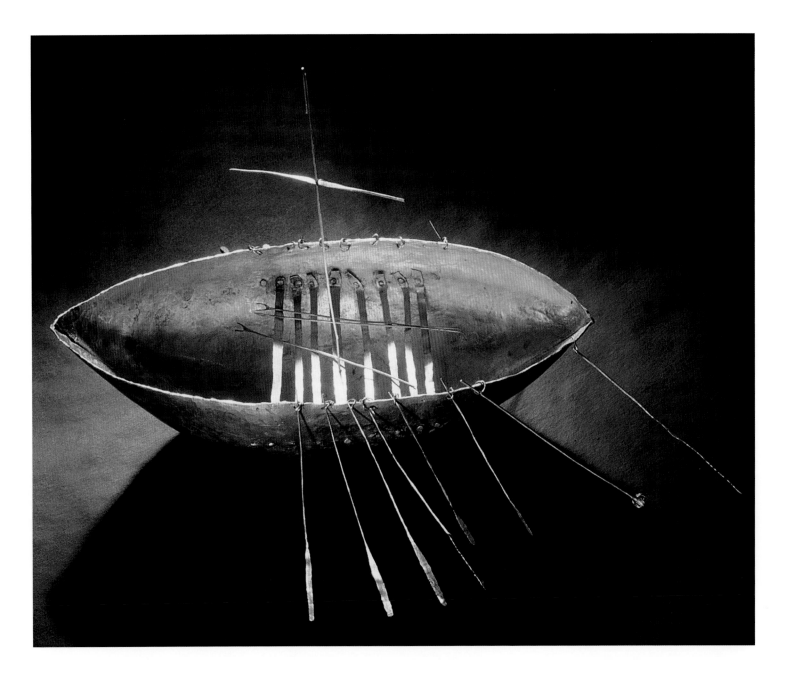

were manufactured in continental Europe by goldsmiths who were either trained by Romans or Romans themselves, but their form and style show they were made for Celts. The neighbouring settlement of Owslebury was obtaining wine from the Roman world in the first century BC when the jewellery was made. It seems likely that the objects had been commissioned or imported as unusual finery to aid the competitive ostentation of a local chief or king, and later buried here as a votive offering.

THE BROIGHTER HOARD

In 1896 ploughing near the shores of Lough Foyle in County Derry uncovered what proved to be Ireland's richest Iron Age gold hoard. As well as two necklaces of loose chains and two torcs of twisted wire, the hoard contained a gold basin and a much more massive hollow torc decorated all over with repoussé designs. The centrepiece was an exquisitely made golden boat, complete with mast, steering oar, rowers' benches and oars. A major dispute arose over the nature of this hoard. Was it composed of personal valuables buried with the intention of recovery? Or was it a votive offering thrown into the waters of Lough Foyle, which had formerly covered the spot? The difference was crucial: if it was an offering, then the finder could proceed with the hoard's planned sale to the British Museum, but if the original owner had intended to recover it, then it was "treasure trove" and thus became the property of the Crown (all Ireland at that time being under British rule). In the end it was decided that the latter was the case and King Edward VII gave it to the Royal Irish Academy, which placed it in the National Museum of Ireland, thus ending the British Museum's hopes of acquiring it.

Above: *The Broighter gold boat formed part of a hoard of superb Celtic goldwork. This model is one of the earliest pieces of evidence for sailing ships in northern Europe, although clearly it could also be propelled by rowers.*

Opposite: *Perhaps worn by a Celtic king and queen, these matching sets of jewellery, found near Winchester, reflect Roman trade with Britain, whose exports included slaves, hunting dogs and waterproof woollen capes.*

CAST UPON THE WATERS

Rivers, springs, bogs and lakes had a special sacred significance for the Celts and their Germanic neighbours in central and northern Europe. Precious offerings were ritually deposited in them on many occasions – as thank-offerings for military victories, for example, or as part of fertility rites. Llyn Cerrig Bach, a former lake on Anglesey, the island stronghold of the British Druids, received a great quantity of such offerings, including weapons, horse trappings, part of a war trumpet and a slave chain (there existed a flourishing trade in slaves, generally war captives, for whom there was a ready market in the Roman world). Beautifully decorated parade armour and weapons were thrown into rivers such as the Thames, including the magnificent Battersea Shield, a decorative bronze facing from a wooden shield, with superb enamelled bronze bosses.

GODS AND SACRIFICES

One of the most magnificent offerings to the Celtic gods was a huge gilded silver cauldron, found near Gundestrup in Denmark. Recovered from land that is now a bog, this was dry ground at the time of the offering: the cauldron, dismantled into its component parts, had just been laid in the grass. It was probably made for a Celtic patron by a Thracian silversmith in the second century BC. Many different cultural influences can be seen in its designs but the greater part of the subject matter of the decorative panels that run around this splendid object is Celtic. There is a line of Celtic warriors with shields and spears accompanied by three who blow carnyxes: the long, animal-headed war trumpets that were supposed to strike terror into the hearts of their enemies. A cross-legged figure in knee-length trousers sports horns on his head: probably the Celtic god Cernunnos. Another god is seen in the act of drowning a victim in a bucket, symbolizing the human sacrifices that were performed in these watery places.

Quite a few such sacrificial victims have been discovered in bogs in northern Europe. Although these were both men and women and included young and older individuals, they all had certain features in common. One was that they appeared, from the fine state of their hands and nails, to have done little manual work, implying that they were chosen for sacrifice well in advance of the occasion and led a specially privileged life of ease from their selection until their death. Another common feature was their last meal (known to archaeologists from their well-preserved stomach contents), which seems to have been a ritual concoction containing a wide variety of plants, perhaps chosen to symbolize spring. Bog sacrifices were usually committed naked to their watery grave. And in almost every case these victims were killed in several ways: knocked on the head, the neck broken, strangled, the throat cut, stabbed in the chest, beheaded; most had suffered two or three of these fates, for what ritual reason we can only guess.

Above: *Panels on the outside of the silver Gundestrup bowl depict gods between whose raised arms mortals perform ritual activities, while whole ritual scenes run around the inside of the piece*

Opposite top: *The Battersea shield is decorated in typical Celtic style, with geometric and swirling patterns and brightly coloured enamelling. The Celts invented the type of sealing-wax red glass found on this shield.*

Opposite bottom: *This young girl was sacrificed and buried in the bog at Windeby in Schleswig, Germany.*

TREASURES FROM ETRUSCAN TOMBS

ETRUSCAN CITIES OF THE DEAD

Etruscan tombs in central Italy began to be discovered in the sixteenth century and soon they were being regularly looted for the fine pottery and metalwork that they contained, which were avidly collected by the wealthy to adorn their mansions. Etruscan pottery inspired the English potter, Josiah Wedgwood, to produce new styles along antique lines and in 1769 to name his new works at Hanley, Staffordshire, "Etruria". Ironically, much of this pottery was not Etruscan but Greek, for the Etruscans were keen importers of fine Greek pottery.

Official investigations of these tombs were greatly assisted by the work of Carlo Lerici, who in the 1940s developed a technique of looking into tombs using a periscope with a camera attached to photograph their contents and the wonderful paintings that occasionally decked their walls. Despite Italy's strict antiquity laws, tomb robbers are still active in the region, some of them exceptionally skilled at locating and entering tombs.

The Etruscan cities were at their height between 700 and 500 BC. Like Greece, Etruria consisted of a series of city states, culturally but not politically united. From their homeland in central Italy the Etruscans expanded southwards into Campania and north into the Po plain, and for a while controlled Rome. During the fifth century BC, however, their lands were progressively lost to Gauls in the north, Greeks in the south and the growing power of the Romans. Control of the rich iron-ore sources on the island of Elba gave the Etruscans considerable wealth in this newly iron-using age, and they were great sea traders. Their rich arable lands provided abundant agricultural wealth and they were highly skilled engineers, building fine roads, ambitious bridges and monumental gateways and city walls.

But the Etruscans are best known for their tombs. They constructed great cities of the dead: rock-cut chambers in hillsides, free-standing stone edifices often enclosed in massive tumuli, and underground rooms, often mirroring the houses of the living in detail. The façades of these tombs were often carved to look like house doorways opening off carefully laid-out streets. Frequently the tombs contained furniture carved in stone, particularly couches on which the dead were laid, as if attending banquets in the underworld. The Etruscans scandalized their Greek neighbours by their style of living and feasting, men and women mixing freely.

COLOURFUL PAINTINGS

A small proportion of the Etruscan tombs are decorated with vibrant paintings that give a wonderful glimpse of their lives. Here we see a farmer at his plough, fishermen hauling in their lines while boys dive from rocks among the fish and birds fly overhead. Close to nature and deeply appreciative of it, the Etruscans saw auguries for the future in the flight of birds, as also in other natural phenomena such as thunder and lightning. Priests carefully examined the livers of sacrificial animals to discover the will of the gods.

Many paintings depicted the celebrations that accompanied Etruscan funerals. We see chariot races, wrestling matches and other funeral games, including a combat between a blindfold man and a savage dog. Crowns await the victors of these contests. Processions of musicians and dancers crowd the walls. Men and women exuberantly twirl their bodies, gracefully waving their arms and vigorously stamping their feet. One man moves in a stately fashion, holding a large shallow bowl of wine while another swings a wine jug as he matches his partner's enthusiastic high-stepping capers. Other dancers accompany themselves on double pipes or lyres or snap castanets.

Elsewhere the scene changes to a funeral feast. A huge bronze jar stands to one side, filled with wine mixed with water and beside it a scoop with which to serve the diners. Men and women recline on couches, eating and drinking. One holds up an egg, symbol of fertility: rebirth and renewal were an integral theme in the celebration of death and burial.

Opposite: *Paintings in the "Tomb of the Leopards" depict a funeral banquet. Men and women recline on couches, eating and drinking, and one holds up an egg, the Etruscan symbol of fertility.*

Below left: *This gold plaque from Pyrgi in Italy is inscribed in Phoenician, reflecting the cosmopolitan nature of this Etruscan port.*

Below right: *These elaborate Etruscan earrings incorporate portrait busts in the pendants.*

GOLDEN OFFERINGS

One tomb was decorated with plaster replicas of many of the possessions of the deceased. More often the tombs contain the actual treasures of the departed: high-quality Greek pottery but also many objects of superb native workmanship. Particularly remarkable are the bronze mirrors, inscribed with fine line-drawings of scenes from Etruscan and Greek mythology. Etruscan goldwork reached a pinnacle of skill, and even today it is not known how they achieved the finest granulation, forming a surface that looks powdered, as a background for exquisite figured decoration.

One of the most richly furnished Etruscan tombs was opened in 1836 by Archpriest Regolini and General Galassi in the Banditaccia cemetery at Cerveteri, one of the largest and most splendid Etruscan necropolises. The tomb lay within an enormous tumulus. In the main burial chamber an Etruscan lady was laid out on a stone couch, covered by a golden shroud, while a man lay on a bronze couch in the antechamber, along with the remains of a wagon finely decorated in bronze. The offerings placed with them included Greek vases, a number of gilded silver bowls and a quantity of gold jewellery.

The city of Cerveteri was 6.5 kilometres (4 miles) from the sea but was well served by coastal harbours from which to conduct its seatrade. The principal port was at Pyrgi and it was here that one of the most interesting Etruscan finds was made – three gold plaques, two inscribed in Etruscan, the third in Phoenician giving similar information. Although the Etruscans used a modified version of the Greek script, their language is still largely unknown, and this find provided a major step forward in understanding it. The plaques refer to a dedication by Thefarie Velianas, ruler of Cerveteri, to the Etruscan mother-goddess Uni and the Phoenician fertility goddess Astarte.

An extraordinary object discovered in the 1940s only became publicly known some 60 years later. A man dug it out of a tomb in south-west Bulgaria in his youth, and in 2003, aged 87, he donated it to the Bulgarian National Museum. It is a book of six pages, bound together like the pages in a ring binder, and is the earliest known example of a paginated book, created at a time when books were made as continuous scrolls. It has illustrations and a text in Etruscan. What makes it even more remarkable is that all six pages are of sheet gold.

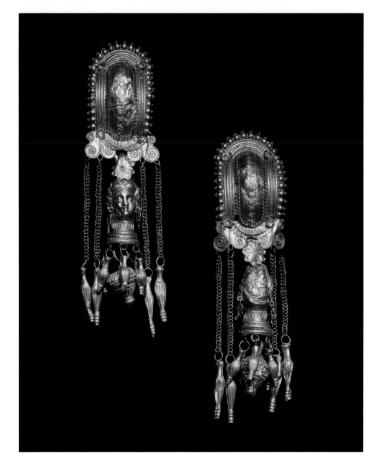

SUDDEN DESTRUCTION: THE ERUPTION OF VESUVIUS

FIRE FROM THE UNDERWORLD

The Bay of Naples was a popular Roman resort and retirement home due to its mild winters and balmy summers. Many villas were dotted around it and there were several flourishing towns: Misenum at the head of the bay, the major port and market centre at Pompeii and the quiet resort of Herculaneum with its fishermen and elderly refugees from the bustle of Rome. The long-inactive volcano Vesuvius, which overlooked these towns, had in the past deposited volcanic ash, producing exceptionally fertile soil on which grew luscious grapes that made excellent wine.

The occasional incident disturbed the peaceful lives of the bay's inhabitants. In AD 59 a brawl in the amphitheatre led the senate to close it for a decade; three years later an earth tremor rocked Pompeii, causing considerable damage. But in August of 79 most citizens had put these unpleasant matters behind them: the buildings damaged in the earthquake were being repaired and people looked forward to the Festival of the Divine Augustus toward the end of the month.

Some people were a little unsettled by a series of minor rumblings that occurred as the month went on. They packed their possessions and left, but most were untroubled and stayed on. Then the animals began behaving curiously – the birds fell silent, all the cats left town and the dogs barked without reason – and several sources of water dried up. On August 20 an earth tremor shook Pompeii, with a sound like distant thunder, but the next day things seemed to be back to normal. Everyone had just settled down again when catastrophe struck.

Around lunchtime on August 24, a public holiday, a sudden almighty explosion was heard and the ground shook violently. Over at Misenum, well out of range, the writer Pliny and his uncle, an admiral, observed broad sheets of fire rising from Vesuvius and a mushroom cloud of soil, ash, pumice and other debris hanging over it.

PERILOUS LOVE OF POSSESSIONS

Wide-awake citizens of Pompeii dropped everything and fled at once. The vast majority got out of the city, though many died in the countryside as they struggled to put distance between themselves and disaster. Quite a few people, however, fatally delayed: they searched for members of their family off celebrating in other parts of town; they went home and packed up everything they could carry; they set off but turned back to collect something they had forgotten. Some thought they would be safe in their cellars, out of the full force of the blast.

Disaster rapidly overtook them: a blanket of stifling ashes and a hail of stones fell on those in the open, while poisonous gases overcame those who remained under cover. Soon all were dead. The horrified citizens of neighbouring Herculaneum watched the terrible eruption and thanked the gods that they had been spared all but a scattering of ash and pumice. Not for long, however. Around midnight a tide of volcanic mud burst from Vesuvius and poured down on Herculaneum, engulfing it completely. More than 150 people went down to the town's boatsheds and tried to escape by sea, but the eruption had

Left: *This extraordinary Etruscan book, made entirely of gold, is said to have come from a Bulgarian tomb, presumably acquired as an import by the Thracian noble buried there.*

Opposite: *Pompeii's disastrous end ensured the remarkable preservation of its buildings. This is the entrance hall of the House of Paquius Proculus, lavishly decorated with mosaics and wall paintings.*

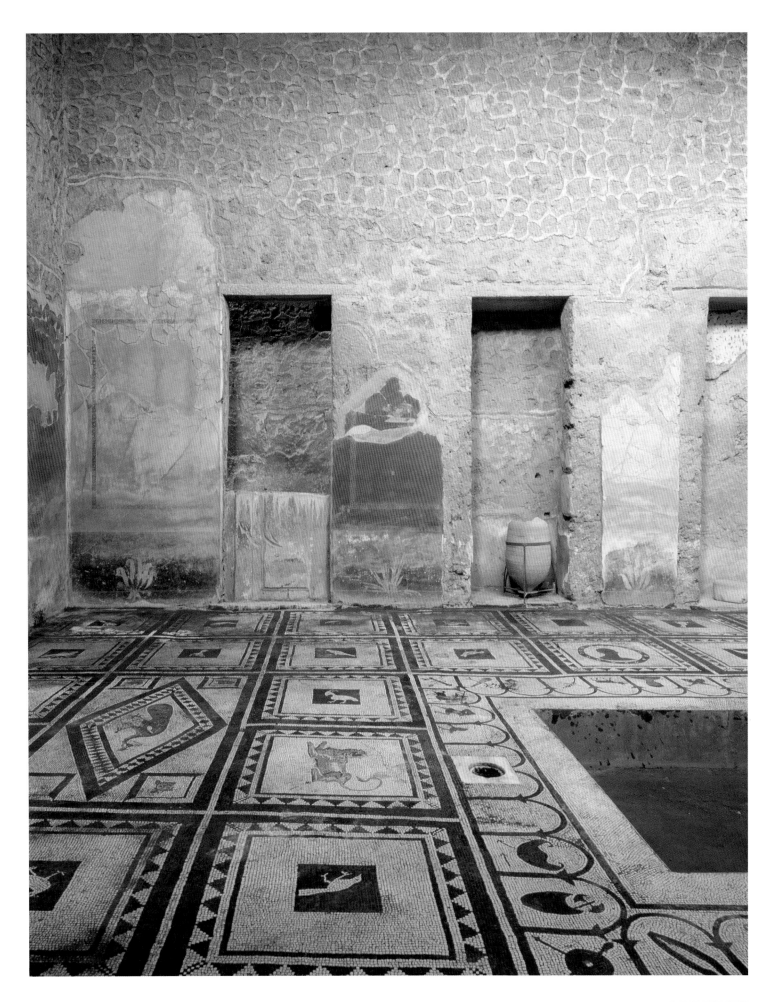

churned up the water and any boats that put out capsized. The horrified crowd was overwhelmed by the gases, mud and ash that poured down on them. One richly dressed woman fell dead beneath an archway, to be rediscovered in recent times along with her golden rings, bracelets and earrings. Pliny the admiral took his warships to attempt a rescue but was unable to get close to either city. He landed at nearby Stabiae and encouraged his friends there to flee with him as soon as a favourable wind arose. Before this could happen, however, he collapsed and died on the beach, overcome by the drifting fumes.

REDISCOVERY

The earthquake of AD 62 and the eruption of 79 so soon after made it seem inadvisable to return to the area, and the emperor sanctioned a massive resettlement programme, housing refugees in nearby towns such as Neapolis (Naples). Many people returned once the eruption had passed, to salvage what they could of their possessions. Pompeians managed to dig many things out of the wreckage of their homes but Herculaneum was completely inaccessible beneath its solidifying blanket of volcanic mud and ash. Gradually the deserted towns passed into history and were then forgotten.

In 1709 a peasant digging a well at Resina, the new town built over Herculaneum, found a quantity of carved stone. An Austrian, Prince d'Elboeuf, bought some of the land and began tunnelling into the ruins, bringing out many beautifully preserved Roman remains. The King of Naples came to hear of the site and he too began investigations: still by tunnelling, though rather more systematically. Within a decade he also initiated work at Pompeii. Eighteenth-century travellers on the Grand Tour visited

---

Below: *Bejewelled gold rings deck the fingers of this unfortunate victim of the mudslide that engulfed the town of Herculaneum on the night of August 24, AD 79.*

the excavations and rambled through the tunnels, observing the labourers mining the rooms for objects. Beautiful vases decorated with relief mouldings and fine marble statues were not only appreciated by the sponsors of the excavations but found a ready market when offered for sale among the avid collectors of the time. Many a noble home in Britain, Italy and France was adorned with objects mined from these and other sites.

In the mid-nineteenth century Giuseppe Fiorelli was appointed to excavate Pompeii and began the systematic uncovering of the buildings, carefully recording his finds. At Pompeii he invented an ingenious technique to recover the form of the long-decayed bodies of the inhabitants. At the time of the eruption Pompeians who died were encased in the falling ash, which gradually hardened. Although their bodies had decayed away, leaving nothing but bones, a void was left in the solidified ash and this acted as a mould into which Fiorelli poured plaster, recovering the form of the body, complete with clothing.

TREASURES RE-EMERGE

As the years have passed, excavation techniques have improved, and work at Pompeii and adjacent sites has reaped the benefit. Nevertheless, the sheer scale of the preserved remains has made the task of excavation a daunting one, fraught with problems. Herculaneum, situated

as it is beneath a modern town, has been particularly hard to investigate, the immensely hard tufa in which it is encased presenting a major challenge.

Many of the inhabitants of Pompeii, Herculaneum and the surrounding villas were wealthy people, their houses resplendent with vessels of silver and fine mosaics. Some people escaped with their personal finery as well as their lives and others returned to retrieve their treasured possessions; but many failed and their treasures lie where they were left. The priests of the temple of Isis prayed to the goddess before packing up a sack of money, statuettes and sacred vessels. They entrusted this to one of their number and he set off, but before he got far he was overwhelmed by a hail of volcanic rocks. Many others died in this way in the streets, burdened with treasures that could now do them no good.

In some houses families had got as far as gathering their finest possessions before they too were overcome by the fumes. Others packed their treasures and left them in hopeful safety as they abandoned their houses. In the huge dwelling of Quintus Poppaeus (now known as the House of Menander) at Pompeii a wooden box had been used to hold 118 pieces of household treasure. These included silver mirrors, the front plain and highly polished, the back tastefully decorated – one bears a fine portrait of a lady. There was also tableware, including

silver eggcups and dishes, and many pieces of gold and silver jewellery. In the villa at Boscoreale, outside Pompeii, a slave was sent to conceal a sack of family silver and gold. Making her way into the industrial quarters of the estate, where wine and olive oil were pressed, she dumped her burden in a well but was not quick enough to make her own escape. When rediscovered in 1895, the hoard was found to include 1,000 gold coins, gold and silver jewellery and a number of silver dishes. One dish had a solid bust of a man in its centre – perhaps the owner of the house.

Tables had been laid in many houses in preparation for the midday meal. In the house now known as the House of the Philosopher, guests were expected and fine silver cups had been set out on the table – but no one ever came to eat.

Above left: *The vast house of Quintus Poppaeus and his family was more like a country villa than a town mansion. A wooden box in its storeroom was packed with treasures of silverwork, including this beautiful mirror.*

Above right: *A number of elaborate silver dishes with raised decoration were among the treasures packed together in the villa at Boscoreale. One shows a woman personifying Africa, another this elderly man.*

ROMAN SILVER HOARDS

HIDDEN FROM DANGER

The eruptions at Pompeii and Herculaneum were a stupendous catastrophe in which nature rather than people buried an unusually rich selection of Roman treasures. But there were also many occasions when individuals felt the need to bury their valuables until a safer time and never succeeded in retrieving them.

One such hoard was probably concealed by a wealthy officer on campaign in Germany at the time of Augustus in the early first century AD. Engaged against the untamed Germanic tribes beyond the imperial borders, he had with him a silver folding table and more than 60 pieces of silver tableware: goblets with chunky relief decoration, larger cups – each with a gilded medallion in their centre, to be glimpsed and gradually revealed by the drinker – silver dishes, including one with hollows to hold 12 eggs, a large krater in which the rich wine was mixed with water and a ladle with which to serve it. This hoard was discovered in 1868 during construction work at Hildesheim, near Hanover.

PEPPER POTS AND COINS

A far more recent find comes from Hoxne in Suffolk, England. On November 16, 1992 Eric Lawes was looking for a lost hammer when he discovered a hoard of Roman material. He reported it immediately and the next day a team of archaeologists excavated and removed the hoard, recovering a great deal of fragile and elusive evidence that would have been lost by casual removal of the material from the ground. As the objects were of gold and silver and had been buried with the intention of recovery, the Hoxne hoard counted as treasure trove. This meant that they belonged to the Crown but that their full market value, nearly £2 million, was paid to the finder as a reward.

The original owner, a Roman who perhaps lived in the small settlement at Scole, some 3 kilometres (2 miles) from the find spot, had buried the treasure carefully, clearly expecting to retrieve it. Everything had been stacked within a wooden box with iron fittings. Hay had been used to separate some pieces and textiles wrapped around others. A number had been

Above: *These are two of the 14,865 gold, silver and bronze coins found in the Hoxne treasure. The lower one was issued by the imperial usurper Eugenius (392–94).*

Below: *Two pieces from the Hildesheim hoard: on the left, a silver dish with a gilded depiction of the goddess Athena and her owl; on the right, a silver flagon with vegetal decoration.*

Above: *This exquisite silver pepperpot has many of its details delicately picked out in gold. It may represent the empress Helena, mother of Constantine, or it could be a generic portrait of an empress.*

placed within smaller inner caskets of wood or ivory, several with silver padlocks.

More than 14,000 coins of gold and silver formed part of the hoard, along with 24 of bronze. These were very useful for dating: they all belonged to the fourth and early fifth centuries, the latest being coins of Constantine III (AD 407–11). This suggests the hoard was buried around or shortly after the time when the last Roman legions were withdrawn from Britain, in AD 410. On the other hand, many of the silver coins were clipped: some of the edge had been removed, reducing their size. People in Britain no longer had access to silver for manufacturing new coins, so they took silver from existing coins and used it to make forgeries of existing issues. At least 178 of the silver coins in the Hoxne hoard are such forgeries so the hoard dates to sometime between 410 and 450, when coinage ceased to be used in Britain.

The hoard also contained 29 beautiful pieces of gold jewellery: bracelets in the form of thick bands decorated with attractive scenes, others made in a lacy punched openwork style. One bore the name of its owner, Juliana. There were also rings that had once held jewels – the latter had been removed before the hoard was buried – necklaces and an elaborate chain. This was worn looped over the shoulders and under the arms, fastened by a large central brooch on the back and chest.

Most of the remaining items were silver tableware, much of it gilded: ladles, spoons, a striped tigress which had once been the handle of a large jug. But the most unusual and interesting pieces were four gilded silver pepperpots. Pepper was an extremely valuable commodity at the time, imported from India in exchange for gold from the first century AD onward. Two of the pepperpots were of sheet silver, in the form of an ibex and a dog chasing a hare. A third showed Hercules fighting a giant, while the fourth was the bust of an empress, perhaps St Helena,

Below: *Two very small silver vases with intricate decoration in the form of foliage were found in the Hoxne hoard, along with five bowls and many spoons and ladles.*

mother of the emperor Constantine the Great (reigned AD 307–337). Constantine gave official acceptance to Christianity, and his mother was a devout Christian. This and several other pieces in the Hoxne hoard show the owners had been Christians, as many Romans were by the fifth century AD.

AVOIDING PERSECUTION

In contrast, the owners of the Water Newton treasure were among the secret followers of Christianity in the days when it was forbidden by Roman law. Although the Romans were generally tolerant of other religions and themselves embraced imported religions on the principle of hedging their bets, they were firmly opposed to any monotheistic sect that refused to pay lip service to the cult of the divine emperor, as did the Christians and the Jews. Some emperors actively persecuted Christians, others were more lenient. But it was safer to practise the Christian rites strictly under cover, worshipping in the private houses of the secret congregation. Participants in these ceremonies used sacred objects that could be disguised as domestic utensils, and communicated with secret signs, such as alpha and omega (the first and last letters of the Greek alphabet, symbolizing God, the Beginning and the End) or the Chi-Rho, a sign combining the Greek letters CH and R, the beginning of Christ's name.

A set of silver church plate used in such secret worship was found at Water Newton in Cambridgeshire in 1975. This small town, near modern Peterborough, was a centre of Britain's pottery-making industry in Roman times, with potteries strung out along the banks of the River Nene, an important waterway which brought in raw materials and took away the finished goods. The Water Newton hoard was deposited around AD 350. It contains 28 pieces: a jug, bowls, cups, a wine strainer, a gold coin and a number of triangular silver plaques bearing the Chi-Rho symbol. Such plaques were common votive offerings among many religions of the time, promised to the gods in exchange for divine favours, and these Christian examples adapted the pagan tradition to their own ends.

REVOLTING NATIVES, TREACHEROUS COMPATRIOTS

The periods of political trouble during the Roman Empire frequently induced wealthy people to hide their belongings for safe keeping. The Iceni, a Celtic people who had settled in East Anglia on the eastern side of England, had started their involvement with the empire as its allies, a client kingdom in the newly conquered province of Britain. Appalling mismanagement within the province and particularly inept and high-handed treatment of the Iceni brought about the

---

Below: *Some of the silver vessels used by secret Christian worshippers in the Roman town of Durobrivae (modern Water Newton in England). The triangular plaque is inscribed with a large Chi-Rho and a small Alpha and Omega.*

---

great revolt led by the tribe's newly widowed queen, Boudicca (Boadicea), in AD 60. The army of liberation swept all before it, but by 61 the tide had turned as the Roman army's superior training told against the mass of the courageous but undisciplined Britons. One member of the native force who did not return home was the wealthy individual who had concealed his treasure of 860 Iceni silver coins in a pot in the Fens near modern March. It was rediscovered in 1982.

Numerous third-century hoards found in France reflect a time of considerable troubles within the empire, when barbarian invasions undermined the stability of the state and individual generals seized their opportunity to make a bid for the imperial throne or establish breakaway kingdoms, as did Carausius and his murderous successor Allectus, who controlled Britain and part of Gaul from AD 286 to 296. In these unsettled times many people hid their valuables, jewellery, small art objects and coins, the latter often including coins struck by the false emperors. A hoard found at Beaurains near Arras, probably the savings of an officer in the Roman army, included a coin of Carausius and a gold medallion of Constantius Chlorus who defeated Allectus and brought the region back under Roman rule. The medallion, one of 40 in the hoard, was struck by Constantius, then a Caesar (deputy emperor) to commemorate his victory. It shows London personified as a woman, kneeling before Constantius in gratitude at her liberation from the usurpers.

TODAY'S UNFOUND TREASURES

ATTILA

Barbarian attacks on the Roman Empire reached their height when the ferocious Huns from Central Asia were united under the charismatic leadership of Attila in AD 434. At first they terrorized the Eastern Empire, but in 450 the accession of a stronger emperor, Marcian, caused the Huns to turn their attentions to the west. However, after laying waste much of Gaul, they were brought to battle in 451 near Tours. The result was inconclusive, the first setback that Attila had received and a blow to his prestige. The Huns moved the following year into Italy, where their considerable successes were tempered by many deaths from disease, and in the autumn they withdrew to their base in Hungary. Here, early in 453, Attila suddenly died from a haemorrhage on the night of his wedding to a new young bride. His devastated followers gave him a lavish funeral, placing him in a golden casket within a silver coffin inside one of iron, and sacrificing many servants and horses to accompany him. They dammed the River Tisza and buried him deep within its bed, breaking the dam and returning the river to its course afterwards, in order that his grave should never be found. And despite much searching, it never has been.

Above: *A detail from a French tapestry that imaginatively depicts the confrontation between Attila and Pope Leo I outside Rome.*

THE PAGAN HORDES

BARBARIAN INVADERS

In the bitter winter of AD 406 the Rhine froze over near the Roman city of Moguntiacum (modern Mainz) and the Germanic barbarians who dwelt on the river's eastern bank poured across it into the Roman Empire, raping, destroying, murdering and plundering. Hordes of Vandals and other tribes continued their ferocious progress through the lands of the decaying Western Empire, settling in Gaul, Spain and eventually North Africa.

Troubles with their warlike and uncivilized neighbours were nothing new for the Romans, but initially the undisciplined though courageous barbarian warriors had been no match for the tight and efficient organization of the Roman legions. However, by the third century many barbarians were becoming united in huge confederacies, overwhelming Roman forces by their sheer numbers. The Romans swelled the ranks of their army by employing many barbarians in their auxiliary forces, and in parts of the empire where populations were declining – for example, border regions such as the Balkans and Belgium – they encouraged tribal groups to settle, creating Romanized barbarian buffer zones.

ALARIC THE GOTH

While these tribes learned to appreciate the benefits of civilization and kept their hostile cousins at bay, they were also something of a liability. Discontented groups could suddenly turn on their Roman masters and wreak havoc. During power struggles between rival emperors in the 390s, Visigoths under their king, Alaric, were entrusted with the defence of the north-western Balkans. As troubles piled up elsewhere in the empire, Alaric went on the rampage in Italy, demanding vast sums to call off his troops, and in 410 he sacked Rome. Marching on through southern Italy, aiming for the rich grainlands of North Africa, the king suddenly died of an illness, to the Romans' relief.

Alaric was given a magnificent send-off by his people. Captives were forced to divert a river, the Busentinus, that flowed around the city of Consentia (modern Cosenza) and he was laid to rest in its bed, surrounded by the magnificent spoils taken in the sack of Rome. The captives returned the river to its bed, hiding the king's tomb, and were all slaughtered to guard the secret of its location. To this day no one has succeeded in locating Alaric's tomb with its fabulous treasures.

CHILDERIC THE FRANK

Several royal barbarian burials have reappeared in other lands, however. In 1653 a richly furnished grave was discovered by chance in a Roman cemetery at Tournai in Belgium. Warrior trappings were prominent among the grave furnishings, including an iron throwing axe, a horse and a sword. The sword's hilt and scabbard were magnificently decorated and there were also many pieces of jewellery, all formed of gold cells enclosing pieces of garnet (cloisonné).

Hundreds of coins were among the other grave goods, and a fur cape, ornamented with 300 gold bees. A gold signet ring identified the deceased: it read "Childerici Regis" – "of king Childeric". Childeric, who died in AD 481, was the father of King Clovis (reigned 481–511), a convert to Christianity who founded the Frankish kingdom around 500, expelling the Romans from Gaul and driving away other barbarian groups. His deeds were recorded by Bishop Gregory of Tours, who contrasted his godliness (however bloodthirsty) with the debauched lifestyle of his father.

Childeric had been the ruler of a much smaller state, centred on Tournai. The remarkable find of his burial was published with admirable rapidity in 1655. In 1831, however, the majority of these treasures were stolen and probably melted down, leaving only drawings and casts from which we can still get some impression of their magnificence.

The grave of Clovis' daughter-in-law, Arnegunde, was discovered in 1958 in the church of St Denis in Paris, within a stone coffin. She also had gold and garnet jewellery and was identified by her signet ring. She was dressed in silk, embroidered with gold thread.

Above: *Arnegunde's gold ring, inscribed "Arnegundis Regina". Her belt fittings were also made of gold, gold and garnet pins and brooches fastened her silk clothing, and her garters and shoes had silver strap ends.*

THE VISIGOTHS

One of the groups evicted from Gaul by Clovis was the Visigoths. After Alaric's death in 410, they left Italy and by 418 had established themselves in Aquitaine in south-west France, where they settled. Gradually they absorbed much of the civilized way of life of the Roman inhabitants of the area. By the 470s the Visigoths had conquered much neighbouring territory and controlled a kingdom that embraced both south-west France and the greater part of Spain. When Clovis drove them from France they consolidated their hold on Spain. The Roman Empire, now reduced to its eastern half centred on Constantinople, wrested the Mediterranean regions from them in the mid-sixth century but the Visigothic kingdom otherwise prospered until it fell to the Arabs in the early eighth century. Among its kings was Recceswinth (reigned 653–672), whose magnificent votive crown of gold inlaid with jewels was among treasures concealed near Toledo, probably during the Arab invasion. The hoard, the Treasure of Guarrazar, was rediscovered in 1859. The crown, which was a religious offering, is decorated with suspended jewelled letters that spell out the king's name.

EASTERN BARBARIANS

While the eastern Roman lands did not, like the Western Empire, go under, they did endure wave after wave of invaders from northern and central Europe and from the steppe to the east. Among these were the Goths, whom the Romans in turn repelled by force and held off with bribes. It was probably during one of the third-century Gothic attacks that the largest known hoard of Roman silver coins, some 81,000 in number, dated between AD 64 and 238, were concealed by a Roman in what is now Reka Devnia in Bulgaria: it was rediscovered in 1929.

The Goths settled in the Balkans, creating a buffer zone between the Romans and other barbarian groups. In AD 376, however, the Goths failed to repel attacks by the Huns, ferocious and warlike nomads from the steppe, and thousands of Gothic refugees threw themselves on the mercy of the Romans, who reluctantly helped them cross the Danube to safety. They proved bad guests, however, soon turning on the Romans, defeating and destroying the major part of the Roman army at Hadrianople in 378 and killing the emperor.

The former ruler of the Goths, Athanaric, deposed when many of his subjects fled to the Romans, had moved with his loyal followers into the Carpathian mountains.

He later travelled to Constantinople as the guest of the new Roman emperor, Theodosius. At some point, perhaps before taking to the mountains, he may have buried a royal treasure in his fortress at Pietroasa. Some scholars, however, do not believe that the treasure was linked to Athanaric but suggest it was composed of votive offerings, concealed in 376 within a sacred enclosure in anticipation of the Hunnish invasion.

The hoard was rediscovered in 1837 by two workmen quarrying stone. Twenty-two gold objects were found, including a large dish with relief decoration of Gothic gods dressed as Greeks and a three-dimensional central figure of a seated goddess; a 12-sided cup and other vessels; and a number of pieces of jewellery. Principal among these were a large brooch in the form of an eagle inlaid with semi-precious stones and three smaller similar brooches. The Romanians, who came to regard this hoard as a national treasure, nicknamed these "the Hen and Her Golden Chicks".

The treasure has had a chequered history since its discovery. Believing them to be of copper, the finders sold the objects for a pittance to a building contractor who recognized that they were gold but failed to appreciate the value of the jewels, which for ease of transport he pried out

and discarded. However, news of the find eventually reached the authorities, who were able to recover 12 of the objects and sent them to Paris for repair. Thereafter they were displayed in the National Museum, from which they were stolen in 1875, though quickly recovered. During the First World War when Romania was threatened by German invasion, the treasure was entrusted to Tsarist Russia for safety – only to be overtaken by the Russian revolution. It was 40 years before the Romanians were able to persuade the Russians to return the treasures.

GEPID PRINCES AND A PRINCESS

The Huns dominated central Europe in the late fourth and early fifth centuries, with many other groups their subordinate allies. Among these were the Gepids, who gained control of Transylvania when the Hunnish hegemony collapsed

---

Below: *These sword hilt and scabbard fittings are among the few surviving treasures from Childeric's magnificently furnished burial. Of the 300 gold bees on his fur cape only these two remain.*

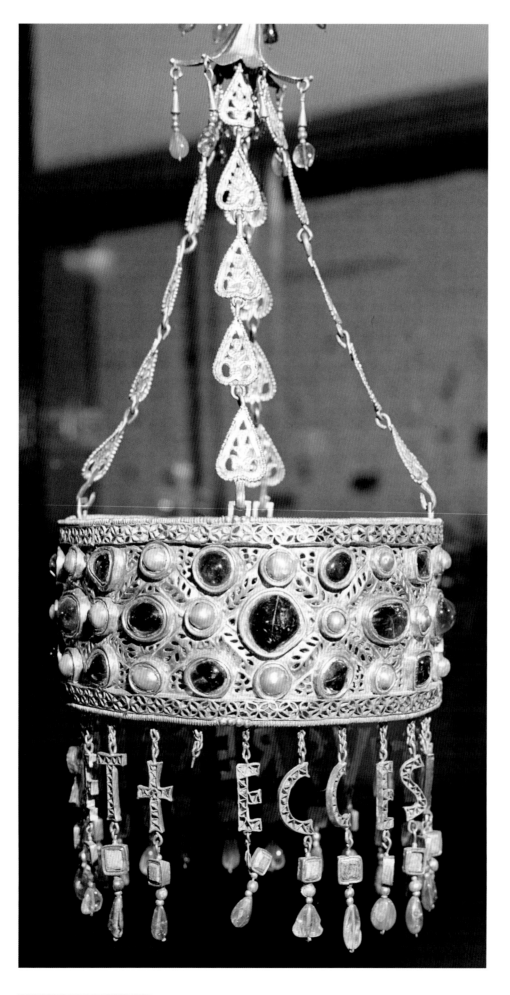

following Attila's death, maintaining their rule until defeated by the Avars and Lombards in AD 567.

In 1889 a rich burial was discovered at Apahida, which proved to be the Gepid royal cemetery. This prince was buried in a wooden coffin with an iron clasp. Among his grave goods were gold and garnet brooches, very similar to those found with Childeric, as well as two silver jugs, cups with golden handles, a glass bottle with gold decoration, a bracelet of solid gold, three gold belt buckles with cloisonné decoration, three gold rings and six gold pendants decorated with boars' heads. One of the rings bore a name or title: "Omharius", a Latinized version of the Germanic name "Audomharjaz", meaning "lord of the army". Crosses on several of the rings show that he was a Christian.

A second burial discovered nearby in 1968 was equally richly furnished. Both burials had been disturbed and partially looted, but this later discovery less so: among the remaining objects was a fine sword in a sheath decorated with cloisonné gold panels, a gold cloisonné belt buckle and a purse with a gold cloisonné cover plate. Other grave goods included a glass goblet with a gold band and the golden handle from a cup. A wooden chest beside the prince contained superbly decorated horse equipment, also with gold and cloisonné decorative elements, including a pair of saddle mounts in the shape of eagles. A stray cloisonné gold buckle found nearby in 1979 suggests that there may have been other rich burials here, probably disturbed or plundered.

A Gepid princess was discovered in 1996 in the bathhouse of an abandoned Roman fortified camp at Potaissa in the Turda region of Romania: this find is known as the Franziska treasure. Like the Apahida princes, she had been interred with a great deal of gold jewellery, including rings and brooches, but also with more feminine pieces, such as gold earrings, a necklace of amber beads, silver shoe buckles, a mirror and a bone comb. Fragments of her clothing survived, and were decorated with gold embroidery.

Left: *The crown of king Recceswinth, which is made of gold inlaid with rock crystal, pearls and sapphires. The crown was a votive offering to the Toledo church where it would have hung above the altar.*

SAXON KINGS

DARK AGES

Many of the barbarian tribes who entered the Roman Empire had been driven south and west by movements of other groups from the steppe regions and from Scandinavia. By 400 the lands of the north were suffering significantly from increased rainfall, which flooded and reduced cultivable land. As well as moving across the continent into the lands of the crumbling western Roman Empire, the inhabitants of Scandinavia and north Germany – Angles, Saxons, Jutes and Frisians – took to the seas, raiding Britain, one region of the Western Empire that was still enjoying considerable prosperity, where they met fierce resistance. In the south and east of England

they gradually carved out kingdoms for themselves, the eventual prosperity of which can be gauged by the splendour of the burials of their kings at Sutton Hoo and Prittlewell.

THE CURIOUS MOUNDS

Mrs Edith Pretty had an interest in archaeology dating back to her youthful travels in Egypt and her father's excavations on their family estate in Suffolk. Left a widow in 1935, she decided after a time to investigate the enigmatic mounds that lay near her house at Sutton Hoo, a quiet spot on the River Deben. After consulting Guy Maynard of the local museum, she engaged the services of an experienced and

conscientious local amateur archaeologist, Basil Brown. Assisted by two of Mrs Pretty's estate workers, Brown set about investigating the largest mound, denoted mound 1, in June 1938. However, after a short while he persuaded Mrs Pretty that they would do better to look into one of the smaller mounds, and so they turned their attentions to mound 3. This, it turned out,

---

Below: *Iron rivets and a crust in the sand where the timbers had decayed were the only surviving remains of the Sutton Hoo burial ship, skilfully traced and exposed by the excavators.*

---

had already been opened by treasure hunters, as had mound 2, which Brown tackled next. Here, however, he began to find ship rivets and believed he could make out the outline of a ship. Material missed by the grave robbers proved that the burial in mound 2 had been Anglo-Saxon in date. Mound 4 proved likewise to have been robbed, but still contained the remains of a cremation in a bronze bowl.

The following year, 1939, Brown yielded to Mrs Pretty's desire to excavate mound 1 and began work on this substantial task. It was not long before he began to find ship rivets. These were clearly still in situ, although the timbers that they had once held together had long since decayed, leaving only a hard discoloration. Brown decided that he should trace the timbers from the inside, following the rivets, a task which he performed admirably. Maynard, who had been keeping an eye on progress, began discreetly to enquire about other ship burials, rare finds then as now, to provide them with comparative information. Soon rumours began to circulate in the archaeological world that a new ship burial had been discovered, and Charles Phillips from Cambridge University came to take a look.

He was bowled over by what he saw and at once started the process that was to bring in professional archaeologists. This took a month to achieve, however, as Europe was poised on the brink of war. Meanwhile Brown continued his painstaking work, uncovering the ghostly timbers of the great ship, some 27.5 metres (90 feet) long. He came upon the burial chamber and covered it up for later study.

THE PROFESSIONALS STEP IN

On July 8 Phillips returned to the site to direct a team of assorted archaeologists who had been roped in and who were to become some of the most distinguished names in archaeology: Stuart Piggott and his wife (later Margaret Guido), O.G.S. Crawford, William Grimes, assisted on some days by Grahame Clark, John Ward-Perkins and John Brailsford. They began systematically to excavate the interior of the ship and on July 21 the first jewelled object appeared, a beautiful, pyramid-shaped strap mount of gold set with pieces of garnet in a geometric design. The excavators were filled with excitement. More goldwork began to appear the next day, coming thick and fast: a set of decorative plaques of gold, garnet and glass from a purse still surrounding a heap of coins, several gold and garnet mounts from a sword belt and a superb gold buckle decorated all over with interlaced sinuous designs of stylized and elongated animals. Further treasures appeared in the following days and were recorded, lifted and packed. By July 30 the excavation was complete.

A team from the Science Museum in London now stepped in to survey and record the ghostly fabric of the ship, making plans and taking photographs (which, unfortunately, were destroyed the following year in the Blitz). On August 14 a coroner's inquest was held and the material was deemed not to be treasure trove as there had

---

Above: *Like many of the panels on the helmet, the massive gold belt buckle from the Sutton Hoo burial is decorated with sinuous patterns of interlaced animals and birds.*

---

been no intention of recovering it. It was therefore the property of Mrs Pretty, who, with exceptional generosity, donated it to the nation, to be housed in the British Museum, where it is still one of the main attractions.

ANALYZING THE FINDS

On September 3, 1939 war was declared and archaeology had to take a back seat for six years. The Sutton Hoo finds were stored in a disused part of the London Underground, returning to the light in 1945, when they were made the responsibility of a young assistant keeper, Rupert Bruce-Mitford, aided by a team of assistants. Their study was to become his life's work. Many of the pieces were damaged as the wooden burial chamber had collapsed on them in antiquity. Others were of materials such as iron that required skilful conservation to reveal their original appearance. Many objects had partly decayed away, leaving only the arrangement of their non-perishable portion as clues to their original form – for example, the drinking vessels and bottles of horn and wood, of which only the decorations at the mouth survived. Several objects, such as the helmet, were at first wrongly reconstructed, but redone when clues from contemporary material made the correct form clear.

One of the most vexed questions was the apparent absence of a body in the grave. Had this been a cenotaph, erected for a king who died far from home? Opinions varied and speculation was rife. Only in recent years has the answer been given. New excavations at Sutton Hoo were undertaken between 1986 and 1992, uncovering many simple flat graves. These contained "sand bodies" – discoloured and hardened soil replacing the decayed bodies of the dead. Advanced analytical techniques now make it possible to identify where human remains have once been from the chemicals they leave behind. These tests made it possible to establish that the ship burial had originally contained a body.

ROYALLY FURNISHED

The person buried in mound 1 at Sutton Hoo was clearly someone of considerable importance, presumably a king. In order to send him off fittingly to the other world, his followers had dragged a huge ship from the River Deben to the burial ground, already designated an elite cemetery and containing other splendidly furnished graves, including mound 2, in which the burial chamber was covered by a ship. Once the great ship was in place a funerary chamber was constructed within it and offerings hung on the walls. On the east wall were a huge cauldron with a long chain by which to suspend it, two smaller cauldrons and a tub. Against the west wall were placed a great shield, decorated with gilded fittings in the form of dragons and a bird of prey, a stone sceptre surmounted by a bronze ring bearing the figure of a stag, and an iron standard. A bronze hanging bowl and a wooden lyre in a beaver-skin bag were hung on the south wall, against which leaned five spears, three angons (pikes) and a fine bronze Coptic bowl from North Africa or the eastern Mediterranean.

A large wooden coffin was then placed in the chamber and the king's body laid within it. Around him were heaped some of his personal possessions, including a down pillow, shoes and other clothing, a coat of mail, a silver bowl, combs, wooden bottles and many other objects. The coffin was closed with a substantial lid and further offerings placed on top of it. At one end was a heap of silver bowls and two silver spoons. Elsewhere along the top of the coffin were arranged a set of gaming pieces, a huge silver dish that had come from Constantinople, a set of wooden bottles, two massive drinking vessels made from the horns of the huge and ferocious aurochs (European wild cattle) and a quantity of parade armour. This included two spears, a belt with massive golden fittings, from which was suspended the gold and garnet purse, and another belt from which hung his sword, decorated with several gold and garnet mounts. There was also a fabulous helmet, made of iron decorated with bronze plates on which two scenes from Anglo-Saxon legends were shown. Gilded bronze covered the nose and ended in a moustache, making up the body and tail of a bird whose wings were formed by the gilded

eyebrows. Between them was the bird's head, with tiny garnets for eyes, and a beast with a similar head came down to meet it, head to head, from the crest of helmet.

WHO WAS HE?

Various clues in the grave may make it possible to identify the king who was buried here. For a start the burial presented an interesting mixture of Christian and pagan symbolism. The two silver spoons bore the names "Saul" and "Paul" and could have been a christening gift. Some other objects, such as the imported silver bowls, might also have a Christian significance. On the other hand, ship burials were a traditional pagan rite for dead kings, who were sometimes cast adrift on the sea in a ship that had been set on fire.

Another useful clue is the date of the grave goods. The 37 coins found in the purse are Frankish tremisses, all minted between

AD 575 and 625. They were accompanied by three gold coin blanks and it has been suggested that together these made up 40 gold pieces to pay 40 imaginary rowers to row the deceased to the afterlife.

Taken together, we have a picture of a king who had toyed with Christianity but was a pagan at heart and who died in the early seventh century. These considerations make it likely that the body in mound 1 is that of Raedwald, King of East Anglia, a Christian convert who rapidly slipped back into paganism and who died in 625.

Below: *The decorative plaques on this replica of the Sutton Hoo helmet show two scenes, repeated several times: a pair of warriors dancing in one and in the other a mounted warrior riding over a fallen enemy who stabs up at him.*

ANOTHER KING

Remarkably, in 2003 another similar intact royal burial came to light, at Prittlewell near Southend in Essex. A team from the Museum of London was asked to investigate a piece of land before road construction took place. Part of an Anglo-Saxon cemetery had been uncovered nearby in earlier years, so the team was not surprised to find further Saxon burials there. They were amazed, however, when they found the outline of a huge pit, 4 metres (13 feet) wide, and investigated its contents. As they removed the soil they came upon a bronze bowl, apparently lying on its side, but with an iron hook through its handle. It was, in fact, still hanging on the wall of what had been a wooden burial chamber.

All the wood in the chamber had completely disintegrated, as had all the other organic remains, including the body, bones and all, but clues skilfully picked up by the archaeologists allowed them to reconstruct a great deal of the tomb's contents: the iron nails outlining the coffin, for example, the stain left by a decayed wooden lyre and tiny fragments of gold thread tracing the richly decorated neckline of the deceased's garment. The richness of the grave goods, many of which resemble those from Sutton Hoo, showed that here, too, was a royal burial.

Around the chamber walls were arranged many of the king's possessions: a sword and shield; a number of valuable imports including an eastern Mediterranean bronze bowl and elaborate jug and an iron folding stool, a rare and kingly object; four precious glass vessels with trailed floral decoration; wooden bottles with gilded mounts; a set of bone gaming counters along with two large antler dice and many other objects. Aurochs-horn drinking vessels (of which only the gilt mounts survive) and an iron standard are royal objects, matching those from the Sutton Hoo burial.

A magnificent gold belt buckle lay where the king's waist would have been, two Merovingian gold coins were perhaps in his hands, and in the region of his vanished head were two crosses of gold foil, perhaps laid over his eyes. These provide a clue to his identity, for they suggest that he was a Christian; a Byzantine silver spoon, perhaps a baptismal gift, might support this. The gold coins and the style of objects indicate that the king was alive early in the seventh century AD. The most likely identification therefore, is King Sabert of the East Saxons. He was the nephew of Ethelbert, king of Kent, who was converted to Christianity by Saint Augustine, and he himself was also converted. However, when both kings died in 616, Sabert's sons immediately threw off Christianity and

reverted to paganism. This burial seems a plausible expression of an uneasy religious compromise: a pagan tomb rather than a grave in the king's church, a set of appropriately regal grave goods rather than the simplicity of a Christian burial, but the inclusion of Christian symbols.

THE STAFFORDSHIRE HOARD

One day in July 2009 Terry Herbert, a metal detector enthusiast, began to explore a Staffordshire field; he had enjoyed metal detecting for more than a decade but had so far found little of note. But this was to be a day unlike any other: he was on the brink of a discovery that would astound archaeologists, capture the public imagination and have thousands of people queuing for hours for their chance to see a temporary exhibition of his finds.

The farmer who had given him permission to search the field had ploughed it more deeply than usual, penetrating previously

---

Below: *The remains of a gold plaque that depicts two eagles with blue-glass eyes holding a fish between them. This is one of the many fine pieces from the Staffordshire hoard of Anglo-Saxon metalwork.*

---

undisturbed layers of soil and bringing their contents nearer to the surface. To Herbert's astonishment he began to find pieces of gold and silver. He investigated the field for six days, discovering more and more precious objects. Then he carefully packed them up and contacted Duncan Slarke, the local Finds Liaison Officer of the Portable Antiquities Scheme, to report his discovery. The Portable Antiquities Scheme has been a highly successful project, providing an official place for responsible metal detectorists, like Herbert, and other members of the public to report old objects they have discovered, thus enabling archaeologists to record their details and where they were found. This means that the information about an object and its context can be studied, contributing to our knowledge about the past.

Slarke sensed Herbert's excitement but was quite unprepared for the dramatic scale of the find. As Herbert showed him box after box of Anglo-Saxon metalwork, Slarke's amazement grew. Not only was the quantity remarkable but the objects themselves were extraordinary: they belonged to a period from which very little metalwork survives in Britain, and they included no pieces of jewellery, which make up the majority of previously discovered Anglo-Saxon metal objects.

But there was a downside to the find. If word got out about the discovery, hordes of treasure seekers would descend on the field, removing any remaining material and destroying all the contextual evidence that would allow archaeologists to unravel the mystery of this extraordinary collection of objects. A team of archaeologists was quickly assembled and for several months conducted a secret investigation and excavation of the area around the find, ensuring that every possible clue was recovered and every last object removed. Terry Herbert and a trusted friend, sworn to secrecy, watched the operation, their excitement overtopped by that of the archaeologists, who knew they were involved in uncovering a find to rival the wonderful Sutton Hoo ship burial. Remarkably, all the participants managed to conceal their excitement from the outside world and the find remained a complete secret until it was officially announced as headline-grabbing news on 23 September 2009: a hoard of more than 1,300 objects, more than a third of them of gold.

Initially the quantity of gold discovered – 5 kg, in contrast to the 1.7 kg found at Sutton Hoo – and its potential value dominated the reports. The hoard's value has now officially been assessed at £3.285 million, a sum that will be divided between Terry

Herbert, as the finder, and the landowner of the field in which it was found. But soon the sheer beauty of many of the objects and the mystery of their burial overtook the initial excitement about their value and captured the public imagination. What was the story behind this hoard?

Stylistically the objects probably date from the late sixth to early eighth centuries AD, a time when Staffordshire was the heartland of the Anglo-Saxon kingdom of Mercia. For much of this period Mercia controlled most of the Midlands, flanked by other, competing Anglo-Saxon kingdoms: Wessex, East Anglia and others to the south, and its main rival, Northumbria, to the north. At this time Christianity was becoming strongly established in parts of England, including Northumbria, but some kings remained pagans, including the Mercian king Penda, who defeated the Northumbrians in 641. He fell in 655 in another battle with the forces of the Northumbrian king, Oswiu. Many of Penda's children were Christians,

---

Above: *This gold strip from the Staffordshire hoard, with its martial message, may originally have decorated a sword belt, shield or sword hilt, or been attached to a church object.*

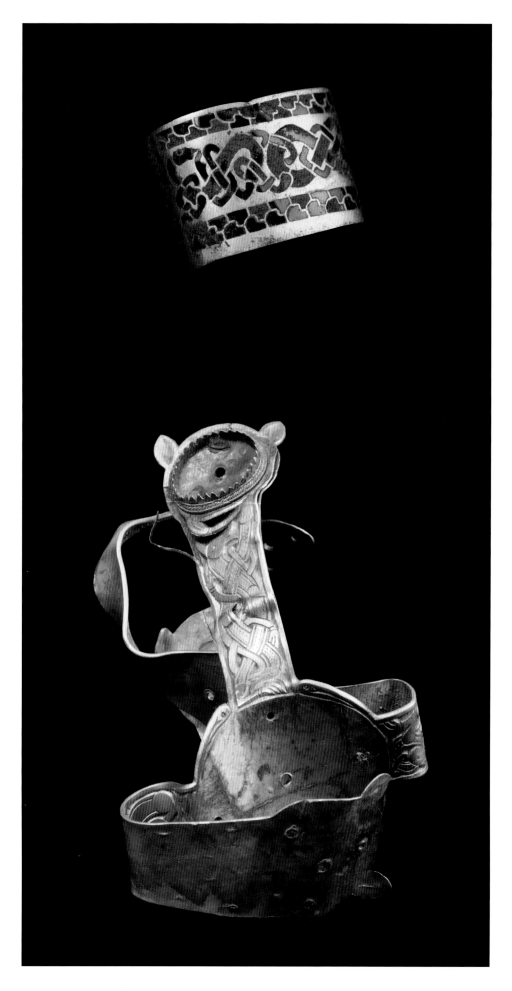

including Wulfhere who became king in 658. He and his brother Aethelred, who succeeded him, continued their father's wars with neighbouring kingdoms, as did their successors.

This is the backdrop to the remarkable Staffordshire hoard. Almost all of the 655 gold and 545 silver objects in the hoard are fittings from weaponry, including 84 pommel caps and 71 hilt collars from swords, as well as fragments from scabbards, helmets and the plates decorating sword hilts. Most are extremely fine works of craftsmanship, decorated with the characteristic Anglo-Saxon patterns of interlaced animals, with garnets skillfully set in cloisonné cells and exquisite filigree work. Such objects must have been stripped from the weapons of royalty and other high nobility. The Anglo-Saxon poem *Beowulf* describes such highly decorated and valuable weaponry elements being seized as trophies after battle and treasured as heirlooms. It is plausible to interpret this amazing collection of military objects as spoils accumulated by Penda or his successors. *Beowulf* also refers to such treasures being placed in the ground. Archaeologists are now speculating that this hoard may have been buried as an offering to the gods or, more prosaically, concealed underground before a military engagement in which the owner (surely a king) perished.

Mixed in among the military gear were other objects, including three gold crosses, folded up to make them easy to stow – unlikely to be the action of a Christian, although Christian kings were not averse to looting the churches of their foes. An inscribed strip of gold, perhaps once attached to a sword-belt, was probably one of the latest objects in the hoard, provisionally dated in the early eighth century: it bore a Latin Biblical text: "Rise up, o Lord, and may thy enemies be scattered and those who hate thee be driven from thy face" – a prayer that seemingly failed to give its owner victory against the Mercian forces.

Above: *This band, taken from a sword hilt, is also from the Staffordshire hoard. It is a skilled example of gold and garnet cloisonné work and is decorated with interwoven, ribbon-like animals.*

Below: *Though most of the Staffordshire pieces were stripped from military equipment, there were also several items of ecclesiastical loot, including this large (folded) gold cross.*

VIKING TREASURES

SCANDINAVIAN TRADERS

Although raiders from Scandinavia and northern Germany plundered Britain and later settled there, many remained in the north. They were farmers but also wide-ranging traders by land and sea. Finds from the island of Helgø in Sweden provide fine evidence of such trade. Although the settlement on the island was similar to many Scandinavian farming villages, it had an unusually large concentration of workshops, producing bronze brooches and other jewellery in moulds, and working iron into tools and weapons. It was probably also an important religious centre. The island's far-flung trading links are underlined by the discovery of a small bronze statuette of the Buddha, an import from India, perhaps acquired in the eastern Mediterranean by a trader or mercenary and brought home. A hoard of gold discovered on the island

contained 47 Roman gold coins and a heavy gold armring probably made by melting down further coins. Such wealth in the area indicates substantial trading, perhaps in furs from the far north.

Other rich finds from Helgø took the form of small plaques of gold foil, depicting figures perhaps from Scandinavian mythology. These were probably votive offerings, buried in the ground. At Sorte Mulde, a probable shrine on the Swedish island of Bornholm, around 2,300 of these plaques were discovered.

The growing power of individual leaders, some of whom now wielded kingly authority, is dramatically shown by the three great tumuli at Gamla Uppsala where the Swedish Svear kings of the sixth century were traditionally said to have been buried. These mounds were investigated in the nineteenth century and the magnificence of the grave offerings in them supported the tradition. Cremation burials had been placed within the mounds, accompanied by jewellery made of gold encrusted with garnets. In other Svear royal graves at Vendel, the royal dead were laid out on boats surrounded by all their valuables, in much the same way as the contemporary burial at Sutton Hoo in England.

BARBARIANS IN BRITAIN

Ferocious Anglo-Saxon raiders and settlers had troubled the shores of Britain since late Roman times, the Romans organizing an efficient coastal defence system against them. Even after the Romans officially withdrew in 410, the Britons continued their fight against barbarian raiders, particularly concentrating in the west, establishing strongholds in hillforts first defended by ramparts in the pre-Roman Iron Age and now refurbished. The Britons were also beset from the north by tribes who had never been conquered by the Romans, among them the Picts from central Scotland and the Dalriada from Ireland, who had settled in south-west Scotland.

By the ninth century many kingdoms were established in Britain, including the Picts, the Saxon kingdoms of eastern England and British realms like Rheged in the west. Christianity was widely practised.

Below left: *This silver bracelet, found in the important Viking trading centre at Helgo in Sweden, is in the form of a curled sea monster with a snake-like head and a pattern of swirling scales engraved on its sides.*

Below right: *A hoard of silver concealed in the seventh century at Norrie's Law in Fife included this fine pair of unusual silver plaques incised with traditional Pictish symbols and possibly dogs' heads.*

Now a new threat began to emerge: in 793 a large band of Vikings from Scandinavia descended upon the monastery of Lindisfarne off the Northumbrian coast and sacked it. This was the first recorded raid on England by bands of warrior seafarers who were beginning to ravage the lands bordering the North Sea. Political turmoil on the European mainland had left these sea lanes virtually empty, encouraging movements by Scandinavian groups who had profited by trade in earlier centuries and who now began to employ the more direct method of helping themselves to the riches of the settled world, particularly those that were beginning to accumulate in Christian holy places such as churches and monasteries. The Swedes continued their lucrative trade through eastern Europe with the Byzantine Empire and the Mediterranean, but the Danes and Norwegians raided and later settled in parts of Scotland, Ireland and northern England, as well as Normandy, whence they came in 1066 to conquer England.

Many hoards deposited in the ninth to the eleventh centuries bear witness to these Viking incursions. Several examples have been discovered in Pictish lands. In the 1840s eight large silver bowls were found, thrust into one of the cells between the two layers of wall in the Broch of Burgar on Orkney, a much earlier fortified structure. Within the bowls were found silver chains, combs and pins and many amber beads. More recently, in 1958, a hoard was found on St Ninian's Isle in Shetland, concealed from Viking raiders beneath a slab in what would have been a church at that time (now incorporated into a later church). It consisted of 28 pieces of silver: hanging bowls, spoons, pins, various mounts for sword and scabbard and 12 beautiful brooches.

LEFT BEHIND

Viking raiders on the rampage also deposited hoards, storing them while continuing their attacks, and occasionally did not return. One such hoard was deposited at Croydon, just south of London, during the winter of 872, when a Viking army wintered here. This consisted of 250 coins of very diverse origins, not only from the Saxon kingdoms of Wessex, Mercia and East Anglia but also from Carolingian Europe and even from the Arab world. The hoard also contained three silver ingots and some scrap silver (known as hack silver) in a cloth bag.

A most impressive Viking hoard was discovered in 1840 in a lead-lined chest at Cuerdale in Lancashire, England. Dating from around 905, one theory is that it was assembled from many Viking sources to finance an expedition against Dublin, from which the Vikings had been evicted in 902. Some of the silver in the hoard had been brought from Ireland, but it also contained numerous coins minted specially in York, another Viking town of the time. The Cuerdale silver hoard weighed about 40 kilograms (88 pounds) and contained around 7,500 coins and approximately 1,000 pieces of hack silver: armrings, brooches, ingots and fragments of broken silverware. Some of the ingots had repeatedly been cut

when suspicious Vikings decided to check that they were genuinely silver all through.

Plenty of treasures were nevertheless carried home to Denmark and Norway. There some suffered a similar fate, being deposited in the ground for safe keeping and never retrieved. This happened to a beautiful deep silver bowl decorated with birds which had been made in the Carolingian Empire in France or Germany during the eighth century and which was buried, along with five smaller silver cups, in a field at Fejø in Jutland, Denmark. Another hoard concealed a century later at Hon in Norway comprised a wealth of beautiful gold jewellery, bead necklaces, silver and coins from Britain, France, Byzantium and the Arab world.

The largest Viking hoard yet known, however, was found in 1999 on Spillings farm on the Swedish island of Gotland near Bogeviken, an important Viking harbour where there was a major trading settlement. Remarkably, more than 700 Viking hoards have been recovered from this small island in modern times. Buried beneath the wooden floor of a Viking hall, the Spillings hoard consisted of three separate heaps, two of silver, weighing 25 kilograms (55 pounds) and 40 kilograms (88 pounds) respectively, and one of bronze, around 20 kg (44 pounds) in weight. The silver hoards were composed of bracelets, rings, armbands and other jewellery of Viking manufacture, ingots and more than 14,000 coins, mainly from the lands of the Arabs, Persians and Khazars with whom the Swedish Vikings traded. The pieces of jewellery were often fastened together into multiples of a mark (a Viking measure of weight, around 200 grams/7 ounces), and were probably payments, perhaps of taxes.

Opposite: *The enormous hoard of silver concealed by Vikings at Cuerdale beside the River Ribble in Lancashire in 905 is made up of a great variety of silver jewellery and dress ornaments as well as hundreds of coins.*

Above: *When the English were successful in defending themselves against Viking raids, the Vikings would turn their attentions on Francia (France), from which one raiding party carried home this fine silver bowl.*

Below: *These silver coins depicting Viking longships were minted in the important trading town of Hedeby in Denmark but were found in Birka, another major trading centre in Sweden.*

The coins' dates and the style of jewellery suggest these hoards were deposited around 870. In contrast, the bronzes were mostly broken pieces of jewellery, made in nearby eastern Baltic lands, from Finland to Lithuania, probably in the seventh century. They had been stowed in a locked wooden chest and had probably been imported as a consignment of scrap metal for reuse.

PREVENTED FROM RESTING IN PEACE

Not all the surviving Viking treasures derive from hoards. An exciting find made in 1904 was a royal burial at Oseberg in Norway. In 834 a queen had been laid to rest here in a trench lined with blue clay; this sealed in moisture, with the result that organic materials survived. A small ship was buried in the trench and behind its mast the burial

chamber was constructed. For additional transport, the queen was provided with a wagon, ornately carved with sinuous patterns, 12 horses and four sledges. Five beds were included, with down- and feather-filled bedding. A great selection of domestic objects were also present, such as wooden buckets, a woollen tapestry wall-hanging, many tools and materials for sewing and weaving, and farming tools as well as two oxen and a bucket of apples. The queen was accompanied by a younger woman, possibly a relative.

Of the valuable jewellery that had undoubtedly been placed in the grave there remained not a scrap. The grave had been robbed in antiquity, probably shortly after the burial took place. The robbers even took the queen's left upper arm and right hand, presumably for the rings and bracelets on

them. Treasure hunting, however, may not have been their only purpose: they may also have aimed to disturb the queen's burial and harm her body, preventing her powerful spirit from continuing to exercise authority beyond the grave.

Opposite: *The remarkable Oseberg ship was probably built as a royal yacht, for river sailing or rowing. Carved panels of interlaced animals decorate the bows and stern.*

Below: *Silver ingots and cut-up jewellery from a ninth-century Viking hoard were found in 2007 near Harrogate, England. They were packed inside an exquisite silver bowl, along with more than 600 silver coins.*

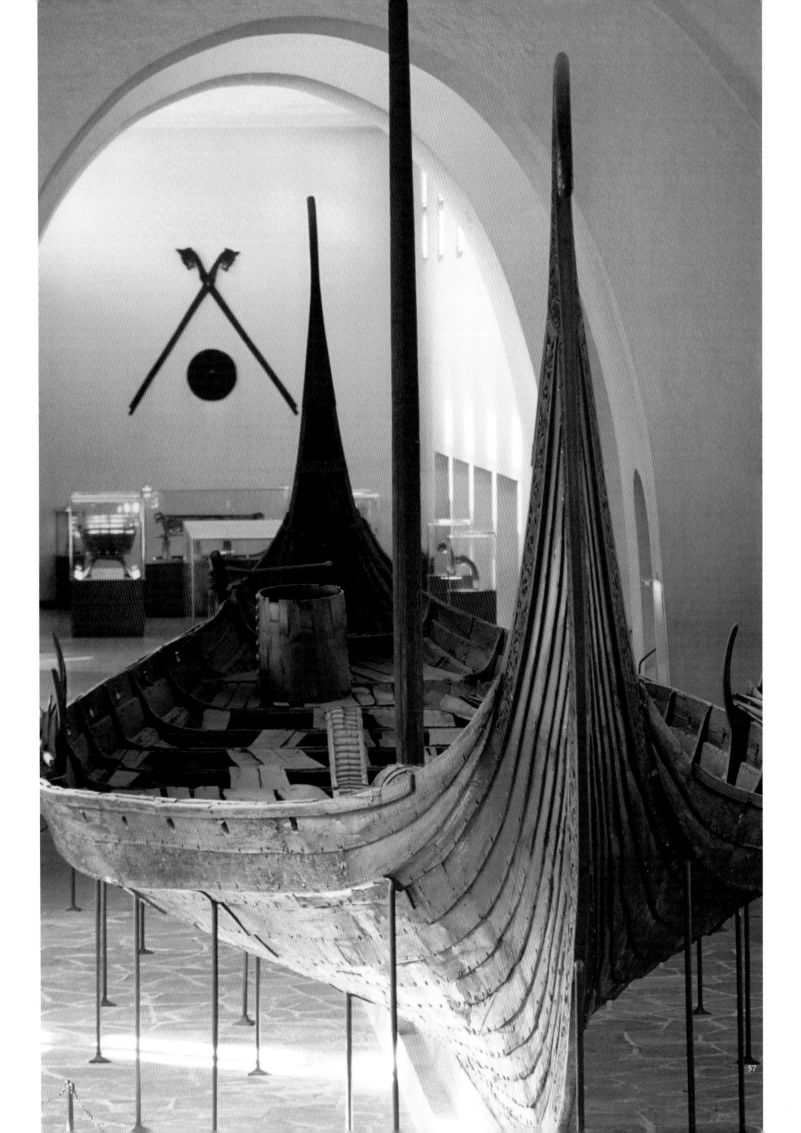

WRECKS OF THE SPANISH ARMADA

SPAIN AGAINST ENGLAND

The close relationship that had existed between England and Spain in the early sixteenth century was shattered by Henry VIII's adoption of the new Reformed (Protestant) Religion and his divorce from his Spanish queen, Katherine of Aragon. His daughter Mary attempted to return England to the Catholic faith and Spain again became involved with England when its king, Philip II, married Mary, a marriage unpopular with her subjects. Her death in 1558 broke this link and under her successor Elizabeth I (reigned 1558–1603), England was again a Protestant land. Almost at once, Philip received a personal rebuff when Elizabeth tactfully declined to marry him. Elizabeth was an extremely shrewd politician and spent the first 30 or so years of her reign skilfully playing off Spain against France. Nevertheless, by 1584 England's relations with Spain were seriously strained. The Netherlands, fighting for independence from Spain, received a measure of support from England; Spain supported the cause of Mary Queen of Scots, who laid claim to the English throne; and English sailors, particularly Sir Francis Drake, were attacking Spanish shipping and Spanish-American colonies, unofficially but with Elizabeth's private approval. The situation came to a head in 1587 when Elizabeth was at last compelled to execute Mary Queen of Scots for treason. Mary named Philip as her heir to the English throne.

Philip now began to prepare for war, counting (wrongly) on the support of many English Catholics. He planned to ship a large army into England, drawn mainly from his troops fighting in the Netherlands under the Duke of Parma, one of the finest soldiers of the time, while the fleet that had carried them swept the English Channel. Spanish preparations were set back when Drake "singed the King of Spain's beard" by raiding Cádiz, capturing a great ship loaded with

Right: *This near-contemporary representation of the sea battle in the English Channel between the large unwieldy Spanish vessels of the Armada and the smaller swifter English ships was painted by the Dutch artist Hendrick Cornelisz Vroom.*

treasure and destroying the barrels needed to carry supplies for the Armada (Spanish fleet). Elizabeth took advantage of the delay, raising militia, erecting a string of beacons around the English coast as an early-warning system and ordering coastal towns to provide ships for their defence. England already had a fine navy, organized and constructed under

the direction of Sir John Hawkins: 25 first-class ships, small but extremely manoeuvrable and armed with long-range guns. Many private merchant vessels provided a naval reserve, ready to defend home waters and often involved in the overseas privateering ventures.

THE ARMADA SAILS

On May 28, 1588 the great Spanish Armada of 130 ships set sail from Lisbon, but was forced by storm damage to put in at Corunna to refit. It set sail again on July 21 and on the 29th was sighted off Devon, south-west England. The Spanish admiral, Medina Sidonia, followed orders to make straight for a rendezvous with

the Duke of Parma. The English fleet of 80 ships, commanded by Lord Howard of Effingham, with Drake, Hawkins and Martin Frobisher under him, snapped at the Spaniards' heels but there was no general engagement. Nevertheless, the Spaniards were already demoralized by these encounters: their huge galleons were difficult to manoeuvre and their tactics of naval warfare were to close with enemy ships, bombard them with heavy fire, grapple on to them and engage in hand-to-hand fighting, where their superior numbers would give them the advantage. It was already clear that these tactics were of little use against the small, fast and manoeuvrable English vessels.

Below: *This chart, painted in 1588 by Auguste Ryther, shows the route taken by the Armada: its invasion through the English Channel and the attempt by surviving ships to return to Spain around Scotland and Ireland. Only half the fleet made it back.*

The Armada anchored off Calais. The English fleet anchored nearby and was joined by more ships, bringing its total to around 140. Medina Sidonia now received a major setback: the Duke of Parma sent a message saying that the Spanish troops required a further fortnight to make preparations before embarking for England. The following night the English attacked the Spaniards with fireships: empty vessels filled with tar, set on fire and designed to explode when left to drift among the enemy. In their haste to escape from these, many Spanish vessels cut their cables instead of weighing anchor and so were unable to anchor again. By the following morning there was a confused mass of tangled ships, only a small proportion of them safely at anchor off Calais, while many were being blown away along the Flanders coast.

DISASTER

Battle was now joined off Gravelines. Many of the scattered Spanish ships succeeded in rejoining the flagship, but the Spanish fleet was dangerously near the shallow waters and sandbanks of the Flanders shore and at a great disadvantage

Above: *Many attempts were made over the years to recover the wrecks of Armada ships and the rich objects carried by many of their officers. These illustrations show eighteenth-century diving equipment in use.*

against the swift English ships. Sadly mauled, short of supplies, with the winds against them, the officers of the Armada decided on August 9 to return to Spain by sailing round Scotland. The English fleet pursued them for a while but turned south on August 13 on reaching the Firth of Forth. By now there was no longer an Armada, only a collection of ships, each operating independently. Rumours flew in Europe, the Spanish proclaiming a great victory; these were gradually overtaken by true reports of their disastrous defeat.

Seven ships of the Spanish fleet had been lost during the fighting and many more were badly mauled. At least eight Spanish ships are known to have been wrecked on Ireland, and in several instances their men were robbed of everything by the peasants and put to the sword by the English garrison. Nineteen or more ships were lost on their way round the

British coast, the last, *San Pedro Mayor*, as it thankfully re-entered the Channel, believing its troubles to be over. A further 35 are unaccounted for. Only 67 ships of the Armada managed to return to Spain. One, *La Urca Doncella*, was wrecked as it reached the Spanish port of Santander – it had no anchor and could not stop.

ON THE TRAIL OF SPANISH TREASURE

The ship carrying the Armada's paymaster-general, the *San Salvador*, had been damaged early in the fighting and had been captured by the English. Nevertheless, many of the other vessels could be expected to have had considerable treasures aboard, including the personal property of the Spanish grandees who took part in the expedition. One ship captured by Drake, the *Rosario*, yielded 55,000 gold ducats. Many were plundered by the inhabitants of the shores on which they were wrecked, but others sank before they could be looted. Numerous attempts have been made over the centuries to locate the missing ships and to recover their treasures. Of those not stripped at the time, five have been investigated and the location of at least four others is known.

EL GRAN GRIFÓN

On September 27, 1588 *El Gran Grifón*, flagship of the Armada's supply squadron, badly damaged in the battles with the English fleet and further savaged by the sea, ran aground on Fair Isle in the far north. Most of the crew were able to escape to land and by December succeeded in hiring a Scottish ship and making their way to Leith, the port of Edinburgh. From here, along with other survivors, they eventually sailed for Spain under safe conduct from Elizabeth but were intercepted by a Dutch fleet and most perished.

The wreck of *El Gran Grifón* remained on the rocks of Stroms Helier at Fair Isle. Many of her valuables were taken off at the time of the wreck and other material salvaged by the locals. Eventually she sank. In 1720 Captain Jacob Rowe patented a new diving device, a brass horn like an enormous diving suit from which the diver's arms protruded. It was enormously uncomfortable but proved effective for depths down to about 32 metres (108 feet). Rowe and a partner, William Evans, decided to work on the

Fair Isle wreck, believing it to be a much more valuable ship, but after raising a couple of cannon they realized the difficulty of the task and abandoned it for the better chance of treasure on the wreck of the *Adelaar* (see page 66).

No further attempt was made to investigate *El Gran Grifón* until 1970, when a team of archaeological divers began work here. They found that nothing remained of the fabric of the ship, but guns and lead ingots still marked its location. Further work in 1977 uncovered a quantity of iron shot used as ammunition on the guns. The violence of the sea in this inlet had destroyed and dispersed virtually every other trace of the ship. Of any treasure that the crew may have left, only one silver coin was recovered.

Above: *An engaging gold and ruby pendant in the form of a salamander was among the objects recovered from the wreck of the* Girona. *The ship was carrying many nobles and their personal treasures.*

THE *SAN JUAN DE SICILIA*

In late September 1588 the badly damaged *San Juan de Sicilia* limped into Tobermory Bay on Mull in the inner Hebrides. Its officers negotiated with the local laird, Lachlan Maclean, for food and water, which he gave them – in return for the loan of 100 men and weapons to help him against his old enemy, Macdonald of Mingary. Maclean spent the next few months terrorizing neighbouring islands. In November an agent of Sir Francis Walsingham (Elizabeth's secretary of state, who ran a superbly efficient secret service) got aboard the ship and blew it up.

The Earls of Argyll, Admirals of the Western Isles, had salvage rights to all shipwrecks in the area, though these were disputed by successive monarchs when the earls' loyalty was suspect or their behaviour treasonable. Rumours of wealth aboard the sunken ship began to grow and several attempts to investigate the wreck were made, using the newly developed but still primitive diving bells: these succeeded in raising a number of guns. In 1677 the job was put in the hands of the distinguished

Swedish salvage engineer Hans Alricht van Treilaben, who produced a description of the wreck and raised more guns, despite being shot at during the operations by discontented Macleans.

New technology giving hope of salvaging more came with Rowe's invention of the diving engine. Rowe, substantially in debt after the *Gran Grifón* and *Adelaar* ventures, offered his services to the 2nd Duke of Argyll, who happily raised the money to salvage the Spanish ship, and work started in 1729. As the ship had previously shown itself to be difficult to get into, Rowe and his associates spent several months systematically blowing it up. Little was left but the hull, and what treasure there was should by now have been exposed. However, Rowe found nothing but ballast and iron shot, and the project was abandoned in 1731.

There now remained almost nothing of the ship and the absence of treasure in what had been basically a troop transporter should by now have been clear. But because no treasure had been recovered people went on hoping. Many more expeditions were mounted to investigate the wreck, the most recent in 1982. One, in 1922, enabled Margaret Naylor to become Britain's first woman diver. Huge sums have been spent on these salvage attempts, but all were in vain.

THE *GIRONA*

Better luck attended the search for the treasure of the *Girona*. Don Alonso de Leiva, the Armada's second in command, was aboard the *Rata Coronada*, which ran aground at Erris, on the north-west coast of Ireland. Unable to refloat her, the Spaniards stripped and burned her and transferred to the *Duquesa Santa Ana*. Heading for neutral Scotland, this ship was wrecked in Glennagiveny Bay, but all her crew of 600 survived. Helped by the local chieftain, they were able to join the crew of the *Girona*, damaged and undergoing repairs at nearby Killybegs, on Donegal Bay. The *Girona* was one of the largest ships of the Armada, with a complement of 1,000 men. Leaving their guns and some of the men, but loaded with 1,300 people, including a number of grandees with their valuable luggage, the *Girona* set sail on October 26, heading again for Scotland. The repairs had not been adequate: they got no further than Lacada Point, rocks off the Giant's Causeway, when the rudder came adrift and the ship struck with the loss of all but five of those on board.

The site of the wreck acquired the name of Port Na Spaniagh, but the reason was forgotten and it was not until 1967 that it was investigated. Robert Stenuit, after years of research, came to the conclusion that this was the probable wreck site of the *Girona*

and with a colleague began diving here in June 1967, continuing work for two years amid the extremely difficult conditions of the area, with its strong currents, dissected seabed and heavy cover of seaweed and algae. They succeeded in recovering many valuables, most of them the personal possessions of the grandees aboard the *Girona*. These included a gold cross of a Knight of Santiago, a high honour, that belonged to de Leiva himself, nearly 50 pieces of gold jewellery such as an exquisite ruby-inlaid golden pendant in the shape of a salamander, a ring inscribed "I have nothing more to give thee", perhaps a parting love gift, as well as 405 gold coins, more than 750 silver coins and several gold chains. These are now displayed in a special room in the Northern Ireland National Museum and the wreck has been designated a protected monument, as have three other Armada wrecks, the *Juliana*, *Lavia* and *Santa Maria de Visón*, found off Streedagh Strand on the north-west coast of Ireland.

Below: *Gold coins recovered from the wreck of the* Girona. *This ship, whose loss was the most serious of the expedition, was one of four galleasses: huge ships powered by sail and oars, and armed with 50 guns.*

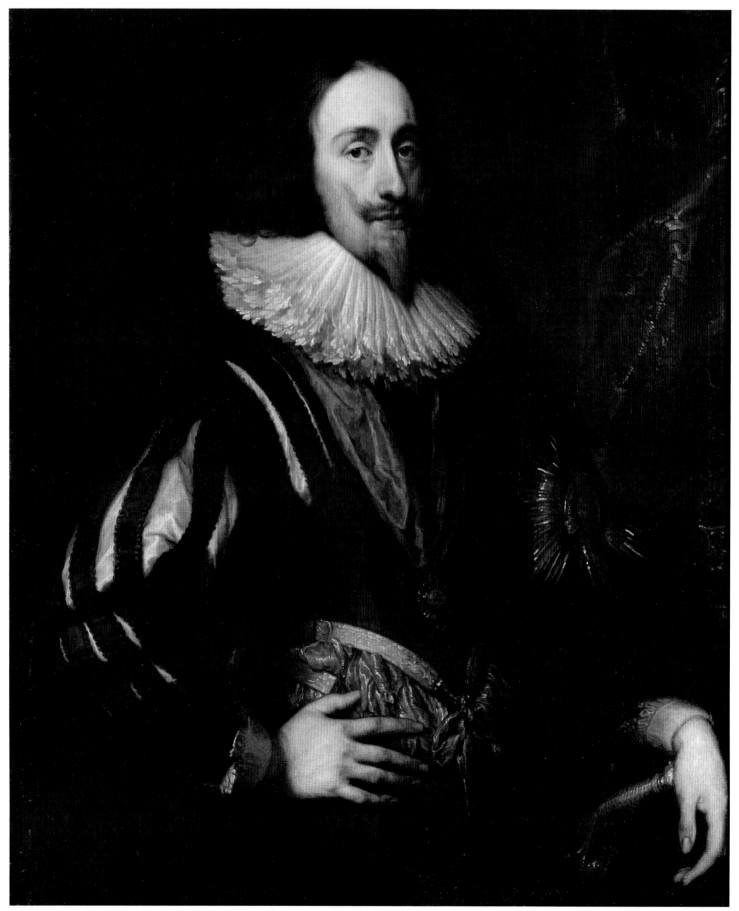

THE KING'S RETURN

When James VI of Scotland became James I of England on the death of Queen Elizabeth I in 1603, he took his family south to England and never revisited his native land. In 1625 James died and his son Charles, who had been little more than a baby when they left Scotland, became king of both realms. Charles I was crowned with great pomp in London, but the Scots required that he be separately crowned king of Scotland as the two countries were not united (and were not to be so for nearly a century). For eight years this remained a bone of contention: Charles was willing to be crowned Scotland's king in England, but the Scots quite reasonably maintained that the ceremony should take place in Edinburgh. At last, in 1633, Charles made preparations to visit his northern kingdom and receive its crown.

In May the king set forth from London accompanied by 150 lords and a huge baggage train. Determined to make an impressive show with his Scottish subjects, Charles took with him many of the royal valuables, including a huge silver dinner service, gold and jewels, tapestries to hang on the walls, church vessels and magnificent robes and garments for the many entertainments that were to take place. Many of the lords in his train were also lavishly equipped, the English determined to impress the Scots with their splendour.

Opposite: *King Charles I.*

The Scots were not to be outdone. Feverish activity had been taking place in Edinburgh for the past year: old buildings were refurbished and new ones constructed, and preparations were made for lavish entertainments such as masques, processions, banquets and displays. The coronation took place in St Giles Cathedral and was followed by great celebrations. Over the following weeks Charles made a royal progress through the Scottish lowlands, being loyally received with lavish gifts by many of his towns and noble subjects. The baggage train, already huge, swelled enormously.

THE *BLESSING OF BURNTISLAND*?

At the end of the tour, the king came to Burntisland at the mouth of the River Forth, from which he was to cross to Leith and thence set off on his homeward journey. The king and his courtiers were to make the crossing in a fine warship, the *Dreadnought*, while the baggage and the rest of his entourage were to be carried in a large ferry boat, the *Blessing of Burntisland*. Shortly after they set out a sudden storm unexpectedly got up. The *Dreadnought* experienced some difficulties but arrived safely in Leith. The *Blessing of Burntisland*, however, was seriously overloaded. A poorly secured cart broke loose and smashed into another, which unbalanced the ferry, and within minutes it had sunk. All but two of the 30 or more on board were drowned and

the king's huge treasure disappeared into 37 metres (120 feet) of water.

A red-headed woman was said to have been heard on the shore just before the fateful voyage, cursing the ferry. Was she a witch? Had she called up the storm? The idea took root and the following spring 19 people were executed as witches for allegedly creating the storm.

For centuries the ferry and its treasures lay irretrievably lost, 1.6 kilometres (1 mile) offshore in the cold, murky silts of the Forth. Modern technology, however, has at last made it possible to investigate such difficult locations and in 1997 the Burntisland Heritage Trust and the Royal Navy teamed up to search for the wreck using side-scan sonar equipment. The following year they located the wreck of a wooden vessel that they believe could be the *Blessing*, interestingly located at the spot where a dowser, Ian Longton, had predicted that it would lie. Sophisticated equipment designed by Dr Colin Stone gave the Trust an enhanced image of the wreck site, a series of bumps on the muddy bed of the Forth, and produced a sub-bottom picture confirming that a wooden wreck lay within the mud. Later divers saw and touched a timber protruding from the mud at the wreck site.

The discovery was officially announced in January 1999 and the site was designated as a protected wreck. Had they really found the *Blessing*? Presumably not, as nearly 10 years later nothing from the ferry's wreck has been recovered. The Forth still guards its secrets.

TODAY'S UNFOUND TREASURES

VIGO GALLEONS

The annual Spanish plate fleet bringing silver from the Americas reached Europe safely in 1702 – only to find that Spain was now at war with the British and Dutch and that its home port of Cádiz was under attack. The Spanish admiral, Velasco, and the commander of the French ships escorting the plate fleet therefore decided to put into Vigo in northern Spain instead. Once in the bay, they erected a boom across the harbour entrance to prevent the enemy fleet getting in. Several forts also guarded the harbour. This was in vain, however,

for when the Anglo-Dutch fleet arrived one of their ships charged and broke the boom while their soldiers on land seized the forts. The plate fleet was not strong enough to take on the British and Dutch, so Velasco gave the order to set the ships on fire and scuttle them. Two ships were captured, but one of them sank on the way back to Britain. Although it is probable that the Spanish had time to recover most of the silver before the ships sank, rumour claimed that the treasure had mainly gone down with them. Salvors have been hunting for it ever since.

Above: *A medal struck to commemorate the British and Dutch victory at Vigo Bay.*

WRECKED OFF EUROPE

THE *ADELAAR*

Early on the morning of March 25, 1728 the inhabitants of the tiny hamlet of Greian on the Hebridean island of Barra flocked to the shore to see if the previous night's storm had brought ashore any interesting flotsam. What they found far outstripped their expectations: a mass of dead bodies littered among pieces of wreckage and smashed casks. The islanders began the salvage at once. It was no time before their chief, Roderick MacNeil, appeared and took over the organization of the salvage, closing the island's shipping so that the word would not leak out. Despite his precautions, however, Macdonald of Boisdale, the local representative of Alexander Mackenzie, the Admiral of the Western Isles, came to hear of the wreck and brought in the forces of authority. He hotfooted it to Barra, where he was told that if he wanted the treasure he could take away the corpses too. He then reached an accommodation with MacNeil that gave him possession of a proportion of what had been recovered.

Mackenzie now sent his brother-in-law, Eugene Fotheringham, to supervise activities on Barra. Fotheringham was obstructed but managed to lay his hands on papers that revealed the ship's identity – she was the *Adelaar*, a VOC (Vereenigde Oost-Indische Compagnie, or Dutch East India Company) ship outward bound from Middleburg to Batavia in Indonesia, via the north coast of Scotland – and these documents gave him an idea of the ship's contents. These included a quantity of coin and general trade goods such as textiles with which to pay the local potentates in Indonesia and China for spices, porcelain and tea.

The law regarding shipwrecks was not entirely clear-cut. Did the *Adelaar*'s contents still belong to the VOC? Lawyers consulted on the matter decided hesitantly against the VOC. Could the admiral's rights be maintained by force? Probably. Mackenzie set off for Barra, backed by a troop supplied by Macdonald of Boisdale, in theory just lightly armed for their own defence on the road. With him were Jacob Rowe, the inventor of the diving engine, and his partner William Evans, frustrated by their lack of success in salvaging *El Gran Grifón* and happy to take a new commission that promised rich rewards.

The sea's strong currents made work on the wreck dangerous and had driven material from the ship into deep gullies that were hard to penetrate. Despite these extreme difficulties, however, Rowe and Evans succeeded in raising most of the treasure: 17 chests containing silver and copper coins and gold bars. It was safely conveyed to Edinburgh, where it was deposited in the Bank of Scotland.

The salvors were not to enjoy their prize, however, for now the VOC stepped in. The Dutch company claimed the salvaged treasure and, contrary to expectation, its claim was upheld in court. Mackenzie was allowed nothing but his expenses and a salvage award, the size of which provoked further dispute, and he ended the proceedings considerably out of pocket. To their disgust, he took out his feelings on Evans and his assistant John Hay, who had spent the winter devotedly continuing the salvage operations.

In 1972 a team of Scottish divers, including Colin Martin of St Andrews University, returned to the wreck and surveyed it, undertaking limited excavation two years later. Nothing was left of the ship by now but they recovered some cannon and a few small personal effects such as pieces of jewellery, as well as a great deal of valuable archaeological evidence.

THE EAST INDIES COMPANIES

France, Britain and the Netherlands were competing in the eighteenth century for control of trade with the valuable lands of the east, source of silks and other fine textiles, spices and tea as well as porcelain. The English East India Company was founded in 1600 and the VOC in 1602. The French were a bit slower to become involved, and other nations, such as Sweden and Denmark, also attempted to secure a share of the trade.

In 1746 one of the French East India Company's ships, the *Prince de Conty*, was on its homeward journey from a voyage to China, Indonesia and Brazil. It was only a few miles short of the Company's base at Lorient

---

Below: *Small ingots of Chinese gold, weighing around 370 grams (13 ounces) each, were among the cargo salvaged from the* Prince de Conty *in 1985.*

---

in Brittany when it struck on the southern headland of the small island of Belle Isle. The Company was able to salvage some of the goods aboard, using a diving bell and assisted by English prisoners. The tea had not only been ruined but had also been dispersed, as had the porcelain, but the heavier guns and the ballast were still in place where they had sunk. In 1985, archaeologists relocated the wreck and began painstaking excavations.

These recovered a quantity of Chinese Qian period porcelain, a finer grade of pottery than had hitherto been found, as well as a few fragments of the chests that had once held the tea, and a number of small gold ingots of the types also recovered from the VOC's *Geldermalsen* shipwreck.

Shipwreck was a common hazard of the time, particularly in certain stretches of the narrow and treacherous English Channel. Two VOC ships went down there on their maiden voyage within six years of each other. The *Amsterdam* was dogged by bad luck from the outset. She attempted twice to set sail in the winter of 1748, only to be driven back by adverse winds. Finally, she managed to set sail on January 8, 1749, but within a day was seized by a terrible 12-day gale and was seriously damaged. Fifty of her crew had died from illness and another 40 were sick, making the ship desperately short-handed. But instead of sinking, on January 26 she ran aground and the crew were able to walk ashore to safety. Most of her cargo was also saved, but within a short time the ship itself had sunk deep into the sands. As a result, however, the fabric of the ship was wonderfully preserved and since its rediscovery in 1969 has been intensively investigated, revealing fascinating details of the construction and furnishing of East Indiamen of the eighteenth century.

In contrast, the fabric of the *Hollandia*, which set sail on July 3, 1743, has disappeared completely. Careful recording by diver Rex Cowan and his team of the way her contents lie on the seabed, however, has made it possible to reconstruct her fate. A severe storm struck the ship while she was in the Channel between July 9–13, and she was blown off course. The captain, Jan Kelder, misjudged his position and turned southward too early, running the ship on to the Gunner Rock off the Scillies. Badly damaged, the

---

Above: *A metre-high (3¼-foot) mound of 35,000 silver coins marked the area off the Scilly Isles where the Dutch vessel* Hollandia *went down after being blown off course in 1743.*

Hollandia sailed on for about a mile then her hull gave way, spilling a trail of cargo and ballast. Sixty metres (197 feet) further on, the ship went down with the loss of all hands, including her distinguished passengers, the Imhoffs, the family of the governor of the Dutch East Indies. Their silver tableware is among the finds recovered from the wreck, along with equipment such as the ship's fire engine and a metre-high (3¼-foot) mound of 35,000 silver coins. Nothing was recovered at the time, despite determined attempts, due to the very poor visibility over the wreck site.

BARBARY PIRATES?

From the 1980s divers in the waters off Salcombe in Devon had been aware of a site where cannons were lying on the seabed. For years the South-West Maritime Archaeological Group used this as a place to train novice divers in underwater archaeological techniques, producing detailed surveys and records of the site, in the hope of pinpointing where the wreck from which the cannon came might lie. They also thoroughly investigated the documentary evidence of local shipwrecks, hoping to identify the wrecked ship, without success. But in 1995 one of the team spotted a gold coin among the underwater rocks. Suddenly they had a new focus for their investigations, and over the following two years scoured the rocks, recovering 400 gold coins, as well as minute gold ingots and pieces of gold jewellery. The coins provided a likely date for the wreck, around 1640, though still no identification. The finds also provided a great surprise: all the goldwork had originated in Morocco. Some Dutch pottery and pewter objects and a fine clay tobacco pipe were also recovered. There is now speculation that the vanished ship may have been that of the Barbary pirates who were an active menace off the southern English coast in the seventeenth century, attacking coastal settlements and occasionally carrying off girls for Moroccan harems: the white slave trade.

Left: *A gold coin, struck by the Moroccan Sa'did dynasty, and two gold snake earrings recovered from the Salcombe wreck site.*

Opposite: *An imaginative nineteenth-century painting of locals stripping the body of Sir Cloudesley Shovell. Legend says his shirt and valuable ring were stolen by two women.*

PLUNDERED WRECKS

Sir Cloudesley Shovell (1650–1707) had a distinguished naval career, which included several brushes with Moroccon pirates. In 1676 he attacked and burned four corsairs' galleys off Tripoli and in 1683 chased a 14-gun pirate ship that had recently captured the *Schiedam*, a Dutch merchant vessel. He recaptured the *Schiedam*, which later took part in a punitive attack on the pirate stronghold in Tangier. After the successful attack, *Schiedam* set sail back to England, laden with guns and horses, but she never arrived. A gale threw her upon rocks off the Lizard, where she sank. She was rediscovered in 1971 when guns, some of her timbers and a number of military artefacts were found.

By 1705, Sir Cloudesley had risen to the rank of rear admiral and was engaged in fighting in the Mediterranean. In 1707 he returned to Britain with four ships, his flagship the *Association* and the *Eagle*, the *Romsey* and the *Firebrand*. In the difficult and dangerous Western Approaches they were beset by fog. Sir Cloudesley's experience was not enough to save them and they were all wrecked upon the Scilly Isles on October 22, 1707. Sir Cloudesley's body was washed ashore and he was buried in Westminster Abbey. It is alleged that he was still alive when he came ashore, but that he was murdered by two local women.

The *Association* was known to have been carrying a considerable amount of gold and silver coinage and was therefore eagerly searched for. In the 1960s the Ministry of Defence granted salvage contracts to three separate salvage companies to recover the *Association* and her bullion. The wreck was located and salvaged in 1967 and the discovery rapidly became international news. Divers from all over the world descended on the site, and it was thoroughly looted and destroyed. Little information could be recovered about this interesting and important wreck. The only records of her contents are the sale catalogues of the auctions through which they were dispersed. This wanton destruction focused public and professional attention upon the need to protect and preserve historic wrecks, the heritage of everyone, and gave rise in the fullness of time to British legislation that controls access to and investigation of designated historic wrecks. For the *Association*, however, it was too late – so little remained of her that it was not thought worthwhile designating her final resting place as an Historic Wreck Site.

THE *KRONAN*

King Karl XI of Sweden commissioned an English shipwright, Francis Sheldon, to construct his flagship, the *Kronan*. Work began in 1665 and the ship was launched in 1668 but not completely finished until 1672. She was a mighty 60 metres (197 feet) in length and with a displacement of more than 2,134 tonnes (2,100 tons) was one of the largest ships of her time, carrying around 128 guns. In 1676 she was the vessel of Baron Lorentz Creutz, the Commander-in-Chief of the fleet defending Sweden against a combined Dutch and Danish fleet, and she carried a crew of 550 along with 300 soldiers. In a battle between the forces in late May, she managed seriously to damage the Dutch flagship. On the morning of June 1 she prepared to engage in battle again. Her gun ports were open, ready to fire on the enemy, when suddenly a freak squall caught her and she heeled over. Water poured in through the open gun ports and at the same moment there was a massive explosion in her magazine. She sank immediately, taking almost all with her. There were 42 survivors: one, Anders Sparrfelt, was blown some 50 metres (164 feet) into the air by the explosion, flew over the ships of the enemy and landed in the sail of a Swedish ship. The bodies of Creutz and many others were washed ashore over the following days. It was a disaster for Sweden.

Anders Franzen is an experienced and dedicated marine engineer. He located and raised another Swedish warship, the *Vasa*, which went down in 1628 and which is now one of Sweden's main tourist attractions.

Once work on the *Vasa* was complete, his interests turned to locating the *Kronan*. As the exact spot where the ship went down was not clearly known, Franzen had to search the area near the long stretch of shore where the bodies of the victims had been washed up. It was not even certain that the remains would be in one place, as the explosion could have scattered them widely. Initially Franzen and his colleagues used side-scan sonar to search for the ship, but abrupt temperature changes at different depths made it impossible for this to give effective results. Then they tried a magnetometer. In 1979 they explored 34 square kilometres (13 square miles) without discovering anything, but the following season their patience was at last rewarded. The magnetometer showed up a massive anomaly which proved to be the *Kronan*.

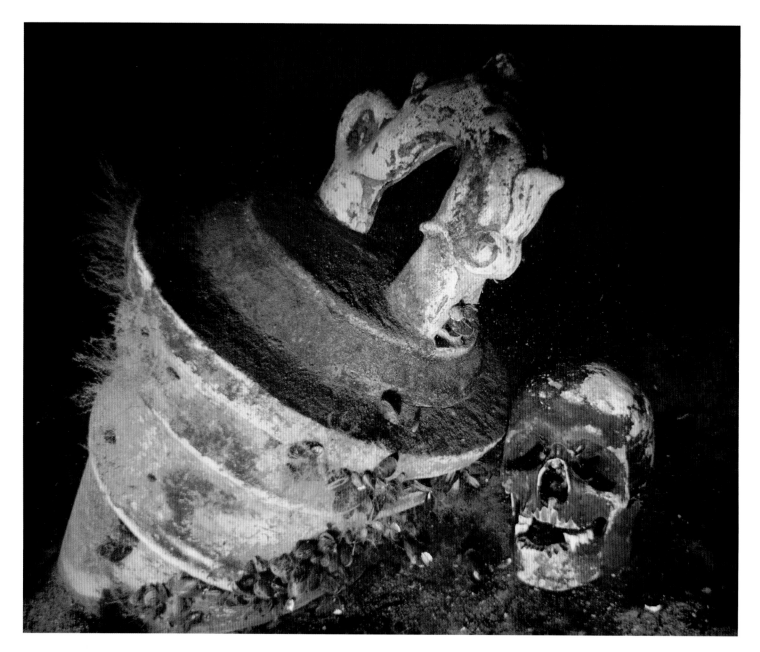

TODAY'S UNFOUND TREASURES

THE *EGYPT*

In May 1922 the P&O liner the *Egypt* was travelling through the English Channel, carrying passengers to Bombay but also loaded with more than 1,000 gold bars, a similar number of silver bars and 37 boxes of gold coins, all securely packed into the strongroom on one of the lower decks. As they passed Ushant, thick fog descended and they began sounding the foghorn at frequent intervals. Despite this precaution, a little farther south the ship collided with another vessel, the French steamer *Seine*, and everyone was forced to abandon ship. The ship sank in very deep water, so Lloyd's, her insurers, decided she could not be salvaged. It was not long, however, before they were approached by hopeful salvors, the Swedish engineer Peter Sandberg, his colleague James Swinburne and the Italian company Sorima, who managed to locate the wreck. To get into the strongroom the salvors adopted the drastic expedient of controlled explosions, directed by an underwater observer. A special grab carried away blasted debris and eventually raised the gold and silver from the strongroom. The salvors called a halt when they had recovered most of the treasure. They left behind scattered gold and silver valued in 1922 at £52,000 – several million pounds at today's prices.

Above: *Members of the Sorima team with gold bars recovered from the wreck of the* Egypt.

Work on the remains of the ship has yielded fascinating details of life in the seventeenth century, from that of Creutz himself down to those of the humble sailors. Creutz's cabin was comfortably furnished, with a leather chair embossed with the initials of himself and his wife. Among his possessions were found 105 gold coins, and a further 150 were discovered elsewhere in the ship. The ship's doctor's medical supplies were also found, along with a golden breastplate that Creutz had worn on ceremonial occasions. Other finds included a number of personal treasures: the gold ring of Creutz's wife, who had died the previous year, altered to fit the finger of her devoted husband, a book of psalms, a pair of leather mitts and a ribbon with a flower. A great

Opposite: *The skull of one of the 800 unfortunates who went down with the* Kronan *in 1676. It lies next to one of the cannons from the ship; because they were captured from various sources, there were of many different types of cannon on board.*

selection of guns from many different sources was also recovered, painting a picture of Sweden's military successes over the previous half century. Not all the ship's guns were present: despite the difficulties, some 60 had been salvaged soon after the disaster, by a team using the diving bell invented by Hans Alricht van Treilaben.

MYSTERY OF THE *BLACK SWAN*

In May 2007 the salvage company Odyssey Marine Exploration amazed the world by announcing the discovery and salvage from a mystery ship, codenamed *Black Swan*, of a cargo including 17 tonnes (18¾ tons) of gold and silver coins that they claimed are worth around $500 million. They disclosed neither the location of the find nor the ship's real identity, though they said the ship was around 400 years old. Rumours placed the ship off the Scilly Isles but outside British territorial waters or off the Spanish Algarve coast. Archaeologists in both countries have expressed dismay at the extraction of treasure from a vessel without proper recording of the historically important information that it must hold. The great advances that

have taken place in underwater exploration technology over recent years now make it possible, though still extremely expensive, to locate and salvage ships from the deep ocean. However, at present there are few laws governing legal ownership of wrecks in international waters and almost no safeguards protecting such ships from being mined for treasure. International agreement on the treatment of such wrecks is an urgent priority.

Meanwhile the Spanish authorities have gone beyond mere words. From the available evidence they think that the *Black Swan* is a Spanish ship, the *Nuestra Señora de la Mercedes*, which exploded when it was attacked by a British warship in 1804 at the Battle of Cape Santa Maria off Portugal. They have therefore taken legal action to reclaim the cargo. Under international law, any military vessel remains the property of its own state, even if sunk in international waters. The Spanish regard the site as a military graveyard since many sailors died in it, so they claim that it should not have been interfered with at all. In June 2009 a US court decided that the evidence showed this was indeed the *Mercedes* and in December

2009 it upheld the Spanish claim. However, the court also granted Odyssey Marine leave to appeal this decision and allowed them to keep the coins until the appeal decision is reached. The results of the complex litigation may set an important precedent, but it is unlikely to be resolved soon. Meanwhile, tensions run high.

Right: *Nicknamed WASP, this revolutionary underwater submersible allows a diver to explore arctic waters and recover material previously inaccessible from wrecks such as the nineteenth-century* Breadalbane.

Below: *An ROV (Remotely Operated Vehicle) is used by Odyssey Marine to investigate wreck sites at depths that are not accessible to manned submersibles. This was taken during investigations of the* Black Swan.

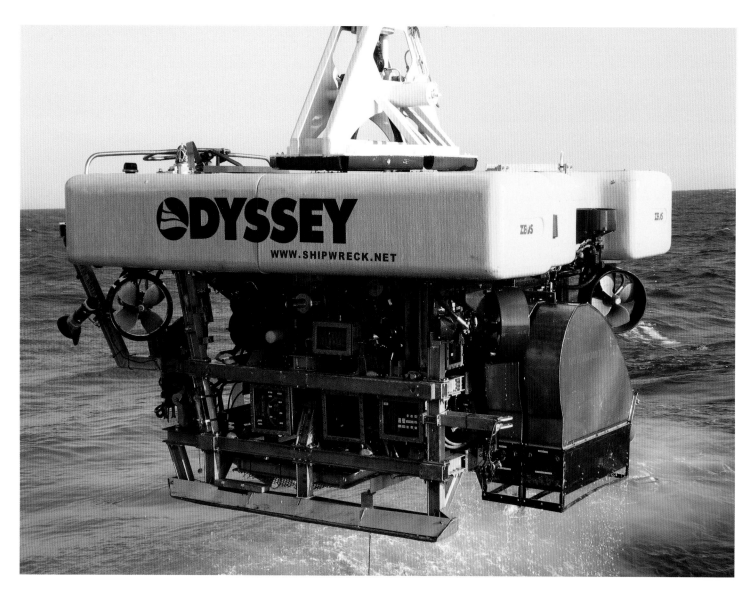

NAZI GOLD AND LOOTED TREASURES

WAR PLUNDER

September 1939. Europe was at war. Hitler and the Nazis inexorably moved forward, occupying Denmark, Norway, Poland, the Netherlands, Belgium, Luxemburg and France, Yugoslavia and Greece. The advancing military machine was accompanied by a Nazi cultural organization of equal efficiency, the ERR, performing the age-old practice of plundering the defeated but executing it with unprecedented thoroughness. Initially restricted to the property of Jews, Freemasons and other groups persecuted by the Nazis, the looting had, by 1940, been officially extended to embrace everyone's valuables. Tens of thousands of paintings, tapestries, manuscripts and other art and cultural treasures, recent and ancient, were seized, taken into "safe keeping" and transported to Berlin. Detailed catalogues of the looted treasures were prepared, running to hundreds of volumes.

In June 1941 the Nazis began to advance on the Soviet Union, their one-time ally. One of their aims, in a campaign of extreme ruthlessness and barbarity, was to wipe St Petersburg (Leningrad) from the face of the earth. Where convenient, works of art and other cultural valuables were to be confiscated but otherwise everything was to be destroyed. In September the official looters reached Peterhof, the magnificent complex of palaces and parks founded by Peter the Great outside St Petersburg, where they found thousands of books and works of art ready crated for them to take: the Russian authorities had ordered these to be packed but failed to take them to safety. Although some of the exquisite furnishings of the palaces were also removed, a great deal was wantonly and deliberately destroyed, as was the case with other palaces around St Petersburg. One of the few survivors was the Amber Room in the Catherine Palace at Tsarskoe Selo (modern Pushkin), regarded as one of the wonders of the modern world.

Below: *Italian sixteenth-century jewellery of diamonds, emeralds and rubies looted from Paris was recovered by the Americans from an Austrian castle.*

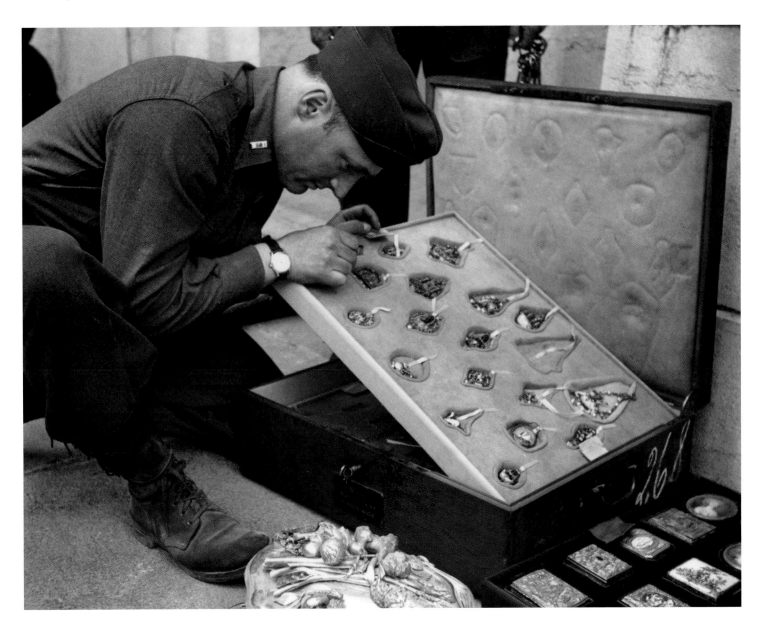

REFLECTED SPLENDOUR

The Amber Room had already had a curious wandering history. Andreas Schlüter, court architect to the kings of Prussia, first proposed the idea of a room decorated with amber to his patron, King Frederick I. Gottfried Wolfram, amber master to the Danish king, was invited to Prussia and in 1701 began work on an Amber Room in which windows would be separated by amber panels. The project had its ups and downs and Schlüter and Wolfram were both separately dismissed. The king transferred the idea to his castle at Charlottenburg, Berlin, in 1707 and in five years the room was ready. However, Frederick died the following year and his successor, Frederick William I, had the Amber Room dismantled.

The Tsar of Russia, Peter the Great, had heard of the celebrated room and when he visited Prussia in 1716 he expressed an interest in it. Frederick William presented it to him as a diplomatic gift. The following year it was transferred to St Petersburg in eight carts, packed in 18 boxes. The room proved difficult to reassemble and so the pieces were taken to the city's Summer Palace and virtually forgotten. When Peter's daughter, Elizabeth, became empress she decided to reinstate the Amber Room. There were not enough pieces for the chosen room, so she had her court architect, Bartolomeo Francesco Rastrelli, construct further mirrored pilasters to go between the amber panels. For a while the Amber Room was used for receptions.

ON THE MOVE AGAIN

In 1755 Elizabeth began work on expanding and improving the Catherine Palace and decided to install the Amber Room there. So it was again dismantled and Rastrelli supervised its installation in its new setting. This was a larger room, so again Rastrelli added new pieces: gilded sculptures, mirrors, pilasters – and canvas panels painted to look like amber. Later Catherine the Great replaced these fake panels with ones of real amber, work that was completed in 1770. The Amber Room was now in its final, glorious form. Three walls of the room were covered in amber panels arranged in three tiers. The eight large central panels included four decorated with Florentine mosaics made in tiny pieces of precious stone, depicting scenes inspired by the five senses. The whole room sparkled as the panels were reflected in the mirrors on the walls and pillars.

As the Nazis approached St Petersburg in 1941 it was decided that the Amber Room's panels were too fragile to be moved, so they were carefully covered in paper and cloth.

However, the room's fame made it an obvious target for the official Nazi art collectors. A group from the ERR supervised the packing up of the panels, a task which took several days, and these were shipped in 28 crates to Königsberg near the Polish border, the regional headquarters of the SS. Here they were displayed in Königsberg Castle as German treasures finally restored to their homeland and here they remained until 1944, when they were packed up – and subsequently vanished.

This is the last that is known of the panels from the Amber Room, despite many attempts to trace them. It seems most likely that they were consumed when Königsberg Castle was destroyed by fire, though many hopefuls continue the search, with frequent announcements that the panels' location has been identified and is about to be explored. In 1979 the Russians began constructing a replacement Amber Room within the Catherine Palace, and this was formally opened in 2003.

This is not quite the end of the story, however. In 2000 one of the additional marble and onyx panels commissioned by Catherine the Great reappeared and was offered for sale at a staggering $2.5 million. This panel, it seems, was abstracted in 1941 by one of the German officers responsible for conveying the Amber Room from St Petersburg to Königsberg. Recovered by the German police, it was formally handed over to the Russians in 2001.

Although the Allies set up a special branch of the military that successfully recovered many stolen art objects and archives and restored them to their owners, many other plundered treasures have never been recovered. Undoubtedly some were destroyed during the frenzied days of liberation, while others must have found their way into private collections. Occasionally some of these surface, as did five paintings that had belonged to an Italian Jewish family. These were found in 1999 in the possession of a New Zealand art gallery, legitimately acquired from a family who had purchased them in 1946 in an Italian market, where presumably they were being offered for sale by looters.

Right: *A watercolour gives some impression of the former splendour of the Amber Room set up in the Catherine Palace at St Petersburg.*

Overleaf: *The works of many famous artists, such as this French impressionist painting by Edouard Manet entitled "Wintergarden", were hidden by the Nazis and rediscovered by American soldiers in the Merkers saltmine.*

THE TIDE TURNS

By November 1942, despite the huge numbers of Russians who had been killed and the immense suffering of the beleaguered people of Stalingrad, dogged Soviet resistance to the Nazis was beginning to take effect. Gradually the Nazis were driven back and the Soviets advanced toward the German border. The tide was also turning in other arenas: by the middle of 1943 the Allies were in control of North Africa and in the autumn began to advance through Italy. When they landed in Normandy in June 1944 they started to slowly beat back the Nazis from the west.

The Nazis began to be concerned for the safety of both their own possessions and the foreign treasures they had looted. It was time to hide away the spoils and put their valuables beyond the enemy's reach. The paintings and furniture in particular posed a problem as it was necessary to store them in a suitable atmosphere. Salt mines, cold and with a constant humidity, made ideal hiding places and many paintings were transferred to them. So was a huge quantity of gold.

The Reichsbank in Berlin suffered a direct hit by a bomb on February 3, 1945. Although this left the safes intact, it was felt that such a narrow escape was not worth risking again and that the huge reserves of gold bullion, much of it stolen from occupied nations, should be taken somewhere less vulnerable and less accessible. It was decided that the gold and dollar reserves should be hidden in the huge Kaiseroda potassium mine at Merkers in Thuringia. The task was successfully completed by February 18.

REDISCOVERED TREASURES

But already the Allied troops had advanced well into Germany and it was not long before the Nazi authorities decided they had made a mistake. They began to transfer the more portable paper currency from the mine back to Berlin and had succeeded in moving about half when the Allies reached a point too close for comfort. Abandoning the rest of the hoard, the bank officials fled. On April 4 Merkers fell to the Americans, who had responsibility for liberating and occupying this portion of the Nazi domains. At first the goods concealed in the mine went unsuspected, but it was not long before a chance remark let slip the secret.

Immediately steps were taken to guard the mine. Going in on April 7, the Americans found themselves face to face with the remaining sacks of paper currency, placed ready to move in the main passageway but abandoned in the haste of withdrawal. After blasting away a heavy steel door that had been placed to close the passage, they found themselves in a room full of sacks of gold bars, worth more than $315,000. In addition they discovered 400 tonnes (441 tons) of paintings and other works of art, including works by Titian, Rembrandt and Raphael and the famous bust of Nefertiti, wife of the heretical Egyptian pharaoh Akhenaten, created more than 3,000 years earlier.

LOST GOLD

The Nazis still had substantial gold reserves. To safeguard these and keep them from the Allies, it was proposed that they be hidden in the National Redoubt, an area of some 52,000 square kilometres (20,000 square miles) in the Alps, where Hitler had his mountain retreat known as the Berghof. With considerable difficulty, the gold and currency were transported by road and rail to the village of Mittenwald in the National Redoubt, where they were handed over to Colonel Franz Wilhelm Pfeiffer, head of the local Alpine mountain troops. He and his men concealed the gold in carefully dug pits in the wooded mountain slopes near Lake Walchen, north of Innsbruck. Several times part of the treasure was lifted and hidden in new holes. There was a certain amount of confusion about the quantities that had been concealed and which consignments had been placed where. In all the anxiety and haste of the time it would have been easy for those involved in the transport and concealment of the treasure to remove a certain amount to line their own pockets, and there seems no doubt that some did, although the majority were worthy of their trust – and were made to suffer for it.

Rumours and incomplete tales led the Americans inexorably toward the hidden gold. Finally on June 7, led by a Nazi officer who had cracked, they were taken to the site of a series of holes from which they recovered 728 bars of gold weighing a total of 9.1 tonnes (9 tons). The delighted American soldiers posed for a group photograph, gold bars prominently displayed. Then they handed the gold over to their officers, who in great secrecy took them to the Reichsbank in Frankfurt, where they were safely stored.

Another cache of 25 boxes containing 100 gold bars was recovered from a bunker on another part of the mountain, as the result of a tip-off. The sergeant in charge of the recovery handed over the boxes, which were loaded on to trucks. These were driven off by two supposed American intelligence officers with two guards – and were never seen again.

NORTH
ATLANTIC
OCEAN

Strait of Gibraltar

Mediterranean Sea

Canary Islands

MOROCCO

TUNISIA

ALGERIA

LIBYA

EGYPT

Red Se

MAURITANIA

MALI

NIGER

CHAD

SUDAN

SENEGAL

GAMBIA

GUINEA-BISSAU

GUINEA

BURKINA FASO

SIERRA LEONE

LIBERIA

IVORY COAST

GHANA

TOGO

BENIN

ASANTE

NIGERIA

CAMEROON

CENTRAL AFRICAN REPUBLIC

ETHIO

Gulf of Guinea

EQUATORIAL GUINEA

GABON

CONGO

(DEM. REP. OF THE)
CONGO

UGANDA

Lake Victoria

KENY

RWANDA

BURUNDI

TANZANIA

1   TANIS
2   DASHUR
3   BAHARIYA OASIS
4   VALLEY OF THE KINGS
5   THEBES
6   *HARTWELL*
7   IGBO UKWU
8   *WITTE LEEUW*
9   *BOM JESUS*
10 DODINGTON
11 GROSVENOR
12 THULAMELA
13 MAPUNGUBWE
14 GREAT ZIMBABWE
15 *SAO JOSE*
16 *ESPADARTE*

ANGOLA

ZAMBIA

MALAWI

NAMIBIA

ZIMBABWE

BOTSWANA

MOZAMBIQUE

SOUTH
ATLANTIC
OCEAN

SWAZILAND

SOUTH
AFRICA

LESOTHO

Cape of Good Hope

INDIAN
OCEAN

AFRICA

Above: *The* Dodington, *one of many rich ships wrecked off the African coast.*

GOLD OF THE PHARAOHS

The ancient Egyptians believed the bodies of the dead had to be preserved for all eternity as the home of their spirit and so they mummified them. They also considered it necessary to furnish the deceased with everything that they would require in the other world: models and paintings of their servants and many of their possessions.

PROTECTING THE ROYAL DEAD

In the tombs of the pharaohs (kings), many of these offerings were made of gold and jewels. Originally pharaohs were buried within pyramids, placed near the mortuary temple where offerings were made for the benefit of their spirits. These conspicuous monuments attracted tomb robbers who, despite elaborate precautions, often succeeded in penetrating the burial chamber, carrying off the valuables on which the pharaoh depended for his eternal comfort and in many cases damaging the royal mummy in the process.

Amenhotep I (1525–1504 BC) made the first break with this tradition, being buried at some distance from his mortuary temple, and his successor, Thutmose I (1504–1492 BC), began the new practice of creating a tomb in the hills overlooking the traditional necropolis at Thebes. Here in the Valley of the Kings (actually two separate valleys) most pharaohs of the New Kingdom (sixteenth to eleventh century BC) were buried. Their tombs took the form of long, rock-cut corridors and chambers, many elaborately painted. Some queens and princes were buried nearby in the Valley of the Queens, while other parts of the hills, including Dra Aboul Naga and Deir el-Bahri, housed the tombs of important officials.

The new system proved no more effective than the old in guarding against robbers. During the troubled period of the Twenty-first Dynasty (1069–945 BC) many earlier royal mummies were moved to a place of safety in an older tomb at Deir el-Bahri to prevent further desecration. The pharaohs of this period were buried far to the north at Tanis in underground tombs of stone and brick.

Left: *The Valley of the Kings in 1922, during Howard Carter's famous investigations. The tomb of Tutankhamun can be seen in the foreground, and behind it is the entrance to Ramesses VI's tomb.*

REDISCOVERING THE PHARAOHS

Interest in ancient Egypt never really died and for many centuries mummies were ground up to make a medicine thought to have powerful properties. By the eighteenth century there was considerable scholarly and popular interest in ancient Egypt and travellers began to visit the Valley of the Kings, by this time the stronghold of bandits.

Giovanni Belzoni went to Egypt in 1815 and spent five years investigating ancient Egyptian remains, hunting for papyrus manuscripts and collecting other antiquities. He explored the Valley of the Kings and satisfied himself that he had discovered every tomb it contained. Among these was the magnificently decorated tomb of Seti I (1294–1279 BC), which contained the pharaoh's alabaster coffin. All the graves Belzoni explored had been plundered in the past, and wooden statues and broken pieces of funerary equipment were their only remaining contents.

Several other explorers investigated the Valley of the Kings during the nineteenth century and in 1898 Victor Loret discovered a cache of 13 royal mummies placed for safety in the tomb of Amenhotep III (1390–1352 BC). Like other tombs in the Valley, it had been thoroughly looted of everything saleable. Many of the Valley's tombs also suffered from flooding which damaged and disturbed their contents. In 1902 an official permit allowing exclusive exploration of the Valley of the Kings was granted to a wealthy American, Theodore M. Davis, a high-handed individual who ground down the archaeologists he engaged to excavate for him. The first of these was Howard Carter, then an Inspector of Antiquities for the Egyptian government, who located and explored several tombs, uncovering mummies and revealing wonderful tomb paintings. Davis struck lucky when his explorations revealed the well-preserved

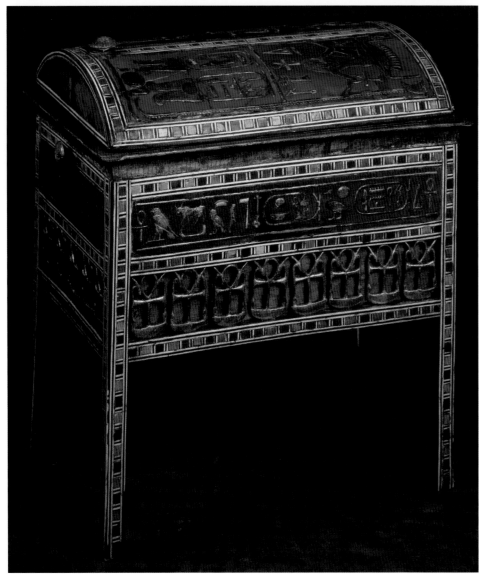

Above: *Found with other jewellery in the "Gold Tomb" in the Valley of the Kings, this earring is inscribed with the name of Tawosret, principal wife of Sety II. The small tomb was probably that of their child.*

Left: *A jewellery box of gilded wood, inlaid with ebony, ivory and faience. This probably belonged to the queen Tiye, the mother of Akhenaten, or perhaps to queen Tiye's own mother, Tuya, in whose tomb it was found.*

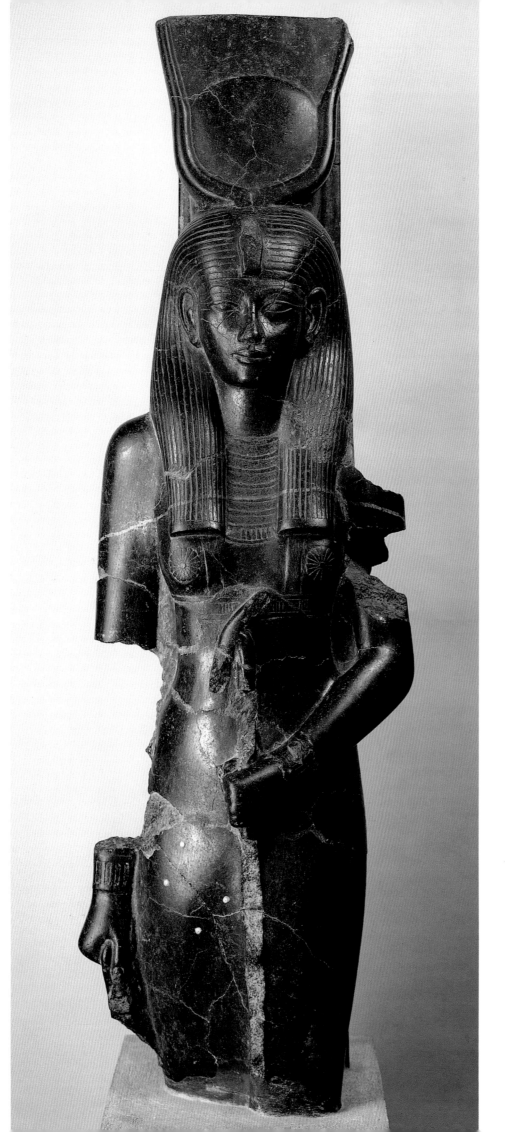

tomb of Tuyu and Yuya, parents of Queen Tiye, wife of the pharaoh Amenhotep III. Though robbed, it still contained gilded coffins and furniture. Another tomb (KV55), badly disturbed, held some objects bearing Queen Tiye's name but the mummy in the tomb was male. Splendid gold and silver jewellery was found in the fill of a small tomb, perhaps the disintegrated remains of a royal infant's burial. By 1914, however, Davis had decided that the Valley had yielded all its secrets and that no unplundered tomb could be found.

By this time Carter was working with another wealthy patron of Egyptology, the Englishman Lord Carnarvon. They were not convinced that the Valley of the Kings was exhausted. Over the years a few things had been found bearing the name of King Tutankhamun, including objects from his funerary feast and mummification rites. This pharaoh, who ruled between 1336 and 1327 BC, had come to the throne at the age of 9. He had been born during the revolutionary period when Akhenaten abandoned the Egyptian traditional gods and introduced the monotheistic worship of the Aten, the orb of the sun. Akhenaten's successor (or late co-ruler), Smenkhkare, had continued this heretical cult but when Tutankhamun succeeded him the Aten cult was swept aside and monuments bearing references to the Aten, Akhenaten or his wife Nefertiti were mutilated. Little was known of Tutankhamun and his grave had never been found. Could it still lie concealed in the Valley?

LAST CHANCE

Carter and Carnarvon secured the concession to work in the Valley of the Kings in 1914, but war broke out almost at once and it was not until 1917 that Carter could start substantial investigations here. Over the following years he looked at a number of places in and around the

Left: *A stone statue of queen Tiye in the form of Hathor, goddess of the heavens, divine mother and goddess of women. The horned headdress worn by the queen represents Hathor as a cow, in which form the goddess acted as royal protector and nurse.*

Right: *The beautiful back of Tutankhamun's throne, covered with inlaid gold and silver sheet. It sensitively portrays the young king and his wife, Ankhesenamen, beneath the rays of the sun-god, Aten.*

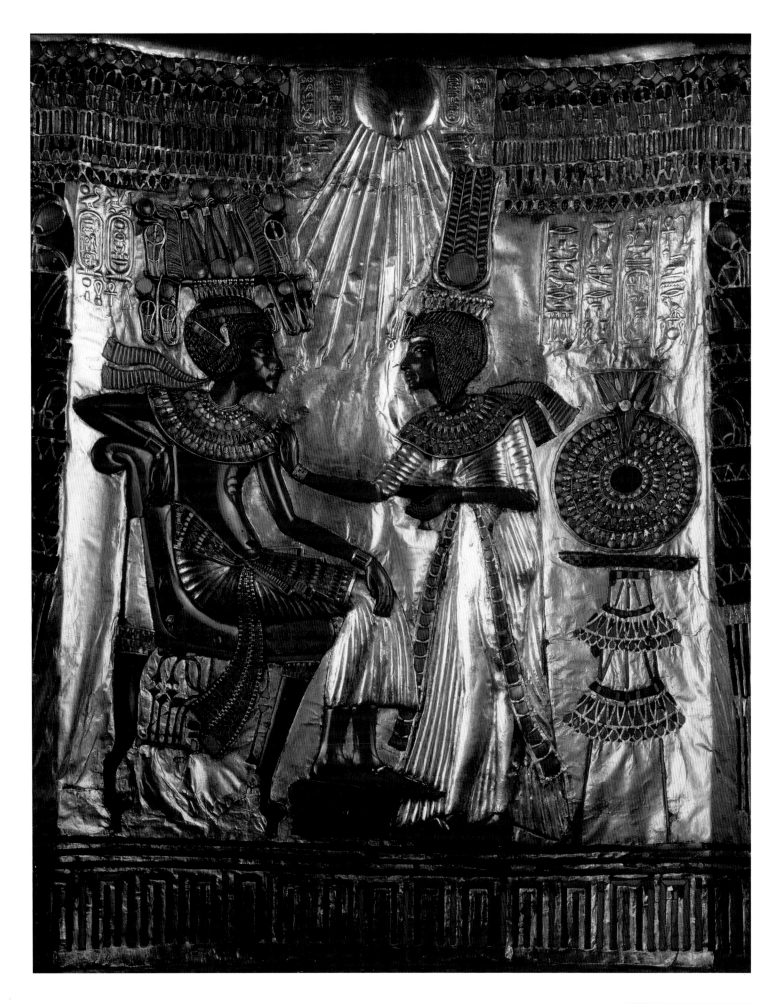

Valley, returning at intervals to an area he considered very promising, a triangle of uninvestigated ground between three tombs that had previously been emptied, those of Merneptah, Ramesses II and Ramesses VI. This area had been used as a dumping ground for debris removed in clearing the adjacent tombs and had therefore been ignored. When Carter cleared the debris he came upon the remains of a little village of stone slab huts, the homes of the workmen who constructed Ramesses VI's tomb. The patch of ground beneath the village was therefore untouched since the twelfth century BC: might it conceal a tomb?

Carter was very hopeful. He therefore saved this small area until 1922, when Carnarvon began to tire of the unrewarding work in the Valley, and used the slim possibility of an undiscovered tomb to revive Carnarvon's flagging interest. Carnarvon decided it was worth trying, as a final piece of work before relinquishing his concession in the Valley. So on November 1, 1922, Carter began the excavation and removal of part of the workmen's village. Three days into the excavation his workmen came upon a step: the entrance to a tomb. Was it a completed tomb or merely the abandoned beginning of one? If it was a finished tomb, had it been looted by the ancient robbers?

To find out, Carter and his workmen cleared the stairway down to the twelfth step – and came upon a sealed doorway. Carter examined it and realized that it had been broken into. But it had been resealed by priests at the time and not subsequently damaged. What lay behind the sealed door? Carter made a small hole and squinted in – a tunnel full of rubble met his eye.

SUSPENSE

Carter now knew he was facing the strong possibility of an undisturbed tomb. Carnarvon was in England and not due at the site for some months. Restraining his impatience and excitement, Carter filled in the staircase again, posted a guard on the tomb and telegraphed Carnarvon, who said he would come soon. For three anxious and nail-biting weeks Carter waited for him to arrive by boat.

On November 23 Carnarvon reached Luxor and work recommenced the following day. The staircase was cleared and the doorway fully exposed, revealing a seal bearing the name of Tutankhamun. But mixed debris in the rubble also contained the names of other kings and the door seemed small for a genuine tomb entrance. Would this prove to be merely a cache of material collected from disturbed tombs?

Excited but apprehensive, the two men cleared the debris from the passage and came to an inner door. The door seals showed again that the chamber had been disturbed but resealed by priests of the necropolis. The excavators fully cleared this door, then Carter made a tiny hole in it, inserted a candle and peered in. As his eyes adjusted to the dim light he was struck dumb by what he saw. Behind him, Carnarvon waited impatiently; to his anxious enquiry, Carter could only manage to reply that he saw "wonderful things".

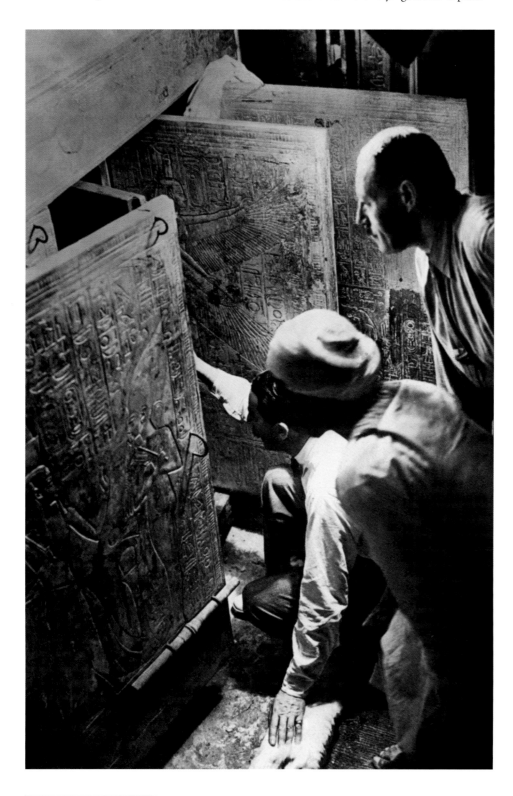

Left: *Howard Carter and his colleagues opening the gilded wooden shrines containing the stone sarcophagus and golden coffins of Tutankhamun.*

ROYALLY FURNISHED

They had discovered an intact tomb: one whose contents have never ceased to astonish the world since then. So many wonderful things were indeed there that it was 10 years before Carter and his many helpers could complete the work of investigating and recording the objects in the tomb, and conserving and removing them.

The door to which they had come opened into an antechamber with three gilt couches, a golden throne, four dismantled chariots and a beautiful chest decorated with a scene of Tutankhamun hunting, as well as many other splendid objects, their arrangement slightly upset by the activities of robbers. The priests who resealed the tomb managed to tidy this chamber, but in the adjacent annexe there was chaos: the jumbled, smashed mess left by the robbers in their haste.

Beyond the antechamber was the door to another chamber, flanked by two life-size statues of Tutankhamun. On February 17, 1923 Carter opened it and saw a breathtaking sight. The small chamber was entirely filled by a gilded shrine. Within this was a nested arrangement of further shrines enclosing a magnificent stone sarcophagus. This contained three nested coffins, two of gilded wood and one of solid gold. Over the face of the young pharaoh was a mask made of gold inlaid with lapis lazuli.

Below: *This painting, by Douglas Macpherson, shows the entrance to the inner room, which housed the gilded shrine containing Tutankhamun's nested sarcophagi. Gilded guardian statues of the king flank the doorway.*

Beyond this chamber lay another, packed with treasures that had belonged to the young ruler. The room was dominated by an exquisite gilded shrine within which was an alabaster chest containing Tutankhamun's embalmed viscera. There were also gilded boxes full of *shabti* figures, model people placed there to work for their king in the afterworld. In this chamber too were signs of disorder caused by the robbers.

NO STONE UNTURNED?

Tutankhamun's tomb was poorly furnished in comparison with those of his more important predecessors and successors: the grave goods in a great king's tomb would beggar imagination. But the chances of finding another such tomb intact are extremely small, so Tutankhamun's treasures are likely to remain the most splendid ever to be found on Egyptian soil.

Had the Valley of the Kings now yielded its last secret? It seems not. In the 1990s an American team headed by Professor Kent Weeks relocated a tomb which had been slightly explored in 1825, and discovered that the known portion actually led into an enormous complex of chambers, the largest discovered in the Valley of the Kings, containing the burials of about 50 sons of Ramesses II – robbed, but still fascinating. As modern survey and reconnaissance techniques are brought into play, the Valley, thought many times over the last century to have been fully explored, continues to offer a tantalizing promise of further discoveries.

In 2000 Nicholas Reeves, using ground-penetrating radar, identified two possible new burial chambers deep underground near Tutankhamun's tomb. One has yet to be investigated, the other has been under excavation since 2006 by Otto Schaden of Memphis University, revealing gilded coffins containing a large quantity of funerary paraphernalia, such as floral collars and embalming materials – but no mummies.

This small piece of ground may yet hold the answer to one of the abiding mysteries of Egyptology: the last resting place of the heretical pharaoh Akhenaten and his family. They were originally buried in a splendid tomb near Akhenaten's capital, Amarna (ancient Akhetaten), but this city was abandoned after his death. At some time during Tutankhamun's reign the royal mummies were probably moved to the Valley of the Kings, along with the more portable of their grave goods. Some of these were buried in tomb KV55, including a gold-sheathed shrine of Akhenaten's mother, Queen Tiye, and the elaborate

---

Above: *Dismantled chariots lie along one side of Tutankhamun's antechamber, while the other is packed with furniture, including elegant animals that formed the sides of three couches.*

Opposite: *Tutankhamun's innermost coffin, in which his mummy lay, was made of solid gold. It represented the youthful king in the guise of Osiris, god of death and resurrection. The king holds a crook and flail, symbols of royalty.*

---

coffin of his lesser wife, Kiya. Could the male mummy placed in this coffin, with the identifying name erased, be that of Akhenaten? Genetic fingerprinting shows he is probably Tutankhamun's father and the "Younger Lady" in tomb KV35 probably his sister and Tutankhamin's mother. However, there is disagreement on whether he is Akhenaten; he may be Smenkhkare. The mystery of Akhenaten's last resting place is still unresolved: perhaps he lies in the newly discovered, unexcavated tomb?

Left: *On the side of this painted wooden chest, Tutankhamun rides his chariot into battle against his Syrian enemies, while on the lid he is hunting birds and animals in the desert.*

Below: *Workmen carry out the coffins from the Theban tomb of the noble Mentuemhet. He was a high priest and governor of Upper Egypt in the seventh century* BC.

MURDER VICTIM OR BOY RACER?

When Tutankhamun's mummy was examined in 1968, apparent damage to his skull suggested that he had suffered a blow to the back of his head: accident or murder? Tutankhamun was succeeded as king by the court official Ay, possibly Nefertiti's father, who exercised great power during Tutankhamun's reign. Might Ay have resorted to murder when the teenaged king began to assert his independence?

In 2005 Tutankhamun's mummy was CAT-scanned, revealing that the damage to his skull had happened after his death. But it also disclosed a bad leg injury, evidence of a terrible accident. It is now suggested that Tutankhamun was the victim of his own recklessness when out hunting in his chariot: he overturned it at high speed, breaking his leg above the knee, probably rupturing a major blood vessel and creating an open wound that rapidly became infected, so that he died of gangrene within a few days.

BEYOND THE VALLEY OF THE KINGS

The Valley of the Kings is not the only place in Egypt with rich burials. It is only a small part of a much larger New Kingdom necropolis at Thebes, with the tombs of royal ladies in the adjacent Valley of the Queens and noble burials elsewhere within it. Earlier Egyptian royalty were interred in pyramid complexes at Giza, Abusir, Dahshur and elsewhere, while many later kings lie in cemeteries in the Nile Delta. Before the discovery of Tutankhamun's tomb one of the most spectacular finds was a cache of gold jewellery belonging to Twelfth Dynasty princesses, found in 1894 by Jacques de Morgan at Dahshur. This jewellery may have been abandoned by tomb robbers or deliberately concealed by the priests to outwit them. The following year de Morgan discovered the unplundered grave of Princess Khnemit, replete with jewellery of gold, carnelian and lapis lazuli, including two magnificent golden crowns inlaid with gems.

Overshadowed by Tutankhamun's splendours and later by the outbreak of the Second World War, the excavations by Pierre Montet in 1921–1951 at Tanis, capital of some of Egypt's late pharaohs, are often overlooked. Within the precinct of the temple of Amun these kings were entombed in small chambers, modestly furnished in comparison with the magnificence of earlier burials. Here in 1939 Montet found six largely unplundered tombs, that of Psusennes (1039–991 BC) being the most impressive: the king wore a gold mask and was interred in a silver coffin placed inside a granite coffin and sarcophagus, and was accompanied by

Above: Tutankhamun's well-preserved, shaven head. When it was first unwrapped, it was so firmly wedged inside the golden mask that Carter considered using a hammer and chisel to separate them.

Below left: The gilded, bronze funerary mask of the short-lived king, Amenemope. He was buried at Tanis, alongside his mother, in the tomb of his father, Psusennes I.

Below right: The silver coffin of the ninth century BC king Sheshonq II was found in the antechamber of Psusennes' tomb at Tanis. It contained his mummy, wearing this golden mask.

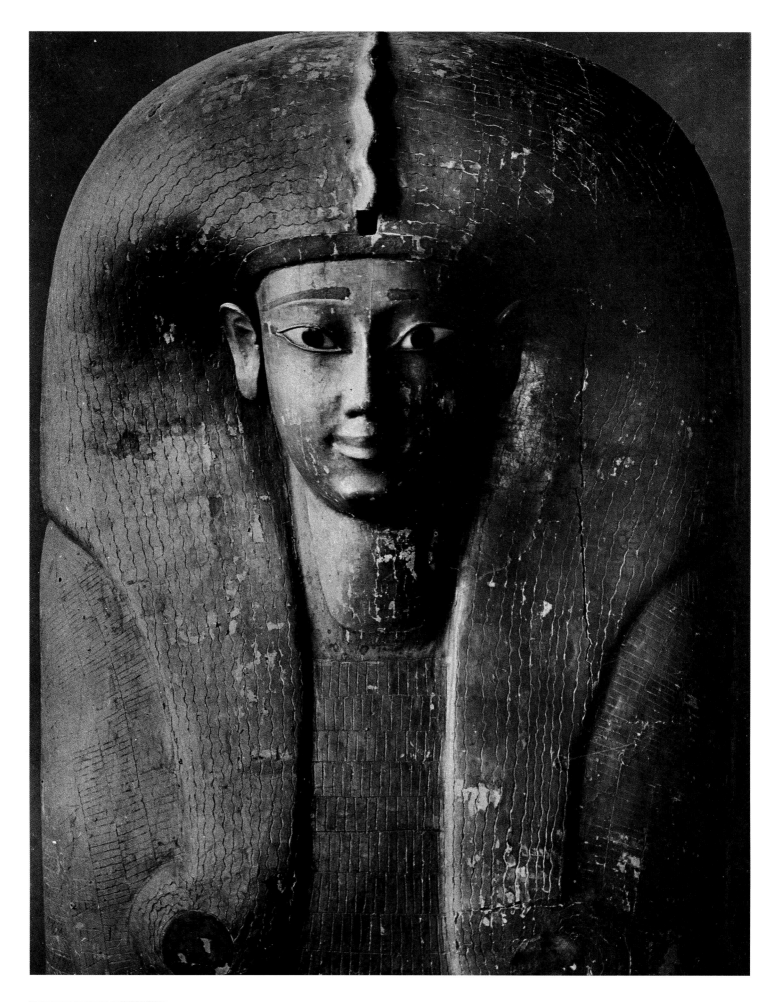

many gold and silver vessels. Other treasures from these tombs included jewellery of gold inlaid with lapis lazuli, carnelian and coloured faience.

DRIVING OUT THE USURPERS

One of the most poignant of ancient Egyptian treasures is a gold necklace found in the coffin of a queen, Ahhotep, with three pendants, the "Flies of Valour", awarded for military bravery. Ahhotep belonged to the impoverished Seventeenth Dynasty (1650–1550 BC), who ruled Upper Egypt from Thebes while the powerful Hyksos Dynasty, who were of foreign origin, controlled Lower Egypt. Following thinly veiled threats from the Hyksos king, hundreds of miles away in Avaris, who ordered that the Theban royal family deal with their hippopotami, whose noise prevented him from sleeping, the Theban king Seqenenra Taa II led a rebellion against the Hyksos. Seqenenra died from horrific battle injuries, but his widow, Ahhotep, and his children continued the fight. His elder son Kamose defeated the Hyksos, but died young; Ahmose, the younger son, completed their expulsion. A stele at Karnak commemorates the important military role played by Ahhotep. The coffin containing the "Flies of Valour" may be hers, though another that definately belonged to her was found elsewhere; alternatively it may belong to another Ahhotep, perhaps the wife of Kamose who was buried nearby. Other objects found in the coffin include a gilded axe depicting Ahmose smiting a Hyksos captive, beautiful beaded gold bracelets and a miniature silver boat.

Above right: *This gold necklace from Ahhotep's burial includes three "Flies of Valour", a high military decoration that was usually awarded to a successful military commander for bravery on the battlefield.*

Right: *A ceremonial axe showing Ahmose I, founder of the Eighteenth Dynasty, in a traditional pose – killing an enemy while grasping him by the hair. Unusually, he is using a dagger instead of the traditional mace.*

Opposite: *The gilded and inlaid wooden sarcophagus of Ahhotep, which was found in 1859 at Dra Aboul Naga, near the Valley of the Kings. Her mummy was inside, but unfortunately was discarded by its finders.*

GOLDEN MUMMIES OF THE OASIS

The Bahariya Oasis, well to the west of the Nile, was an important wine-growing area in ancient Egyptian and later times. Here in 1996, antiquities' guard Abdul Maugoud made a spectacular discovery. On his way home from work his donkey accidentally put its foot in a hole. Peering into this Maugoud saw something shining. He immediately contacted the local antiquities officer, Ashry Shaker, who investigated, revealing a tomb, full of "beautiful mummies". The news was quickly passed to Zahi Hawass, the archaeological director responsible for the region, who began excavations there in 1999, revealing a cemetery of tombs cut into the sandstone beneath the desert sands.

In the first tomb he opened, eight steps descended through an antechamber into a pair of chambers with niches around their walls. In these were arranged rows of mummies, 43 in all, some stacked above others and a few even on the floor: this was presumably a family tomb, used over a long period. Most of the other tombs investigated were similarly full; Hawass believes that the cemetery may contain more than 10,000 bodies and may take 50 years to excavate completely. The first mummy examined was that of a woman, her face and chest covered by a long golden mask that modelled her face, hair and breasts and had panels of embossed and painted decoration, depicting gods associated with death and the afterlife and other funerary themes. Beside her was a man in a similar mask and between them two small mummies, probably their children. Hawass suggests that the husband died first: his wife's golden mask was modelled so that her face was turned affectionately toward him.

The necropolis dates from the period in the early centuries AD when Egypt had fallen under Roman rule. By now the mummification process was simpler than in earlier times: the body was coated in resin and bound in strips of linen arranged in a pattern, with sticks laid alongside the body for reinforcement. Well-to-do individuals then had a coffin of cartonnage (layers of linen or papyrus, coated in plaster) moulded over their body, realistically rendering their features. The

wealthiest people had a thin layer of gold over the cartonnage, covering the face and often the chest. These burials were well furnished with grave goods, including many figurines of benevolent gods and goddesses, and mourners covering their eyes; necklaces, earrings, bracelets and other jewellery of faience, gold, silver, copper, glass and ivory; jars of wine; and other valuables, including in one case a coin of Cleopatra. Clay animals and other toys accompanied the children.

Opposite: The magnificent gilded cartonnage coffin of Sheshonq I, a strong ruler who reunited Egypt. The hawk's head on the coffin represents Horus, god of kingship.

Top: *The gilded mummy of a man, wearing a headband inlaid with faience and gemstones. Decorations on the chestplate depict various gods, including the winged goddess Maat (Truth).*

Below: *A workman carefully uncovers mummies in one of the Bahariya Oasis tombs, while a conservator treats one that has already been exposed, to preserve its fragile surface.*

THE GOLD OF AFRICA

WEST AFRICAN GOLD

Herodotus, the fifth-century BC Greek ethnographer and historian, tells of a curious ancient trade in gold dust. Carthaginian seafarers would come ashore at traditional places of exchange on the West African coast and set out the goods they had to offer. After lighting a signal fire they would return to their ships. The natives would appear, lay down gold in exchange and then retire. The Carthaginian traders would return to assess the quantity of gold. This process continued until both sides were satisfied but at no time did they ever meet.

In later times Arab traders from North Africa employed camel caravans to cross the Sahara desert and obtain gold, ivory and slaves, in exchange for manufactured goods. From the tenth to the sixteenth century AD, West Africa was Europe's main source of gold. The wealth of West African kingdoms became legendary, with reports that even the kings' dogs wore collars of gold. Many prosperous inland towns developed as a result of trade links across the Sahara, and their riches can be gauged by the occasional discovery of wealthy burials.

BRONZES AND GOLD

In 1959 the archaeologist Thurstan Shaw was invited to excavate at Igbo Ukwu, a site in southern Nigeria where superb bronzes had previously been discovered. The excavation proved a nerve-racking experience for Shaw. Not only was he suffering ill health but when he found the first of the site's bronze treasures someone attempted to steal it from under his bed as he slept. His work revealed the richly endowed burial of a local chief who died in the ninth century AD. The chief had been interred in a wooden chamber, seated on a stool dressed in his regalia. With him were buried three magnificent ivory tusks and many bronze objects, including a beautiful shell with intricate geometric patterns over its entire surface.

Several West African states manufactured superb bronze and brass sculptures, of which the most outstanding works were created by the Ife and the Benin. The Asante were the richest in gold and produced fine goldwork, especially royal regalia: much of the gold they obtained from subjugated neighbours. All goldsmiths were obliged to work in the Asante capital, Kumasi, under close supervision. When European traders first came to this coast in the fifteenth century, they were anxious to acquire both slaves and gold, for which they traded not only manufactured luxuries but also guns and ammunition. Initially the African kingdoms had the whip hand, for their centres lay inland and European traders penetrated there only with official permission and backing.

Below left: *The kingdoms of West Africa produced magnificent bronze and brass sculptures and reliefs like this seventeenth-century Benin warrior.*

Below right: *This gold head was probably the death mask of an Asante ruler.*

By the ninteenth century, however, Europeans controlled much of the West African coast and were penetrating the African interior. The British in the Gold Coast came into conflict with the powerful Asante kingdom. In 1874, in retaliation for an Asante attack on their fort at El Mina, the British mounted a successful military expedition against Kumasi. The defeated Asante king was forced to pay an indemnity of 50,000 ounces (1.55 tonnes/1¾ tons) of gold: to raise this vast amount he had to hand over much of his personal wealth, including court regalia such as the cast gold pectoral discs worn by important royal officials as badges of offices.

EASTERN TRADERS

Arab merchants traded by sea with East Africa. Coastal towns here imported spices, fine pottery and textiles and in return exported slaves, ivory and gold obtained from the interior. The gold came mainly from the Zimbabwe plateau, where, in the eleventh century AD, the Shona state established its capital on top of a steep hill at Mapungubwe on the Limpopo River. Around 1250 the capital was moved further north to Great Zimbabwe. Here, to house the king and his

court, a series of magnificent stone-walled enclosures was constructed, surrounded by a substantial town which flourished into the fifteenth century.

By the seventeenth century, when Europeans began to establish bases in southern Africa, the equality of earlier trading relations had gone, a victim of the degrading effect of the slave trade. Africans were now viewed as culturally and intellectually inferior to Europeans, incapable of great artistic or architectural works. By the nineteenth century missionaries, explorers and prospectors were penetrating many parts of the African interior. One, a young geologist called Carl Mauch, learned of impressive ruins: the massive fortified settlement at Great Zimbabwe. Visiting them, he published an account of what he had seen. In the climate of nineteenth-century thought it was not considered possible that Great Zimbabwe had been erected by native Africans. Instead Mauch and his contemporaries speculated that it represented the remains of some kingdom known in antiquity – perhaps the palace of the Queen of Sheba. This was an exciting prospect, for it was thought that the ancient gold mines of King Solomon in Ophir should lie nearby.

KING SOLOMON'S MINES

Solomon (c.1015–977 BC), King of Israel, made his capital, Jerusalem, a place of great splendour, reserving his most magnificent efforts for the Temple. He is said to have obtained 120 talents of gold for these works from the distant land of Ophir, to which he sent a naval expedition. When the Queen of Sheba heard of Solomon's glory, she decided to pay him a state visit and was apparently greatly impressed both by the city and by the king himself. Her gifts were themselves splendid in the extreme and included spices, gems and tonnes of gold.

Where were Sheba and Ophir? Clearly they lay to the south of Israel. The discovery of Great Zimbabwe seemed to raise the possibility that Sheba and Ophir lay in southern Africa. The idea rapidly developed and many Europeans embarked on expeditions to southern Africa, searching for the legendary mines of gold and diamonds;

Above: *This bowl, from a royal burial at Mapungubwe, was made by covering a wooden bowl with sheet gold. Agriculture, gold mining and trade made Mapungubwe prosperous.*

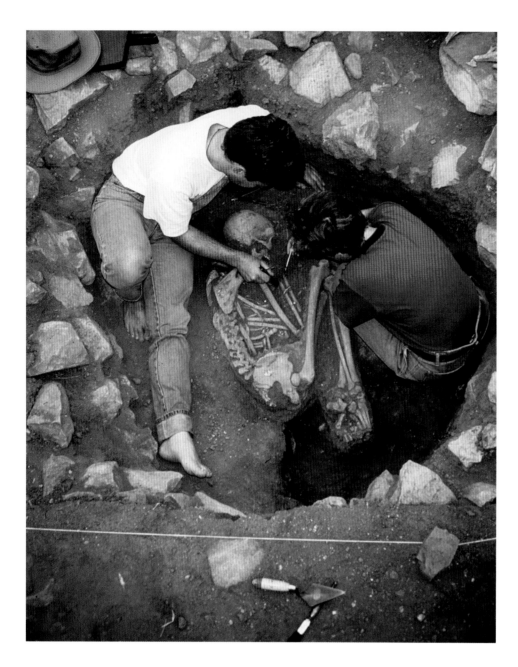

both gold and diamonds were eventually found. The legend inspired literature such as Rider Haggard's influential novel *King Solomon's Mines* (1885), and this in turn fed the quest for gold and treasure.

Excavations by Gertrude Caton-Thomson in the 1930s demonstrated that Great Zimbabwe was the creation of local Shona people. The 1930s also saw the discovery of rich burials at Mapungubwe, containing many valuable imported glass beads, along with copper and gold ornaments and a sceptre, wooden vessels and a model rhinoceros, all plated in gold. Three individuals buried in an upright position were probably kings. One was buried with 100 gold bracelets and more than 12,000 gold beads. This cemetery, now protected by law, is still under investigation. Occasionally other similarly rich graves are discovered in southern Africa, including several at Thulamela Stone Citadel, a royal enclosure located near a tributary of the Limpopo River, occupied AD 1250–1700. Here a woman's skeleton was found, wearing a bracelet of twisted gold wire and another bracelet from which nearly 300 gold beads survive. Nearby was a burial mound containing the disarticulated bones of a man with at least seven gold wire bracelets, beads of gold and ostrich eggshell, and other gold objects.

Left: *The grave of Thulamela's queen being investigated by a team that specialises in excavating skeletons. Aged 43 to 50 years, she was old for her time, but enjoyed very good health.*

SHIPS WRECKED OFF AFRICA

THE INTREPID PORTUGUESE

From the early fifteenth century Portuguese seamen, encouraged by Prince Henry the Navigator, began to explore the African coastline, initially searching for the source of the gold brought across the Sahara by Arab traders. Later they also sought a sea passage to the silks, spices and porcelain of India and China, an alternative to the overland routes controlled by the Islamic world and their Mediterranean competitors, especially the Genoese and Venetians.

In 1487 Bartolomeu Dias sailed round the Cape of Good Hope and entered the Indian Ocean. Ten years later Vasco da Gama went further along this route, sailing up the East African coast and crossing to Calicut, initiating the lucrative Portuguese sea trade with India. By 1515 the Portuguese had established fortified trading posts along the Indian coast, notably at Goa, and had penetrated beyond India to South East Asia, making regular use of the sea route around southern Africa.

Recent excavations off Mozambique have uncovered several early Portuguese shipwrecks. In 1622 Vasco da Gama's great-grandson, Francisco, was sailing to India as governor of the Portuguese possessions there. His ships were attacked by a fleet of the Dutch and English who were by now trading competitors of the Portuguese. One of the Portuguese ships, *São José*, carrying nine chests of silver coins, was badly damaged and ran aground; only a small proportion of the ship's valuables were rescued before it sank. Some 25,000 silver coins as well as bronze cannons, trade beads, rosaries and other personal possessions of the passengers have been recovered from the excavation of the *São José* wreck.

Some years earlier, around 1558, the *Espadarte* was wrecked outside the San Sebastian fort while travelling back from India to Portugal. A rich cargo of Chinese Ming porcelain dating to the reign of Jiajing

(1522–66) and spices – pepper, nutmeg and mace – recovered from the wreck show it played an active part in Portugal's lucrative trade with the east. The ship also yielded a private hoard of gold, in small ingots, nuggets and gold dust.

A BIG SURPRISE FOR THE DIAMOND HUNTERS

Early in 2008, the Namdeb Diamond Corporation constructed an earthen cofferdam off a stretch of the Namibian coast to explore a section of the seabed for diamonds. To their surprise they discovered some copper ingots, which they showed to the company's archaeologist, Dieter Noli. Diamond prospection was suspended while he examined the site of the find. He soon discovered cannon, other weapons, ivory, gold and silver coins. Clearly these were the contents of a wrecked ship, now largely destroyed by the sea. Calling in the help of the veteran marine archaeologist Bruno Werz, Noli continued the excavations until October 10, 2008, a deadline imposed both by the enormous costs of maintaining the cofferdam and by the seasonal conditions of the sea. The pair succeeded in completing their investigation, recovering a cargo of around 20 tonnes (22 tons) of copper ingots, 50 ivory tusks and thousands of gold and silver coins, as well as naval equipment and pewter tableware. Lead patches and signs of marine worm in the surviving timbers suggested that the vessel was in poor condition when she sank. A preliminary analysis of the coins showed it was a Portuguese vessel that sank in the early sixteenth century – the oldest European shipwreck known in the southern hemisphere. The cargo, including copper ingots stamped with the mark of the Fuggers banking house, shows that the ship was outward bound, but had already traded with Africa for ivory.

Research since the excavations has answered some questions, although there is still much to learn. It seems likely that the ship was the *Bom Jesus*, lost on its maiden voyage in 1533. Approaching the southern tip of Africa on a journey to obtain spices from the Indies, it was driven off course by a storm and foundered on rocks near the mouth of the Orange River. *The Bom Jesus* had set sail from Lisbon on March 7, 1533, part of an expedition bound for Portugals' recently established trading posts in India. Its cargo included a large consignment of Spanish gold coins, the investment of a group of Spanish merchants, and a quantity of newly minted coins of the Portuguese king João III, who owned the ship.

The recovery of a wooden block from the ship some three miles from the wreck indicates that it broke up after it struck, although the heavy cargo probably pinned down much of the vessel in the spot where it met its fate. Although the archaeologists found its cargo, they recovered few human bones, suggesting that many of the crew survived, although none managed to return home.

TODAY'S UNFOUND TREASURES

SEYCHELLES TREASURE

Olivier Le Vasseur, "the Buzzard", began his career as a privateer commissioned by France to prey on enemy shipping in the Caribbean. When peace came in 1713 he turned to private unlicenced piracy, moving in 1720 to the Indian Ocean. Here he seized the *Nossa Senhora do Cabo*, a Portuguese ship carrying a quantity of treasure, including an enormous jewel-studded cross known as the Fiery Cross of Goa.

In 1730 Le Vasseur was captured and hanged. From the gallows he flung papers into the crowd containing clues to where his vast hoard of treasure was concealed. He had made the island of Mahé in the Seychelles his base and here he seems to have constructed a gigantic puzzle whose solution would lead to the treasure. Cryptic clues in the papers may link with curiously carved boulders on Mahé's Bel Ombre beach. At first these were investigated by the local Savy family, but in 1948 an Englishman, Reginald Cruise-Wilkins, became involved and he devoted the rest of his life to unravelling the puzzle. He believed that Le Vasseur had linked the clues to the treasure's location with the ancient Greek story of the Labours of Hercules. Since his death in 1977 Cruise-Wilkins' son John and an American, Robert Graf, have continued the quest.

Above: *For some people, the attractions of the beautiful Seycelle islands are enhanced by the lure of pirate treasures that are reputedly hidden here.*

THE *WITTE LEEUW*

In 1613 the galleon *Witte Leeuw* (*White Lion*), owned by the VOC (Vereenigde Oost-Indische Compagnie, or Dutch East India Company), was returning home from a successful trading expedition to Indonesia, in consort with three other VOC merchantmen and two English ships. They rounded the Cape of Good Hope and put in at St Helena for provisions, anchoring in Jamestown Bay. While they were there, two Portuguese carracks were sighted.

At this time the Portuguese and Dutch were in conflict over rights in the East Indies. The Dutch therefore gave battle, while the neutral English ships stood by watching. The Portuguese captain, seriously outnumbered but commanding a disciplined and efficient crew, held his position and battered the Dutch ships with his guns. Suddenly something went wrong on the *Witte Leeuw*

– perhaps a gun exploded over the magazine. The ship blew apart and sank. One of the other Dutch ships had been sadly mauled and the remaining ships fled.

The Belgian diver Robert Stenuit's researches on post-medieval wrecks kept turning up references to the *Witte Leeuw*. Intrigued, in 1976 he decided to search for it. Investigating places in Jamestown Bay marked as foul anchorage sites, where obstructive debris lay on the seabed, Stenuit and his collaborators found a group of six cannons. Raising one to the surface, they were gratified to discover that it bore the insignia of the VOC – their investigation was on the right lines.

The wreck proved to be deeply buried beneath a substantial deposit of more recent debris of all sorts. When they finally uncovered remains of the *Witte Leeuw* they received a big surprise. Stenuit had seen the ship's manifest and was expecting a cargo of spices and gems

– 15,171 bags of pepper and 1,311 diamonds were listed. But instead the first thing they found was fine porcelain, which obviously had been included without the knowledge of the company officials back home.

During a seven-month season Stenuit and his colleagues recovered a considerable quantity of porcelain, much of it undamaged, due to the cushioning effects of peppercorns that had also survived. But they found no diamonds. These would have been kept secure in the captain's cabin and when the ship blew up they were all dispersed beyond any hope of recovery.

Above: *Dividers, used to measure distances on naval charts, and Spanish gold and Portuguese silver coins were among early finds from the "Diamond wreck," now identified as probably the* Bom Jesus, *lost in 1533.*

The Dodington East Indiaman.

THE *DODINGTON*

Robert Clive had gone out to Madras in 1743 as an impoverished clerk with Britain's East India Company, but his military genius soon brought him to prominence in his country's hostile encounters with the French on Indian soil. In 1753 he returned to Britain an extremely wealthy man and was commissioned as a lieutenant-colonel. He was sent out to India again to take command of the British trading station at Fort St David and to lead a combined naval and army expedition against the French.

The expeditionary force was a substantial one. Seven ships sailed from Britain in April 1755, loaded with hundreds of soldiers as well as munitions and food for the troops. One vessel, the *Dodington*, was carrying a company of 200 Royal Artillery soldiers and a quantity of valuables, including Clive's own treasure chest containing around £3,000 in gold, an enormous sum at the time.

After the convoy had rounded the Cape of Good Hope, the *Dodington* became separated from the other ships. Navigation in the area was dangerous as the coast was not properly charted at that time. During a serious storm on July 16 the *Dodington* ran on to rocks forming part of Bird Island, which appeared on charts of that time as "Chaos Island" or "Confused Island" because its location was uncertain. Many men were washed overboard at once and as the ship broke up more were drowned. Only 23 managed to reach the island.

Fortunately many of the ship's stores were washed ashore. Along with fresh fish and eggs, these enabled the men to survive on the island for seven months. Some of the valuables from the ship were also saved: silver coins belonging to the East India Company and silver plate belonging to a Mr Boddam. The castaways were able to gather enough smashed timber to construct a boat in which to escape, which they called the *Happy Deliverance*. In this they finally came to shore in Mozambique.

Above: *An engraving, by an unknown artist. of the moment when the* Dodington *was wrecked off South Africa, with the loss of 247 lives. After she struck, the ship quickly broke up.*

SHARK-INFESTED WATERS

There was talk at the time of salvaging the *Dodington*, but nothing came of it. It was not until 1977 that two South Africans, David Allen and Gerry van Niekirk, began seriously to search for the wreck. They had a detailed account by the *Dodington's* mate, Evan Jones, to guide them to the site, but his directions were not clear and the island had seen many shipwrecks, making it difficult to pinpoint an individual wreck. Huge swells impeded work and made positional recording virtually impossible with the technology of the time. (Modern equipment and techniques have recently enabled the wreck of the *Dodington* to be surveyed in detail.) In addition, the waters around the island are full of fish and therefore support many seals, which in turn attract large numbers of Great White sharks. Although not usually aggressive toward humans, the sharks can easily mistake divers for seals and attack them, inevitably inflicting very serious wounds.

Working in great secrecy to avoid the problematic publicity and competition that they had previously suffered during salvage work, but with a proper salvage permit and keeping in touch with the director and the historian of the Port Elizabeth Museum, the team explored these waters until they located promising remains, including guns that finally identified the wreck as the *Dodington*. From it they salvaged a quantity of copper, silver "pieces of eight" coins and one of the guns, leaving the iron cannon on the site. Of Clive's gold, however, there was no trace.

This was not the end of the story. In 1997, sharp-eyed staff at the South Africa Heritage Resources Agency (SAHRA) in Johannesburg noticed that a London auction house was advertising "Clive's gold" for sale – a consignment of 1,200 gold coins offered by an anonymous seller. Successfully arguing that the gold had been illegally recovered from South African waters, following a four-year legal battle SAHRA obtained an out-of-court settlement that gave them a third of this treasure: 405 gold coins, now in the Bayworld (Port Elizabeth) Museum. Nothing is known about who recovered the gold and how, though the finders' representatives claimed that the gold came from a pirate ship that had salvaged it from the *Dodington* before she went down and had then, conveniently for the salvors, itself sunk just outside the 38.6-kilometre (24-mile) limit of South African territorial waters – an unlikely tale, since the sea at this distance off the coast is at least 200 metres (656 feet) deep: discovering and salvaging a ship here would have required a very sophisticated diving operation that could hardly have taken place unnoticed.

THE *GROSVENOR*

The British East India Company ship the *Grosvenor* left Sri Lanka on June 13, 1782, laden with Company goods, including a considerable quantity of diamonds and

TODAY'S UNFOUND TREASURES

ALEXANDER

When Alexander the Great returned to Babylon in 323 BC after conquering Persia and northern India, he made plans for new campaigns in Arabia and the Mediterranean. These were cut short by his sudden death, perhaps from malaria though many at the time believed that he had been poisoned. His body was embalmed and lay in state in Babylon while an elaborate funerary chariot was constructed: a golden coffin and golden lid under a pillared canopy with a jewelled golden ceiling, decorated with painted scenes from Alexander's life. The following year the chariot, drawn by 64 mules, and funerary cortege began their journey back to Alexander's ancestral home in Macedon. On the way the chariot and cortege were hijacked by his general and friend Ptolemy, satrap and later king of Egypt, who took them back to Memphis, Egypt's ancient capital. Alexander's golden coffin was later moved to the new capital, Alexandria, where it was laid in a magnificent tomb within the Ptolemies' royal burial enclosure. This remained a famous monument and shrine well into imperial Roman times, visited by emperors including Caligula, who reputedly stole Alexander's breastplate, and Caracalla, who heaped the sarcophagus with the valuables he was wearing. The tomb was subsequently destroyed or forgotten and attempts to relocate it have so far failed.

Right: *Alexander fighting at the Battle of Issus where, in 333 BC, he defeated the Persian king, Darius III. This Roman mosaic is a copy of a painting by one of Alexander's contemporaries.*

the private property of its officers: tidy sums in gold and silver. After nearly two months of open sea, on August 4 several seamen thought they glimpsed land, but their observations were ignored and the *Grosvenor* ran aground on rocks off the mouth of the River Tezani in southern Africa. About 100 people drowned as the ship sank and, of the 123 who managed to scramble ashore, only a handful survived the long gruelling trek to the nearest Dutch settlement.

In 1880 gold and silver coins on the beach alerted Sydney Turner, a shipowner, to the location of the wreck, and he attempted to obtain more by using dynamite, but with little success. As time passed both the reputed size of the treasure and the ambitious designs

Above: The latest in diving equipment was employed by the eighteenth-century salvors of the Hartwell.

of the treasure seekers grew – among these were proposals to construct a breakwater around the wreck site and a salvage attempt using a special large crane. In 2000, however, a Hungarian team of archaeological divers finally located the wreck and succeeded in recovering canon, gold and silver coins and many personal effects of the passengers and crew – but no trace of the mythical great treasures said to have been on board, which reputedly included the Peacock Throne of the Indian emperor Shah Jehan.

SALVAGING THE *HARTWELL*

The *Hartwell* was on its maiden voyage to China in 1787, laden with British East India Company silver for buying eastern porcelain, tea and spices, and with consignments of private merchandise. Conditions on board were not happy and the men eventually mutinied. Deprived of sleep during the three days it took to bring the mutiny under control, the captain made fatal navigational errors and the ship was driven on to a reef

in the Cape Verde islands. No one died but nothing was saved of the ship's valuable contents.

The East India Company soon engaged the services of William and John Braithwaite to salvage the cargo, nearly 6,000 kilograms (13,230 pounds) of silver. This proved a difficult task as the packing chests had broken open, widely scattering the coins. Nevertheless, over two years the brothers managed to raise a considerable quantity, worth 11,000 Spanish dollars – only to be attacked by pirates who carried off the lot. The Braithwaites began again, using the latest diving equipment brought out from Britain. This time they were more successful and within the year they had brought up a great quantity of silver coins – to a value of nearly 100,000 dollars. At this point they decided to stop, although by no means all the treasure had been recovered.

In 1993 the Cape Verde government licensed a new investigation of the *Hartwell*. Further silver coins and a number of other objects were recovered, including a fine gilded telescope.

ARCTIC

EUROPE

Black Sea

KAZAKSTAN

MONGOLIA

TURKEY

GEORGIA

ARMENIA

AZERBAIJAN

Caspian Sea

UZBEKISTAN

TURKMENISTAN

KYRGYSTAN

TAJIKISTAN

LEBANON

SYRIA

ISRAEL

JORDAN

IRAQ

IRAN

AFGHANISTAN

CHINA

SAUDI
ARABIA

PAKISTAN

NEPAL

BHUTAN

YEMEN

OMAN

INDIA

BURMA

Arabian
Sea

Bay of
Bengal

LAOS

THAILAND

CAMBODIA

VIETNAM

SRI LANKA

South China Sea

MALAYSIA

INDON

ISRAEL

JORDAN

1	*HMS EDINBURGH*	7	SARDIS
2	RYZHANOVKA	8	ALACA HOYUK
3	TROY	9	ULU BURUN
4	TOPTEPE	10	VANI
5	KUL OBA	11	UGARIT
6	HALICARNASSUS	12	BYBLOS

RTH
REA

JAPAN

5
46
48

TAIWAN

PHILIPPINES

PAPUA NEW

GUINEA

55

I A

ASIA

Above: *Direct trade between Asia and Atlantic Europe began in the sixteenth century, using ships like this Portuguese carrack.*

ROYAL TOMBS OF UR

In 1922 Sir Leonard Woolley began excavations in the ancient city of Ur in southern Mesopotamia (Iraq), famous as the birthplace of the biblical patriarch Abraham. He started work in the area where an earlier excavator had uncovered part of the wall of the sacred precinct and at once found burials, with pottery, bronze objects and stone beads.

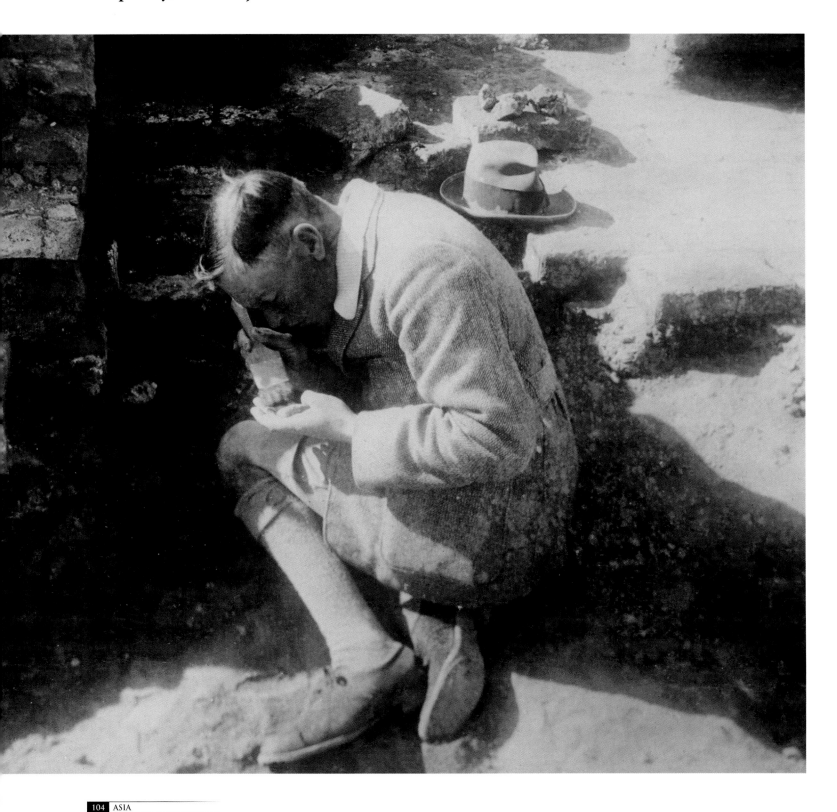

THE GLEAM OF GOLD

Woolley was expecting gold beads too, but the workmen found none. He therefore offered baksheesh (a bribe) for every gold bead found. The next day suddenly many gold beads appeared. The workmen had been selling them to the local goldsmith, but had bought them back as Woolley was offering a much better price.

The cemetery, on which Woolley began serious work in 1927, was dug into the soft ground where rubbish had been dumped in the early days of the city. People were buried here in the period from 2600 to 2450 BC, when Ur was one of the principal cities of Mesopotamia, for a while being regarded as the city in which the gods had vested supreme authority.

Several thousand individuals were buried in the cemetery during this period. Most were placed in a wooden coffin or wrapped in a mat and their personal possessions buried with them – a few pots, some pieces of jewellery, a knife or a dagger and sometimes a cylindrical seal bearing their own name or symbol, to be rolled on clay sealings or tablets as their "signature".

One grave stood out. The burial pit contained a large number of pots, bronze vessels and weapons, including a number of spears stuck into the ground in a row at the head of the grave, and some of these objects were of gold. When the earth was removed from the coffin, it revealed that the body was covered in jewellery of gold and lapis lazuli, along with golden bowls. Two of these bore a name – Meskalamdug, one of Ur's early kings. The finest object was an exquisite helmet in the shape of a wig, made of beaten electrum (an alloy of gold and silver). Each strand of hair had been carefully delineated in the decoration on its surface.

ROYALLY FURNISHED

Meskalamdug's grave had been richly furnished but was otherwise like the others in the cemetery. However, Woolley also discovered 16 royal burials that had been treated much more elaborately. Although there was considerable variation in detail, all followed a similar form. The cemetery had been expertly plundered in ancient times, and many graves were badly disturbed.

The best preserved was that of Queen Puabi, probably the wife of an unidentified king, whose burial chamber lay just below her grave pit.

When the Sumerian workmen dug the queen's grave, a pit more than 12 metres (39 feet) long, they could not resist the temptation to plunder the king's burial chamber below. They concealed their nefarious activity by placing the large chest of the queen's clothes over the telltale hole.

At the end of the grave pit they constructed a stone chamber. The dead queen was decked in all her finery – a beautiful gold headdress in the form of three gold wreaths ornamented with flowers, a cloak of beads made of gold and precious stones, gold pins and amulets, and a golden cup in her hands. Lying on her bier, she was carried down the ramp of the grave pit and placed within the chamber. Around her were arranged a number of her valued possessions – a second headdress of lapis lazuli beads decorated with small figures in gold, several cockleshells containing valuable green cosmetics and many vessels of gold and silver.

Other valuable objects were placed in the grave pit outside the chamber. These included a wooden sledge decorated with small lions' heads in gold and silver, drawn by a pair of oxen who had been killed once the sledge was in place. A wooden gaming board inlaid with lapis lazuli, shell and other colourful materials was placed, with its playing counters, near the sledge, and many gold tools and weapons, and vessels of alabaster, silver and other precious materials, were added.

STEPPING INTO ETERNITY

The grooms who led the oxen into the pit remained with them. A dozen young women also made their way into the grave, wearing fine headdresses and necklaces of gold, lapis lazuli and carnelian. One carried a lyre exquisitely decorated with a bull's head made of lapis lazuli and gold. Three other maidens made their way into the queen's burial chamber, and two crouched by the royal bier. Five soldiers took up their station in the ramp leading down into the grave pit.

Each of these attendants carried a cup which must have contained a drugged drink. Lying down, they composed themselves for death and drank the draught. Dead or unconscious, they never moved as mats and earth were piled over them and the grave was sealed.

The same scene took place within the other royal graves. In one, called by Woolley the Great Death Pit, six soldiers and 68 court ladies gave up their lives. One lady, perhaps arriving late, had not had time to put on her silver hair ribbon. Woolley found it, still rolled up, at her side.

All the graves that had not been plundered contained objects equally as wonderful as those in Puabi's tomb. Lapis lazuli, a stone of brilliant blue, was one of the most precious materials at the time, since it had to be imported over thousands of kilometres from the only source known to the Sumerians, in Afghanistan. Two statues in the Great Death Pit had been made of large quantities of lapis lazuli, gold and silver. Each depicted a goat standing on his hind legs to eat a golden bush. Lapis lazuli also formed the background on a mosaic showing two scenes, war and peace, that decorated an object known as the "Standard of Ur", perhaps the soundbox of a musical instrument. A number of instruments, mainly lyres, were found in the graves, all as richly decorated as that in Puabi's grave.

Left: *Beautiful necklaces, earrings and hair ornaments of gold, carnelian and lapis lazuli adorned many of the women who accompanied Queen Puabi into her grave.*

Opposite: *Modelled in wood, this magnificent figure of a goat was covered with silver, gold, shell and lapis lazuli.*

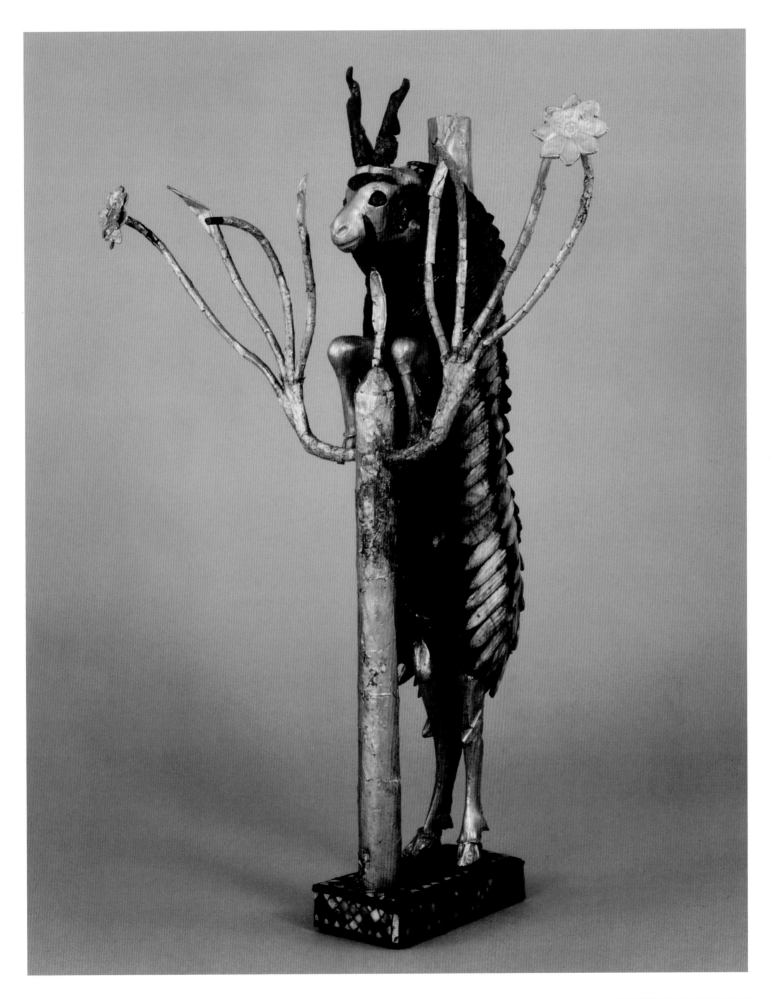

TREASURE OF KING PRIAM

A DREAM OF HEROES

The story of the Trojan War, fought by the Greeks to recover their stolen princess, Helen, the most beautiful woman in the world, and immortalized by the great Greek epic poet Homer, has fired the imagination of many down the ages. Alexander the Great (356–323 BC), beginning his amazing conquest of the Persian Empire, turned aside at Troy to honour the heroes of that ancient conflict. In Germany in the early nineteenth century a small boy who drank up the tales of Homer's heroes from his clergyman father grew into a teenaged grocer's assistant, spellbound one day by the incomprehensible but impassioned recitation of Homer's words by a drunken customer. Young Heinrich Schliemann vowed then that he would learn to understand Homer's epics in their original Greek and that one day he would seek the lost city of the Trojan War, which many people believed to have been only a creation of fiction.

Born in 1822, Schliemann showed a remarkable flair for both languages and business. By the age of 25 he was already established as a prosperous merchant in St Petersburg in Russia and was fluent in eight languages. When he visited the USA in the 1850s, his financial acumen enabled him to accumulate a substantial fortune and his business ventures elsewhere were similarly successful. By 1863 Schliemann was wealthy enough to abandon commerce and pursue his dream.

He prepared himself by travelling widely and studying at the Sorbonne in Paris. In 1868 he visited the Troad – the area of Turkey in which the legendary Trojan War took place – and here he met Frank Calvert, the US vice-consul. At the time, those who believed that Homeric Troy had really existed identified it with a place in the Troad called Bunarbashi, but Calvert was convinced that the mound of Hisarlik was the true location. He had purchased a part of the mound, but lacked the resources to excavate it. Schliemann shared Calvert's view and possessed the funds. In 1870, too impatient

Above: *Heinrich Schliemann was a man with a mission that sustained him for more than 30 years – to prove the historical truth of the story of the legendary Trojan War.*

Below: *Schliemann rapidly published reports on his excavations at Troy, well illustrated with drawings of the remains that he had uncovered, such as this view of the city walls from the south-east.*

Samothrace,
Imbros,

Dr. Schliemann's Houses.

PLATE XIII.

Hellespont.
Plain of Troy.
Scamander.

Greek Tower
(where the
man stands).

a Place where
the Treasure
was found.

Wall of Troy
Scæan Gate,
and
Paved Road
to the
Plain.

Plain of Troy,
seen through
the great
Trench.

Later but
Pre-Hellenic
Buildings,
partly over
the Ruins of
Priam's Palace.

Paved Road.   TOWER   OF   ILIUM.   *Page* 321.

THE SCÆAN GATE AND PAVED ROAD, THE TOWER OF ILIUM, CITY WALL, PALACE OF PRIAM,
AND THE WALLS OF A TOWER OF THE GREEK AGE.
From the South-East.

to await an official permit to excavate, the German began a trial investigation of the Hisarlik mound.

TROJAN GOLD

Official permission caught up with Schliemann and in 1871 he began major excavations in the mound, which was massive, representing many centuries of occupation. He had decided that the city occupied during the Trojan War lay at the bottom, so he wantonly removed walls, houses and other debris in the upper deposits. Later, when experience, criticism and his own discoveries had taught him greater caution and respect for the material he was uncovering, he regretted his first destructive enthusiasm and conducted his excavations more systematically, particularly from 1882, when he was assisted by Wilhelm Dörpfeld, who became one of the finest archaeologists of the age.

By 1873 Schliemann's excavations had revealed the remains of nine superimposed cities on the site of Hisarlik and had convinced many that he had indeed discovered Troy. There were, however, many professional doubters, who were moved by both jealousy and serious reservations about Schliemann's methods, results and honesty. In this they were to some extent justified, for he was a ruthless romantic, given to embroidering the truth and dishonest when it served his ends.

Schliemann identified one of the early levels, Troy II, as the city of King Priam and the Trojan War, partly partly because it had been destroyed by a conflagration. Here he uncovered the remains of massive walls and gates and many objects that had served the people of the time, such as pottery. As the 1873 season approached its end the excavations took a dramatic turn. As was his habit, Schliemann was watching his men at work. Suddenly he dismissed them all, telling the foreman that he had just remembered that it was his birthday and that the men should take an extended break to celebrate. When they had all left, he jumped down to where they had been working – whence his sharp eyes had spotted the glint of gold. Working feverishly with a knife and regardless of the masonry of the wall hanging above him, Schliemann rapidly cut out the treasures and hastily concealed them in his wooden hut. When he came to write his account of the discovery, he recorded that his wife had shared the adventure, but she was, in fact, in Athens at the time.

Later Schliemann was able to examine the treasure more closely. All the objects had been packed tightly together, with many pieces of gold jewellery placed inside a massive silver jar, and this suggested to him that they had been hidden as Troy fell to the Greeks. Their magnificence left him in no doubt that he had found the personal treasure of King Priam and his family – the golden rings, necklaces, bracelets and earrings of Helen, of the Trojan Queen Hecuba and of Prince Hector's wife Andromache, as well as golden cups and silver knife blades. One particularly fine headdress was made up of hundreds of tiny gold leaves hung on linked vertical chains.

Below left and right: *Replicas of gilded silver earrings, which would have been worn in Troy around 2300 BC.*

SUSPICION AND DECEIT

Schliemann's uncharacteristic behaviour that morning had aroused the suspicions of the government agent, Effendi Amin, whose unenviable job it was to watch the excavation, and he demanded to search the excavator's storage chests and cupboards. When Schliemann refused, Amin went off to obtain official support. Schliemann lost no time in enlisting the help of Frank Calvert's brother to smuggle away the gold, without, it seems, revealing what it was – his letter to Calvert refers to broken pottery. The treasure was carried safely to Greece, where Schliemann exhibited it in his house. He took photographs of his young Greek wife, Sophia, dressed in the golden jewellery. The Turks were justifiably outraged, particularly as Schliemann's excavation permit required that he divide his finds equally with the Turkish authorities. They demanded that he pay a fine of 10,000 francs – but Schliemann succeeded in turning away their wrath by handing over 50,000 francs instead, in exchange for outright ownership of the treasure.

WINNING RESPECT

Schliemann next turned his attentions to the home of the Greek heroes, excavating at Mycenae (see page 17), where he was even more spectacularly successful. His methods, amateur even by the standards of the time (although they improved), his showmanship and his lack of transparency made other archaeologists suspicious of his findings, and the fact that he was uncovering new, previously unknown civilizations meant that there was no established material against which to prove that his finds were as ancient as he claimed. Gradually, however, scholars were won over and the Bronze Age civilizations he had discovered were accepted – but throughout his life Schliemann remained touchy about his finds and easily enraged by criticism.

"King Priam's treasure", along with other lesser hoards of gold and silver from Troy, and many other objects such as pottery, had become internationally famous. Many countries vied for the honour of acquiring them from Schliemann. He was torn – Greece was the country of Homer and his dreams; Russia had been his home in the days of his youthful rise to wealth; England had welcomed him with open arms when German scholars had been hostile; but Germany was his native land. Germany began to accord him the acclaim he had always sought, presenting him with honours, and eventually Schliemann chose Berlin as the final home of his treasures.

THE TREASURES VANISH

Schliemann's Trojan collections were installed in Berlin in 1881 with lavish ceremony, and remained there until 1945. During the Second World War the Germans looted a vast number of art treasures and antiquities from the countries that they invaded. In 1945, when the tide of war turned against Germany, many of these looted valuables, along with Germany's own art treasures, were hidden or taken to places of comparative safety. The finds from Troy were dispersed – the lesser pieces were concealed in various places, and after the war some were recovered, while others seem to have disappeared forever. "King Priam's treasure" and the other Trojan gold were packed, with other treasures from Berlin's Museum for Pre- and Early History, in three boxes and taken to the well-fortified flak-tower in the city's zoo, where they were jealously guarded and cared for by Wilhelm Unverzacht, the museum's director. In the final days of the flak-tower's siege, he even slept on the boxes.

On May 1, 1945, the defenders of the flak-tower surrendered to the Russians. Concerned by the looting all around, Unverzacht worked hard to hand over his treasures intact to the Russian authorities. The three boxes were taken with other objects of particular importance and flown to Moscow – where they disappeared.

Left: *Sophia, the Greek girl whom Schliemann had chosen as his wife, was photographed wearing the gold necklaces, earrings and headdress that Schliemann identified as the treasure of King Priam.*

Nothing was known about their subsequent fate, although it was much discussed. The Cold War made international investigation impossible. However, the collapse of communism in the 1980s brought many things to light, including archives which revealed that for half a century Schliemann's gold had been resting in the vaults of the Pushkin Museum in Moscow. In 1996 they at last saw the light again, in a magnificent exhibition in the museum. Recently a government spokesman said that Russia now considers them to be Russian cultural property, part of a large collection of art objects regarded as compensation for its own cultural losses during the Second World War. Germany disputes Russia's claim to these treasures.

NOT PRIAM'S GOLD
Schliemann had resumed excavations at Troy in 1878 and in 1882 was joined by Dörpfeld; they worked together until Schliemann's death in 1890. By this stage much more was known about Greek and Anatolian prehistory than had been in 1870, when Schliemann made his first discoveries. In the final season it became clear to both men that Troy II, which Schliemann had identified as Priam's city, was in fact much earlier. Dörpfeld regarded Troy VI as the city of the Trojan War, around 1200 BC. Later the eminent

American archaeologist Carl Blegen was able finally to pin down the Troy of Homer's epic – Priam, if he existed, had ruled the city of Troy VIIA. Recent excavations have shown that in this period the Trojans crowded within the city's fortified citadel. Slingstones were stockpiled for active defence, but skeletons and weapons lying in the streets bear witness to the city's fall.

Schliemann's spectacular gold finds belonged to a far earlier age – the later third millennium BC. Metallurgy was at that time in its infancy and many cultures of Europe and West Asia created lavish works of gold for their kings and chiefs (see pages 14 and 105). Troy had been a major centre of trade during that period, part of a network of towns that grew wealthy through the exchange of local resources and, in particular, metal ores. The extraordinary goldwork uncovered by Schliemann at Troy was part

---

Below left: *This superbly crafted jug of beaten gold was one of the many rich objects placed in the royal graves at Alaca Höyük.*

Below right: *The bull, portrayed here on a standard from Alaca Höyük, had been prominent in Anatolian art for millennia.*

---

of the wealth of its rulers and included a number of pieces assembled by a craftsman to be melted down to make something else.

ANATOLIA'S TREASURES
Further to the east, in central Anatolia, equally lavish works were being made using local gold and especially silver, for the region was a source of silver highly valued in the ancient world. In the late third millennium BC, the area around Alaca Höyük was home to a prosperous community that buried their leaders in great style, although they lived in a relatively small town.

Fourteen elite burials have been discovered here. Men and women were placed in large rectangular pits, sometimes covered with red ochre, accompanied by jewellery, weapons and vessels made of gold, silver, electrum and copper, including fine spiral-headed pins, belt buckles, goblets with beautifully decorated stems and two daggers of meteoric iron with gold handles – an indication of how highly prized iron was in this period long before iron ore began to be smelted. Some of the graves contained objects of bronze inlaid with silver that have been called "standards" – geometric figures or small animal figurines, such as stags and bulls, with a tang to allow them to be mounted on a pole. It is assumed that these had some religious purpose.

RICH CITIES OF THE LEVANT

AN EXCITING DISCOVERY

George Bass is a pioneer of marine archaeology who has spent his life investigating ancient wrecks. In 1960, early in his career, he excavated the remains of the oldest shipwreck then known – a Bronze Age Syrian cargo boat carrying copper ingots and scrap metal which was wrecked around 1200 BC on Cape Gelidonya off Turkey's southern coast. That wreck had been spotted by sponge divers and Bass kept in close contact with the sponge divers of the region, whose daily work gives them ample opportunities to discover ancient wrecks. To ensure that the sponge divers knew what to watch out for, Bass and his team would give slide shows in the divers' villages to show them what the remains might look like.

One day in 1982 a young sponge diver named Mehmet Çakir noticed some strange objects on the seabed near Ulu Burun off Turkey's southern coast – they looked like "metal biscuits with ears". Recognizing this as a description of ancient copper ingots, the diver's captain reported the find to the Museum of Underwater Archaeology at Bodrum, who contacted Bass. Could this be another early trading vessel? Bass and his team investigated. What they found surpassed their wildest dreams. Not a humble cargo boat, this time, but a ship carrying a royal gift of Bronze Age treasures from the Levant coast to some prince in the Aegean – and at least 100 years earlier than the Cape Gelidonya wreck, making it the earliest shipwreck then known in the world: firewood on board the ship gives a tree-ring date of 1316–05 BC.

Preliminary survey work in 1983 revealed the remains of a ship 9 metres (30 feet) long, outlined by her cargo – hundreds of neatly stacked ox-hide-shaped copper ingots that were typical Bronze Age products of Cyprus, the main exporter of copper at that time. Bass and his team began the arduous business of

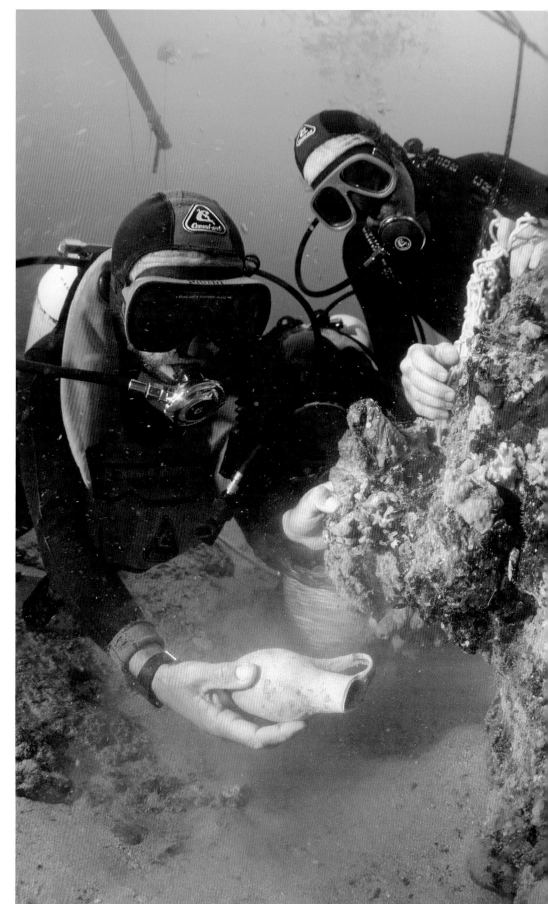

Above: *Divers excavating the Ulu Burun wreck recover a small jug. This was made in Cyprus, where the ship called to take on its main cargo of copper ingots shortly before it sank.*

Opposite: *Golden treasures from the Ulu Burun shipwreck include a Syrian-made pendant, which shows a naked goddess holding a gazelle in each hand.*

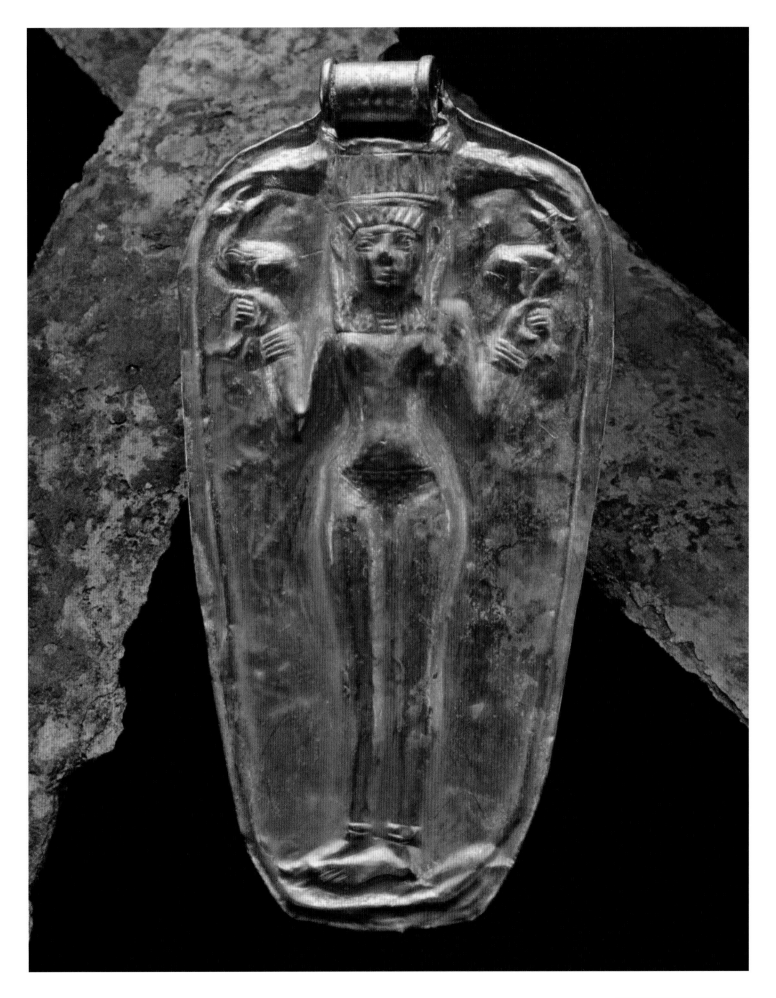

excavating the wreck in 1984 – but it was not until 1994 that the task was completed. The wreck lay in 43 metres (140 feet) of water, sloping steeply downward to 52 metres (170 feet) – a dangerous depth at which to work. Because of the difference in pressure, divers rising too rapidly to the surface after a deep dive can suffer from the "bends", a painful and potentially crippling condition, so, as a precaution, Bass's team initially dived for only five minutes at a time. They learned that they could build up to two 20-minute dives per day so long as they had long periods of decompression using pure oxygen.

In the sandy area around the ship's keel, excavation was relatively easy – the sediments could be sucked away with an airlift. But in the upper portion the archaeologists had the laborious task of chiselling away the concretions that had welded the ship's cargo into a solid mass. Once exposed, the position of every one of the thousands of items in the cargo had to be painstakingly mapped, using stereo-photography and hand-held tapes. The slope of the ground made this a difficult task. Some of the finds were small enough for the divers to carry to the surface. But to lift the massive and heavily encrusted storage jars and stone anchor weights, something stronger than people was required, and for this operation the excavators used nets attached to balloons.

THE ANCIENT MARINERS' LOSS

Copper – 354 ox-hide ingots and 130 round "bun" ingots – formed the major part of the cargo, more than 10 tonnes (10 tons) in all. Tin ingots added another tonne – tin was essential for alloying with copper to form bronze, from which most tools and weapons of the time were manufactured, including the swords, daggers, axes, knives, razors and cauldrons found on the ship. Equally valuable at the time was the consignment of more than 145 Canaanite jars containing the yellow resin of the terebinth shrub (*Pistacia terebinthus*), used in Egypt as incense and by the Mycenaeans of Greece for making perfume. The ship was probably Canaanite, although some of the personal possessions on board show that the crew also included Mycenaeans. The Canaanites, predecessors of the Phoenicians, lived in the Levant and traded a wide range of raw materials, many of which have been recovered from the wreck. These included ivory from hippos and small Syrian elephants (later to become extinct) and blue glass, probably manufactured to a secret recipe known only to the Canaanites. About 175 glass ingots were found in the cargo. These would have been used by their Egyptian and Mycenaean customers to manufacture glass objects.

The cargo also included some scrap metal to be melted down and reused, including part of a gold ring, bits of gold pendants and twisted pieces of silver bangles. A surprising item among the scrap was a gold scarab bearing the name of the Egyptian Queen Nefertiti, wife of the heretical pharaoh Akhenaten and Tutankhamun's mother-in-law. Not all the gold was scrap, however. There were several gold amulets and pendants, perhaps worn for good luck by members of the crew. A fine example shows a goddess holding a gazelle in each hand. One of the most valuable items in the cargo was a magnificent gold chalice. Along with five ram's-head drinking vessels made of faience, the raw ivory and a number of fine cylinder seals, these may have been diplomatic gifts intended for the ruler of the Aegean lands for which the ship was bound when it was wrecked on the treacherous rocks at Ulu Burun.

TRADING CITIES

This was a time of particular prosperity for the cities of the Levant coast. In the early centuries of the second millennium BC, many were strongly influenced by their neighbour, Egypt, which either controlled or claimed to control many of them. Byblos in particular had close ties with Egypt. The tombs of its rulers, excavated in the cliffs along the city's shores, contained many fine objects that may have been diplomatic gifts from the rulers of Egypt. Other objects, such as a beautifully wrought gold pectoral (chest ornament) bearing an image of a hawk (the form in which the Egyptian god Horus was usually depicted), were probably locally made by craftsmen heavily influenced by Egyptian art styles and ideas.

For about a century (c. 1650–1550 BC) Egypt was ruled by a dynasty, the Hyksos, who came from the Levant or who were related to inhabitants of that region. During this time close diplomatic links existed between Egypt and independent Canaanite cities of the Levant. Trade flourished, the city states trading with their neighbours

---

---

in Egypt, Mesopotamia, Anatolia and the islands of the eastern Mediterranean. The prosperity enjoyed by these cities was vividly demonstrated by discoveries at Tell el-'Ajjul in southern Palestine, which was under Hyksos control.

In 1933 the eminent British Egyptologist Flinders Petrie uncovered five substantial hoards of goldwork from the houses of Tell el-'Ajjul and from the city's palace. Further gold treasures were found in the graves of warriors in the cemetery, buried with their horses. Many of the pieces discovered were simple gold pendants in the basic shape of women, with face, breasts and vulva but no limbs. These represented Astarte, the goddess of fertility. Other pendants took the form of a star and there were also rings with gemstones and toggle pins for fastening clothing, objects that were likewise relatively simple in design. The greater part of the jewellery, however, shows the amazing skill and versatility of the craftsmen of this time. Elaborate earrings, pendants and pectorals were created using granulation, a technique in which tiny balls of gold are attached to the surface of a gold object with a glue that contains copper hydroxide. The object is then heated, carbonizing the glue

and reducing the copper hydroxide to metallic copper, which then bonds with the gold. In this way the Tell el-'Ajjul goldsmiths produced beautiful objects, decorated with figures of birds or geometric patterns.

After 1550, Egypt was again ruled by a native dynasty and new power struggles began to develop between the major political powers of the time – Egypt and Mitanni (a state in northern Mesopotamia and Syria) at first and the Hittites in Anatolia from around 1450 BC. All sought to control the rich city states of the Levant, which responded by building massive ramparts around their cities, capable of withstanding sieges. A smooth slope (glacis) of stone or earth covered by plaster was constructed below the city walls, making it difficult to approach the walls with siege engines or scaling ladders and virtually impossible to undermine them. Many cities of the southern Levant, however, fell to the Egyptians, while many of those in the north came under the domination of the Hittites. A degree of peace settled on the region after the inconclusive Battle of Kadesh in 1275 BC. As neither Egypt nor the Hittites had won, both were content to conclude a treaty defining their spheres of influence.

UGARIT

The major trading city of Ugarit (modern Ras Shamra), capital of a flourishing city state on the north Levantine coast, managed to weave a path between the two great powers, acknowledging the authority of both, and enjoying great prosperity during these troubled times. The heart of the city was the palace, a vast complex of more than 100 rooms, including accommodation for craftsmen, foreign merchants and nobles as well as the royal family. Pools and gardens added to its attractions, but it also housed major storerooms and a huge archive of cuneiform tablets dealing with a whole range of matters – diplomatic activities, commerce, legal and administrative records and religion – giving an invaluable insight into life in this city and in the world of its time.

Ugarit traded with Cyprus for copper, the Hittites for gold, tin and silver and the Mycenaean world for fine pottery, in exchange for local produce. This included grain from its fields, wine and olive oil. The surrounding hills supplied timber and grazing for the sheep whose wool supported a flourishing textile industry. Local craftsmen also manufactured fine metalwork and the famous purple dye made from murex shellfish.The wealth of the city's inhabitants can be seen in the many expensive locally made and imported pieces found in their graves and houses. These include a gold plate decorated with a hunting scene in which a noble armed with a bow rides in a light chariot, pursuing a bull and other local game. Cylinder seals of stone were often mounted in looped gold terminals, which acted not only as decoration but also as a convenient means by which they could be worn so as not to lose them.

Around 1200 BC, many states around the eastern Mediterranean suffered attacks from pirates and seaborne invaders. Ugarit seems to have fallen prey to such an attack in about 1170 BC and was never reoccupied.

QATNA

Inland city states were also influenced and threatened by the major states. One of the most important was Qatna (modern Tell el-Mishrifeh, near Homs), which not only sat astride the north–south trade route between Egypt and Anatolia but was also a terminus of the desert route that linked the Levant coast with Mari on the middle Euphrates and Mesopotamia. Qatna was a huge city, around 100 hectares (247 acres) in extent. Documents attest its prosperity. For example, eighteenth-century letters found at Mari refer to diplomatic exchanges between the king of Qatna and Mari's governor, Yasmah-Addu, the ne'er-do-well son of the king of Upper Mesopotamia, Shamshi-Adad. In one letter Shamshi-Adad refers to a gift of 10 talents (300 kilograms/661 pounds) of gold, to Ishi-Addu, king of Qatna, on the occasion of his daughter's marriage to Yasmah-Addu. A later document, from the temple of Qatna's goddess, Belet-ekallim, is an inventory of all the treasures offered to her by devotees over the years. The first mentioned is a statue of the goddess in red gold, holding a sword of yellow gold, and it also lists quantities of jewellery made of gold, lapis lazuli, faience and other valued materials.

The palace at Qatna has been under excavation since 1992. A discovery here in 2002 brought some of the city's treasures to light. A long passage was uncovered leading down to a deep shaft that gave access by ladder to a burial complex 12 metres (39 feet) below ground. This had been untouched since the palace was destroyed, probably by the Hittites, around 1340 BC. Records on cuneiform tablets that had fallen into the passage reflect the constant threat of military action and the need for defence: one, for example, is an order for 18,600 bronze swords.

Two seated stone statues of benevolent figures guarded the tomb door, with bowls for offerings beside them. Through this door was a large central chamber with benches around its walls. Animal bones and pottery found here were perhaps the remains of the annual feasts when the dead were believed to revisit the living. The bodies of the dead were laid here on wooden biers or, in the case of the most recent burial, in a wooden coffin, covered by coloured textiles. Later, the bones were tidied away into stone sarcophagi or piled up in one of the three side-chambers. With the bodies were rich grave goods including gold and gemstone beads and other objects of gold, among them a strange gold hand. A pair of ducks' heads, back to back, part of some larger object, every feather beautifully delineated, demonstrate superb craftsmanship.

Opposite: *In this necklace, from Tell el-'Ajjul, beads of rock crystal and amethyst alternate with tablet-shaped gold beads with Egyptian-style decorative motifs.*

Left: *In the scene on this gold plate from Ugarit the hunter has tied his reins around his waist, leaving both hands free to shoot with his bow at the escaping game.*

SPLENDOURS OF THE PALACE AT NIMRUD

WINGED BEASTS

In 1842 Paul-Émile Botta, French consul at Mosul in Iraq, began desultory investigations of several ancient mounds near the city and found remarkable sculptured reliefs depicting warfare and processions. The French government, impressed by his finds, sponsored excavation and recording of the sites, which were none other than two successive capital cities of the Assyrians, Dur-Sharrukin (modern Khorsabad) and Nineveh.

The British government was slow to develop an interest in the area, but in 1845 Austen Henry Layard, a young diplomat at Constantinople, began work on his own account on a third mound, Nimrud, with financial backing from the British ambassador, Sir Stratford Canning. Tunnelling into the Nimrud mound and following the line of ancient walls, Layard uncovered the spectacular remains of the ancient Assyrian city of Kalhu. He revealed enormous statues of winged bulls flanking the entrance to the throne room of a royal palace, its walls carved with scenes showing the military and sporting achievements of King Ashurnasirpal II (reigned 883–859 BC) – lion hunts, campaigns and sieges. Fired by the magnificence of Layard's discoveries, the British government belatedly began to sponsor his efforts. In subsequent years he uncovered the remains of a second palace, built by a later king, Tiglath-Pileser III (reigned 744–727 BC), and successfully arranged for the monumental statues and reliefs to be shipped to England, where they still dominate the Assyrian collection in the British Museum. The French were less fortunate – many of the sculptures that they had excavated were lost or destroyed while being transported home.

Below: *Layard used methods similar to those of the Assyrians – who had originally brought the winged stone bulls to Nimrud – when he removed the statues from the site to transport them to London.*

THE CONQUERING KINGS

In the tenth century BC, Assyria began to expand its power over Mesopotamia and adjacent areas of West Asia. Ashurnasirpal II pushed the boundaries of the Assyrian Empire still further, boasting that he had washed his weapons in the Great Sea (the Mediterranean). He decided to found a new capital city, Kalhu, which he peopled with displaced inhabitants from many of the lands he conquered. Work was begun in 878 BC on the massive city walls and the king's palace, which took about 15 years to complete. To mark the inauguration of the palace, Ashurnasirpal gave a great feast that lasted 10 days, inviting nearly 70,000 guests, who consumed, among other things, 14,000 sheep, 1,000 deer, 10,000 gerbils, 10,000 loaves of bread and 10,000 skins of wine. To the magnificence of the royal palace, with its throne room, public halls and private chambers, Ashurnasirpal added other splendid public buildings – temples to the goddess Ishtar and to other deities,

On Stone by W.L. Walton.

Frontispiece. Vol. I

LOWERING THE GREAT WINGED BULL.

John Murray Albemarle Street 1848.

Printed by Hullmandel & Walton

a ziggurat and impressive government offices. A large central square was decorated with trophies collected during the king's successful campaigns and monuments commemorating them. The king also had a canal dug from the Upper Hab River to provide water for the orchards and botanic garden that he constructed to adorn his city.

The annual campaigns of Ashurnasirpal and his successors yielded huge quantities of plunder and the defeated peoples were also compelled to pay tribute – gold, silver and other metals, linen and other textiles, timber, ivory, exotic creatures and many other goods. The king's son and successor, Shalmaneser III (reigned 858–824 BC), began work soon after his accession on a new palace to act partly as a treasure-house for all the wealth that was accumulating. Completed in 846 BC, it was also a fortress and an arsenal. Three great courtyards enabled the king to muster

and view his troops, complete with chariots. Workshops for making and replacing armour, weapons and other military equipment flanked the parade ground. The royal residence formed another wing of the complex, and consisted of a great throne room with a massive dais on which stood the king's throne, public ceremonial rooms and private apartments, including a harem.

When Sir Max Mallowan excavated Shalmaneser's palace he uncovered a number of wonderful objects. These included exquisite ivory carvings, some made by local craftsmen, others imported from many lands, including Egypt and Phoenicia. Some pieces were ornaments, such as a procession of tribute bearers leading animals. Others were elements from furniture such as chests, chairs and beds, or ornamental plaques to decorate them, depicting people, plants and animals – sphinxes were a popular motif. Fragments of gold scattered on the floor of the

storeroom show that originally many of the ivory pieces had been gilded.

Mallowan found other treasures in about 100 pottery jars at the base of a deep well. These included an exquisite carved ivory head of a woman whom he called "Mona Lisa", her face bearing an enigmatic smile like that of the famous painting. The same well produced a pair of ivory plaques, only 10 centimetres (4 inches) long, showing a lioness killing a young man. Gold covers his loincloth and highlights his hair and the red and blue papyrus flowers in the background are coloured with lapis lazuli and carnelian inlays.

Below: *This finely carved ivory plaque, inlaid with gold, carnelian and lapis lazuli, found in the Assyrian king's treasure-house, was probably of Phoenician workmanship.*

GOLDEN PRINCESSES

Assyrian texts describe the splendours of their royal burials, but the majority were looted in the past. However, in 1988 Iraqi excavations uncovered an amazing find – a chamber beneath the harem of Ashurnasirpal's palace containing an intact royal burial, complete with priceless grave furnishings, including alabaster vessels. The queen, an elderly woman, had been laid to rest in a terracotta sarcophagus, her head resting on a silver bowl and her body covered with gold jewellery: rings, bracelets, amulets, fibulae, earrings with granulated decoration and necklaces of beads made of gold and gemstones.

But that was not all. Remarkably, over the following two years three more tombs were discovered under different rooms of the harem; one had been looted but the other two were full of treasures. The second tomb bore an inscription identifying it as that of Yaba, wife of Tiglath-Pileser III, and laying a heavy curse on anyone who should disturb or reuse the tomb. Despite this, the stone sarcophagus within the tomb contained two bodies.

Above left: *These two bracelets, from the tomb of queens Yaba and Atalia, are made of gold inlaid with glass and semi-precious stones, including tiger's-eyes, forming sacred trees and tiny winged guardian genies.*

Above right: *This panel, part of an elaborate piece of royal jewellery from Nimrud, was skilfully inlaid to create a miniature mosaic of a date palm, complete with ripe fruit. Gold pomegranates can be seen dangling below.*

Inscribed golden vessels buried with them showed that one was Yaba while the other, buried later, was Atalia, wife of Sargon II, the king who abandoned Nimrud and founded a new capital, Dur-Sharrukin, in 717 BC. As Sargon was a usurper, it is possible that Atalia was Yaba's daughter. Both queens had died in their thirties. They were wearing gold necklaces, earrings and anklets in abundance, as well as a golden crown and an extraordinary diadem of gold ribbon inlaid with tiger's-eye gems and fringed with tiny gold pomegranates. Exquisite gold panels, perhaps from another diadem, were inlaid with beautiful mosaic designs: one depicting a date palm, the other a stylized tree of life. The queens' linen clothes had been sewn with hundreds of gold ornaments in the form of stars and flowers. There were beautiful jars and bowls of gold, alabaster and rock-crystal. Atalia also had precious objects that had

once belonged to Banitu, wife of Sargon's predecessor, Shalmaneser V; one, a cosmetic container, was reinscribed with Atalia's name.

The third tomb had belonged to Mullissu-mukannishat-Ninua, Ashurnasirpal's wife, but it had been broken into. All that remained were an empty stone coffin set into the floor and a few small objects that the looters, in their haste, had dropped. Later, however, the antechamber to the tomb had been repeatedly used. Within it were three large bronze sarcophagi, containing the secondary burials of seven adults and six children and a wealth of grave goods. Perhaps the most extraordinary was a crown worn by a child. The top of this was modelled as a leafy gold vine, with lapis-lazuli grapes hanging from it. A row of gold winged figures supported this, standing on a thick band of gold daisies and pomegranates. Inscribed objects showed that another of the bodies was that of a eunuch,

Shamshi-ilu, who served as commander-in-chief of the army under three successive eighth-century kings.

When Saddam Hussein was overthrown in 2003, the Baghdad Museum was sacked and looted. Many of the well-known pieces that were stolen, such as the famous Warka Vase, were soon returned; but more than 10,000 cuneiform tablets and other small but valuable objects were taken from the museum basements and most are still missing, presumed sold to criminal dealers in stolen antiquities. By great good fortune the Nimrud goldwork survived this plunder: before the first Gulf War in 1990 it was placed for safekeeping in the vaults of the Central Bank, along with the wonderful Nimrud ivories and the treasures from the Ur Royal Cemetery. The bank vaults were flooded during the conflict in 2003. The goldwork was unharmed, but sadly the ivories were badly damaged.

TODAY'S UNFOUND TREASURES

THE *DOURADO*

Louis Dominic de Rienzi had spent many adventurous years exploring and travelling in the Americas, the Mediterranean and much of Asia. He had also taken part in many famous conflicts – Waterloo, the Greek fight for independence from the Turkish Ottoman Empire and Italy's struggles for freedom. He had discovered several important archaeological sites, including Petra, and had visited many others, assembling a great collection of antiquities. This he had with him when in 1829 he embarked from Macao in the East Indies on the *Dourado*, bound for Bombay. Within a week, however, the ship was in serious difficulties. Everyone took to the boats, and Rienzi, by his own account, played a heroic part in rescuing drowning companions. Abandoning the doomed ship, the boats headed for Singapore, not far distant. On arrival, the captain persuaded the authorities to send an immediate salvage team, with armed guards, for the ship contained $500,000 in gold. The salvage ships failed to find the *Dourado*, but within a few days it was reported to have sunk off the island of Bintan. Divers were soon at work but their success was limited to recovering a few small objects. Rienzi returned to Europe, lamenting his loss.

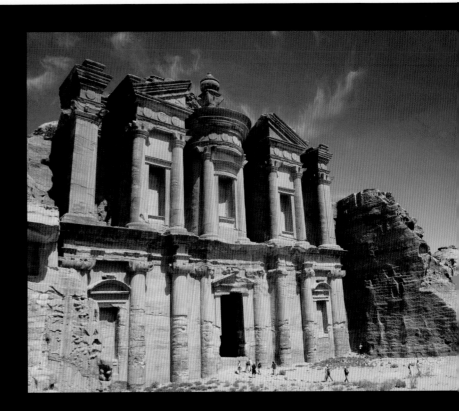

Above: *The magnificent "Monastery" in the ancient Nabataean city of Petra in Jordan: it may have been a tomb or religious meeting place.*

LANDS OF ALLUVIAL GOLD

THE RICHES OF CROESUS

The Kingdom of Lydia rose to prominence in western Anatolia in the seventh century BC and under Croesus (reigned 561–547 BC) it gained control of the whole region, through conquest, diplomacy and intimidation. So confident did Croesus grow that he considered challenging the rapidly expanding Persian Empire. He sent rich gifts to the Delphic oracle, to ask if he would be successful: the oracle replied that, if he attacked Persia, a great empire would fall. Encouraged, Croesus attacked – but it was his own empire that was destroyed.

During the brief period of Lydian pre-eminence, and particularly in the reign of Croesus, the kingdom became internationally famous for its wealth, particularly in gold. Lydia is credited with the invention of coinage, made of electrum, and a little later, probably in the reign of Croesus, the introduction of two separate types of coins, respectively in pure gold and pure silver. The wealth of the region is reflected in the elite barrow cemeteries near Sardis, the capital. Some of the barrows are enormous; generally they cover beautifully constructed chamber tombs of stone and sometimes marble, though there are also more modest burials in cists. Most of the graves have been plundered, but recently several intact cist burials were found, furnished with many fine Greek and Lydian pottery vessels, silver and bronze mirrors, gold and silver containers and all their gold and silver jewellery, including clothing sewn with gold decorations. The grave goods of the kings must have been far more sumptuous. Croesus's gifts to the Delphic oracle were reported by Herodotus to have been of extraordinary richness, including outsize golden bowls, a gold statue 3 cubits (1.5 metres/5 feet) high, couches decorated with gold and silver and more than 200 talents (6,000 kilograms/13,228 pounds) in gold and electrum ingots.

Where did all this gold and silver come from? Some may have been obtained in tribute from kingdoms incorporated into Croesus's empire, but much was said to come from the River Hermus that flowed through Sardis and particularly from its tributary, the Pactolus, that drained nearby Mount Tmolus. Even today gold dust and tiny fragments of gold can be panned from the Pactolus. It has been suggested that under Croesus and his immediate predecessors there was a short period when the gold that had built up in the river through the ages, as the river eroded the gold-bearing mountain, was intensively

---

Opposite top: *This gold coin was issued by King Croesus of Lydia, whose wealth was legendary. On the left is a roaring lion, a design used on earlier Lydian coins, and on the right is a bull.*

Opposite bottom: *The Toptepe treasures, including this hippocamp brooch, were sold by looters to an American museum, but later returned to Turkey. In 2006 the brooch was stolen from the Usak museum.*

TODAY'S UNFOUND TREASURES

THE *SÃO PAULO*

The *São Paulo* was a Portuguese carrack, a huge vessel weighing more than 1,524 tonnes (1,500 tons), plying the trade route to the East Indies. It set sail from Belém in Portugal in April 1560, carrying coins, rich trade goods such as tapestries and many passengers, but illness and adverse weather slowed its journey and a storm brought it to an end the following January, wrecking the ship on a small island just off Sumatra. The passengers and crew managed to recover some goods, including food, and were able to survive while they constructed and repaired boats to take them off the island – though some of their number were captured and eaten by neighbouring cannibals. When they left, the boats were overcrowded since some of the merchants had packed in salvaged goods, but they seized a junk and sailed down the Sumatra coast. Putting in at the River Menencabo, they were deceived by apparently friendly natives who fell on them in the night, capturing or killing around seventy of them. The survivors managed to reach Java, where, weakened, some of them died of overeating. The remaining 250 eventually reached their destination, the trading post of Malacca (Melaka) in July.

Above: *The* São Paulo *would have looked similar to the carrack in the centre of this scene, which was painted a few decades before the* São Paulo's *ill-fated journey.*

exploited by the Lydians and largely used up. This gold was really electrum, containing up to 40 per cent silver and a little copper.

Exciting evidence that local gold was being processed in Sardis was exposed by excavations in the 1990s. A series of bowl hearths (cupels) and furnaces with traces of gold foil and drops of gold were unearthed. These revealed that the metalsmiths of Sardis knew how to separate electrum into its constituent metals. They removed the copper and other impurities by cupellation, heating the electrum with lead in the cupels with a continuous blast of hot air: this produced a slag of base metal oxides and pure electrum. Next they used a technique that they may have been the first to devise – parting by cementation. The electrum was beaten into foil to maximize its surface area and placed in a closed earthenware pot along with common salt (sodium chloride), and heated for a long time at a temperature below the melting point of gold. The salt vapours attacked the silver, which vaporized and formed silver chloride, leaving pure gold. The silver

chloride was deposited on the inside of the vessel or on clay or brick dust that had been mixed in with the salt. It was recovered by smelting the clay and silver chloride with lead and then repeating the cupellation process, to produce lead oxide with a little button of pure silver on the surface.

FUNERARY TREASURES

Elsewhere in Lydia burials have been found that underline the kingdom's wealth. Many were plundered long ago but their walls still preserve wonderful paintings of Lydians enjoying banquets, performing rituals or journeying to the other world accompanied by a procession of servants, horses and chariots. Finds from intact tombs show that banqueting equipment formed a major part of the grave goods: silver bowls and plates, wide silver drinking cups, silver ladles to serve wine and silver, bronze or fine pottery jugs or situlae to hold it.

One burial at Halicarnassus (modern Bodrum) is known as the Carian Princess. Within the tomb chamber was a sarcophagus

containing a woman in her forties, buried wearing a garment covered with gold and blue glass appliqués, gold earrings, three gold and gemstone rings, two necklaces, gold bracelets with terminals in the form of antelope heads and a wreath of golden leaves. Some scholars believe it is the tomb of Ada, sister of King Mausolus of Halicarnassus, whose own tomb, the Mausoleum, was one of the Seven Wonders of the World.

Another intact tomb was discovered under a tumulus at Toptepe near Usak. In it the body had been laid on a stone couch. Among the grave goods were stone vessels containing perfumed oils and all that the deceased would have required for a banquet, including a bronze jug with magnificent animal decoration, a similarly decorated ladle and silver bowls. The deceased was wearing a great deal of valuable jewellery, including glass bracelets with lion's-head terminals and a beautiful gold brooch inlaid with glass, in the form of a hippocamp (a mythical sea creature with a horse's body and a fishy tail).

THE GOLDEN FLEECE

In the ancient Greek kingdom of Iolkos, so the legend goes, a prince married a second wife who threatened the lives of his children. The god Hermes sent a ram with a golden fleece to rescue them. They flew east on its back toward the Black Sea; Helle fell off, giving her name to the Hellespont into whose waters she fell, but her brother Phrixus reached safety in the land of Colchis (in modern Georgia). Here the ram was sacrificed in thanksgiving and its golden fleece hung up in a sacred grove, guarded by a serpent.

Several generations later, Prince Jason and his companions brought their ship, the *Argo*, to Colchis's strand in quest of the Golden Fleece. The king's daughter, Medea, fell in love with Jason and helped him, drugging the guardian snake so that Jason could easily kill it and murdering her own brother to delay the pursuit as she and the Argonauts fled with the treasure. Romance with this unscrupulous princess brought many disasters on Jason but in the short term he returned successful from his quest.

This dramatic tale reflects Greek exploration of the Black Sea, where they found lands that they could colonize or where they could trade for foreign riches, including gold. Behind the legend of the Golden Fleece lies a practice common in this region, and further east in the land of the Scythians, of panning using a woolly fleece as a filter to catch the particles of alluvial gold.

VANI'S GOLD

The gold of Colchis was no legend. Over the years, excavations, erosion and chance discoveries in the Colchian capital (or sacred centre), modern Vani, have uncovered many tombs from the fourth and third centuries BC in which gold was lavishly used for vessels, horse harnesses and, above all, jewellery. Although these objects show the influence of contemporary art in Greece, the Near East and Persia, the Colchians had a style all their own. In particular, they used granulation almost to the point of excess. A charming example of Colchian goldwork is an earring decorated with a model of two men with long spindly arms, wearing a gorytus (bow-case), riding horses with spindly legs, set on a wheeled stand. The men have granulated hair or caps and granulation also creates the detail of elaborate harnesses on the horses. Below the wheeled stand hang many chains, each ending in an acorn, a favourite Colchian symbol. Little birds, representing the Great Mother goddess, were another favourite motif, used as elements in the decoration on jewellery and as appliqués sewn on clothing, as were animals, such as deer, rams and even tortoises. These were frequently used in large numbers, for example as appendages to beads forming long necklaces, and usually they had details picked out in lines of granulation.

Not all the material was of gold. There were also vessels of silver, including small cauldrons (situlae) and cups for drinking the wine that was produced here, and silver jewellery, including necklaces, bracelets and diadems. Two silver belts were decorated with relief scenes of a procession and a feast, respectively. The Colchians were buried within the city, in graves dug into the ground. Often important individuals were buried with horses, dogs and a few servants, all presumably sacrificed. Although the servants were not lavishly bedecked with gold, as their masters were, they were generally wearing some jewellery, of stone beads, silver and even gold. In one rich fifth-century burial, for example, one servant was wearing earrings and necklaces of gold and diadems and bracelets of silver, while the other two had earrings and one of them a gold necklace. The principal burial, however, was a lady smothered in gold and silver jewellery and accompanied by silver and bronze jars and cups and a lovely glass beaker.

Opposite: *Animal-shaped beads were popular in Colchian jewellery. This necklace from grave 6 at Vani is composed of 56 gazelles.*

Below: *A close-up of the fastening on this diadem, found in grave 6 at Vani, shows lion chasing wild boar.*

HIDDEN TREASURES OF THE HOLY LAND

THE OLD OLD TESTAMENT

In 1947 Muhammad adh-Dhib, a shepherd boy of the Beduin Ta'amireh tribe, was searching for a lost goat among the hills west of the Dead Sea. Idly he tossed a pebble into a cave, to rouse the animal if it had strayed inside. He heard a chink as the stone hit pottery – could it be treasure? He fetched two friends and they went in to investigate.

To their disappointment, the cave contained only a series of large storage jars. Smashing these, the boys found they were full of old manuscripts. They took seven away with them, hoping they might be worth a little, and were able to sell them to a shoemaker in Bethlehem nicknamed Kando, who dealt in antiquities.

It was not long before the significance of the find became apparent. These seven scrolls may have been part of an ancient library belonging to a religious community, the Essenes, who had lived at Qumran from the second century BC. In AD 67, when the Holy Land was under Roman rule, the Jews revolted against their oppressors. The Essene community hastily hid their precious manuscripts, at first wrapping them carefully and placing them in large storage jars which they secreted in caves in the nearby cliffs, and then, as the tide of Roman reprisals swept closer, stowing them loose in hiding places near at hand. Alternatively, some or most of the manuscripts may have been brought to this secure and desolate hiding place from elsewhere, most probably Jerusalem.

In 1949 an expedition was mounted to investigate the area where the scrolls had been found. This and later explorations have revealed a large number of manuscripts from several caves, as well as the settlement of the Essenes themselves at Qumran. This was a strict and austere Jewish community whose members renounced worldly riches. Among the scrolls recovered was one detailing the rules by which they lived. Others included copies of books of the Bible – an exciting find because, until these were discovered, the earliest surviving copies of the Bible were only around 1,000 years old. These were twice that age. The texts also included a number of commentaries and other works of scholarship written by the Essenes.

Below: *The Qumran caves, where the Dead Sea Scrolls were discovered.*

THE COPPER SCROLL

One scroll, however, was completely different. Instead of parchment, it was inscribed on copper. The text was written in a form of Hebrew that dates it to the early centuries AD, later than most of the Dead Sea scrolls. It may be a copy of an earlier manuscript, transferred on to copper because this was a more durable material than the parchment or whatever the original had been written on. Much of the text is difficult to read, partly because of the obscurity of the language, partly because there were mistakes in the copying of the text on to the copper scroll but also because its writers deliberately made it cryptic.

But despite the problems, and the differing opinions of scholars on the detail of its meaning, there is no doubt overall about what it is. The Copper Scroll is a list of hidden treasures, giving information about where they were hidden. Most of the treasures were gold and silver bars and vessels but there were also precious oils and unguents, ritual robes and other valuable materials. There has been considerable debate about the quantities, but even the lowest reading of the figures in the text puts them around 100 kilograms (220 pounds) of precious metals. Although some people argue that the treasures may be legendary, the effort involved in engraving the document and the quality and value of the copper used seem to imply that it was a record of genuine concealed treasures.

The presence of the Copper Scroll among the austere Essenes is a mystery. Was it inscribed by them or not? If so, to what did it refer? Some scholars suggest the scroll gives the hiding place of treasures taken from the Temple in Jerusalem before it was sacked by the Romans in AD 68. But the Essenes were on bad terms with the Temple priests so it seems unlikely that they would have been chosen to hide the Temple's wealth. On the other hand, the Essene community was remote from civilization and might have seemed an ideal place to conceal treasure.

Despite numerous attempts, so far no one has succeeded in locating any of the treasures. The places referred to cannot be identified because they are buildings that have now gone, or the descriptions are too general or the place names are unknown. On the other hand, over the centuries people may well have stumbled upon most of them, so there is no guarantee that correctly working out the hiding places will reveal any treasures.

Right: *The unique Dead Sea Scroll inscribed on copper.*

HEROD'S PALACES

The Romans became involved in the affairs of the Holy Land in 64 BC when the two rival claimants to the throne each appealed to Rome for support against the other. Their dispute became caught up in the civil wars between Pompey and Caesar, Antony and Cleopatra and Octavian (Augustus), and eventually Antipater, chief minister of the kingdom, rose to power. In 40 BC the Roman Senate appointed Antipater's son, Herod (74–4 BC), as king of Judaea; he married Mariamne, a daughter of the Judaean royal house, to strengthen his position. When the dust of Rome's own affairs settled, Herod, a skilful politician, was confirmed by Augustus as king.

An often cruel and suspicious man, who executed several members of his own family, Herod was nevertheless a generous and cultured ruler, with a passion for building. His personal wealth and substantial state revenues gave him the means to indulge himself in executing his innovative and brilliant architectural designs, and being on good terms with the Romans, he was able to make use of Roman skills and knowledge in civil engineering. He rebuilt the Temple in Jerusalem, turned a small town into the fine port city of Caesarea, and constructed a number of palaces for himself.

Herod's most ambitious residence was the palace that he had built on the side of the massive rock at Masada. He surrounded the top of the rock with a casemate wall and built storerooms, baths and reservoirs. His palace was constructed on three terraces built out from the northern end of the rock and was lavishly decorated with paintings and mosaics.

Equally unusual in form was the palace complex that Herod built in the Judaean desert and which he named Herodium after himself. A series of palatial buildings, bathhouses and other structures were laid out at ground level, while a small mound was built up to form a conical hill on and into which a circular fortress was constructed. This contained a palace on a grand scale, with a pillared courtyard and gardens as well as luxurious private apartments.

When Herod died in 4 BC, the historian Josephus recounts that he was borne on a solid-gold bier adorned with precious stones, wrapped in crimson cloth and wearing a golden crown and diadem. He was laid to rest at Herodium, which he had designed also as his mausoleum. For a long time investigations of the fortress-palace, begun by Ehud Netzer in 1972, failed to reveal the king's tomb. But in April 2007 fragments of an ornately carved pink limestone sarcophagus were discovered

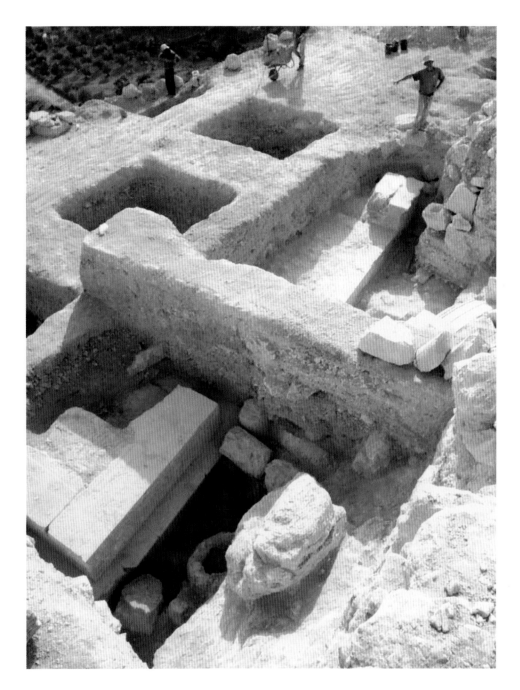

on the slopes of the fortress mound. A monumental stair, mentioned by Josephus, led to this spot, but there was little to suggest a mausoleum, except the remains of a stone plinth. Nevertheless, there seemed a strong possibility that the sarcophagus had belonged to Herod. It may have been smashed and emptied within memory of the king, perhaps during the Jewish Revolt when Herodium was occupied by the rebels who regarded him as a traitor. As there was no conclusive evidence, the scholarly world waited to be convinced.

Netzer continued to work at the site, revealing two more sarcophagi, perhaps belonging to other members of Herod's family. In December 2008 he announced that he had uncovered broken stone

architectural elements from which he believes it is possible to reconstruct the form of the mausoleum, rising through two storeys to a tapering roof 24 metres (80 feet) above. There now seems little doubt that this is Herod's tomb.

Opposite: *An aerial view of the ruins of the Herodium, King Herod's palace in the desert, stongly fortified with a double wall and four towers.*

Above: *Excavations in progress on the stone plinth of Herod's tomb, discovered in 2007 on the Herodium mound.*

THE WEALTH OF PERSIA

ELAM AND SUSA

While cities and empires rose and fell on the plains of Mesopotamia, another civilization flourished on the Iranian plateau. Its chief city was Susa, home of the Elamite kings, who were often in conflict with the peoples of the plain. Many of the finest works of Mesopotamian sculpture were found at Susa, to which they had been taken as the spoils of war. The city had many temples, to a variety of gods but particularly to Susa's patron deity, Inshushinak. Among the votive offerings associated with the shrine is a gold figure of a bearded man carrying a goat, presumably as a sacrificial offering. A matching statuette in silver was found with it. Susa was a major city for thousands of years, still important under the Persian (Achaemenid) Empire (529–330 BC) and continuing as a key centre into much later times.

The tombs of Susa's kings may have been sited somewhere away from the city. Brick-vaulted tombs discovered at Haft Tepe (ancient Kabnak) are thought to be those of Susa's fourteenth-century BC kings, while underground vaulted chambers containing cremated remains found at Choga Zambil (ancient Al-Untash-Napirisha) are probably the resting place of the Elamite kings in the thirteenth century BC. Little remains of the grave offerings that must once have accompanied these burials, owing to the activities of looters. Among these the chief was probably Ashurbanipal, King of Assyria, who sacked the city in 647 BC, breaking open royal tombs and removing not only the treasures but also the bones of the Elamite kings.

MARLIK TEPE

In contrast to these plundered graves, intact burials of great splendour, dated around 1200 BC, were discovered by chance in 1961 at Marlik Tepe near the Caspian Sea. Within a mound were found royal graves, some cut into the rock and others constructed of stone slabs: 53 were excavated. Vessels of pottery, gold and silver, bronze figurines, a great variety of weapons and jewellery of precious stones and metals abounded in the graves, particularly those of royal women and children. Nature had provided inspiration for the local craftsmen, who had created golden jewellery in the shape of pomegranates, pottery vessels in the form of animals, including humped bulls and a charming bear, and gold and silver vases decorated with trees as well as imaginary creatures such as unicorns and winged bulls.

Below left: *This splendid dragon's head of gilded silver was found among the treasures of the temple of Inshushinak, Susa's principal deity. The objects, from various periods, were deposited around 1200 BC.*

Below right: *A beaker decorated with winged bulls from Marlik displays the great skill of the ancient goldsmiths.*

TEPE NUSH-I JAN

While the Assyrians and Elamites were locked in conflict in the west, eastern Iran saw the emergence on to the international stage of two related Indo-Iranian tribes, the Medes and Persians. In 614 BC the Medes made common cause with the Babylonians and together they sacked the Assyrian capital, Nineveh, in 612. Following this success the Medes spread into Anatolia, coming to control a huge empire. Few of their sites have been excavated. One exception is the religious centre at Tepe Nush-i Jan. Here two temples with a pillared hall and courtyards were constructed around 800 BC. The central temple had a fire altar, suggesting that the Medes' beliefs were related to Zoroastrianism, which became the main religion of later Iranian empires. Around 600 BC, a complete reorganization of the site was initiated and the central temple was filled with stones in preparation. The project was abandoned, however, perhaps due to troubled circumstances. A hoard discovered in one of the buildings would support this theory. Hidden around 600 BC and never recovered, it consisted of 321 pieces of silver packed into a bronze bowl. These included rings, spiral beads and pendants as well as small silver bars for use as "money". Some of the pieces had been manufactured much earlier, as far back as 2000 BC.

PERSIAN CITIES

In 559 BC, Cyrus became king of the Persians, at this time subordinate to the Medes. Within a decade, however, he had made himself master of the Medes too, founding the mighty Persian Empire. Cyrus consolidated control of Anatolia, conquering previously independent coastal kingdoms, including Lydia, then turned his attentions to Babylon, which he took unopposed in 539 BC. His son, Cambyses, added Egypt to the empire and his successor, Darius, extended it into Thrace in the west, though he also suffered a humiliating defeat at the hands of the Greeks in 490 BC.

Darius made the ancient Elamite city of Susa his administrative capital, constructing a large and splendid palace there, complete with Apadana (audience hall). But he also built a new capital at Persepolis, beginning work here in 513 BC. A vast stone plinth dominated the site and on this was built a huge Apadana, a sumptuous royal palace and a large number of storerooms in which the imperial treasury was housed. Superb relief carvings on the staircase leading up to the platform show individuals from all regions of the vast empire bringing tribute to swell the treasures stored here – gold torcs, jars containing wine; Bactrians leading camels and Scythians bringing horses; Ethiopians bearing gold, ivory and ebony, and many others.

The Persian Empire fell to Alexander the Great between 334 and 330 BC and he took Persepolis in 330, plundering the royal storerooms of their treasures. He also set fire to the city during a drunken orgy. All but a handful of the gold and silver objects made by the Persians have disappeared, looted from tombs and cities by robbers and conquerors, but the surviving examples show what fine craftsmen the Persians were. For example, they created beautiful silver drinking vessels (rhytons) whose lower end opens out into the body and head of an animal, such as a goat, ibex or bull. Several fine examples in gold, with the forequarters of a winged lion, were reputedly found at Ecbatana (modern Hamadan), the former capital of the Medes.

Left: *Another beaker from Marlik, this time of silver, decorated with spirited parade horses. Real and imaginary animals were frequently depicted on the metal and pottery vessels found at Marlik and other sites.*

GOLDEN TOMBS OF THE SCYTHIAN HORDES

DANGEROUS WORK

Paul Dubrux was a Frenchman who had been driven from his homeland by the French Revolution of 1789. In 1797 he entered the Russian Civil Service. After being posted to Kerch in the Crimea in the 1810s, he took a lively interest in the numerous local funerary mounds of the Scythian nomads who had lived in the region during the first millennium BC. In September 1830 the military in the area were ordered to acquire and transport several hundred stones to build a barracks. Dubrux was invited by Kerch's governor to visit the scene of their labours and recognized that the mound at Kul Oba, from which they were moving a large

number of stones, was a Scythian burial tumulus. So the officer in charge was detailed to keep an eye on their work here.

On September 19 a massive entrance passage made of cut stone was revealed in the side of the mound, leading into a vaulted chamber. Originally the stonework had been held up by wooden posts but these had disintegrated, leaving the stones barely supported by the surrounding earth. Dubrux and his workmen took their lives into their hands when they began to investigate this chamber. On one occasion, Dubrux moved off from a place where he had been standing talking, to remonstrate with someone who had just taken the light away. The next moment, a huge stone block

crashed down upon the very spot where he had been standing.

The dangers of the excavation seemed likely to deter any tomb robbers, but Dubrux was still concerned that the chamber might be looted after work hours. Rightly so, for the minute he had left the site the guards also deserted their post and local villagers moved in to pillage the tomb. As Dubrux had had the tomb entrance blocked with stones, they were unable to do much damage on the first night, but, although a guard was posted on subsequent nights, the robbers got in and removed a quantity of small gold objects. On the fifth night, however, collapsing stones injured some of the robbers and frightened them off. Dubrux was later able to recover some of the gold that the villagers had stolen.

A ROYAL BURIAL

The mound contained four burials, only one of which had been robbed by the villagers. This burial had been placed at a separate level from the rest and was probably not related to them. Of the other three, one was a slave or groom and another a woman who was probably the wife of the principal individual in the grave. This man, who must have been a Scythian king or nobleman, was decked with golden finery – a torc around his throat, its ends decorated with figures of Scythian horsemen, rings and bracelets, and a felt cap decorated with gold. He had been buried in one side of a large timber coffin. In its other compartment were his treasures – a massive sword with a gold hilt, golden leg guards, a golden-handled whip, a gold bowl and five figurines made of gold.

His wife's coffin was also well furnished, containing a bronze mirror with a gold handle and a magnificent electrum vase decorated with scenes of Scythian daily life. She too wore a gold torc and bracelets as

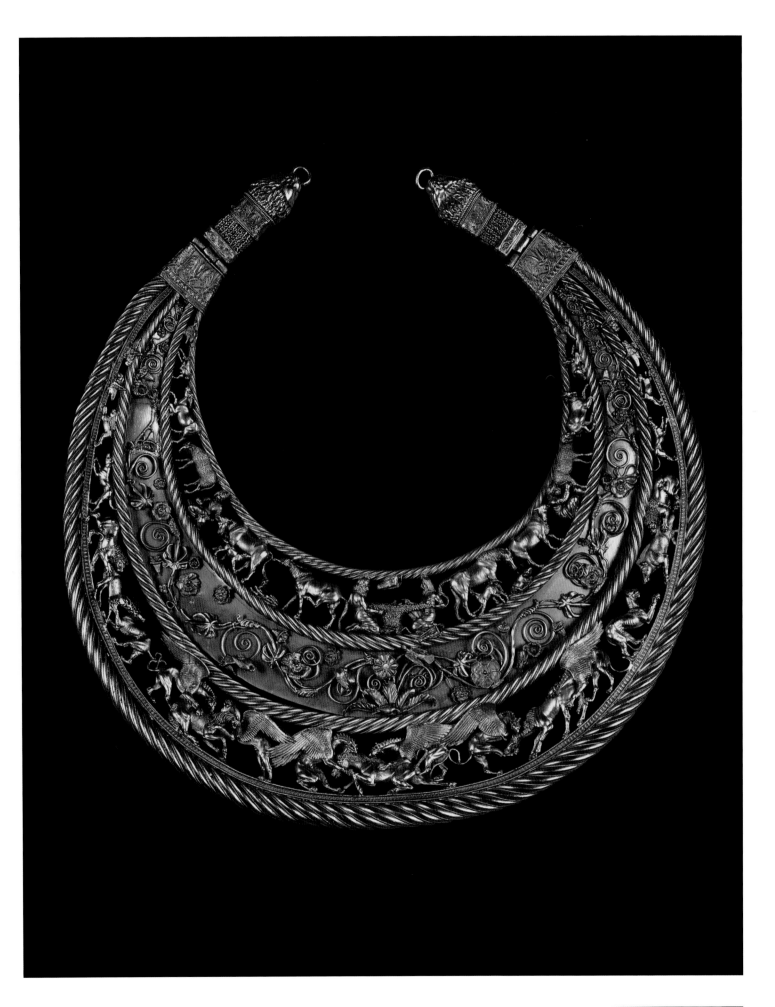

well as gold necklaces and pendants and a headdress of electrum. Elsewhere in the tomb were horse bones, bronze and silver cauldrons and drinking vessels, knives with handles of ivory or gold and the remains of ivory inlay from a coffin, exquisitely decorated. Numerous gold plaques scattered over the floor must have fallen from textiles which had covered the tomb's walls.

NOMADS

The grave at Kul Oba is by no means the wealthiest of the Scythian burial mounds found in the Eurasian steppes. Unfortunately, however, these mounds were often ransacked in antiquity, so many have lost their treasures. We know a great deal about the Scythians who inhabited the area around the Black Sea during the first millennium BC, not only from the graves which have been excavated but also from their neighbours, the Classical Greeks. The great Greek historian and ethnographer Herodotus gave a detailed description of their way of life. Some Scythians, he said, had settled down to farm, living in permanent villages, but the majority of them were nomads who grazed large herds of sheep on the scattered pastures of the steppe. Similar groups lived and moved through the entire steppe region, which stretches to the border of China.

These nomads rode horses and travelled in horse-drawn wagons, living either in the wagons or in tents. Fine artists, they produced colourful woollen clothing, saddle-cloths, rugs and carpets, elaborate wooden carvings, including headdresses for themselves and their horses, and exquisite gold and silver jewellery and vessels. Many were decorated in what has become known as the "Animal Style": swirling designs of real or imaginary beasts, often engaged in combat with one another. One famous example depicts a panther attacking a yak which has seized an eagle, which is pecking the panther. Much Scythian goldwork seems to have been made by Greeks working to Scythian specifications – there was considerable trade between these two very different nations.

Below: *Sharply reining in his horse, this Scythian, apparently riding bareback, prepares to spear his victim, a fallen enemy or an animal at bay, in this lively scene from Kul Oba.*

IMMENSE SACRIFICES

Herodotus also described Scythian royal burial practices. Dead kings were first mummified, their guts removed and replaced with herbs and frankincense and their bodies coated in wax. They were then taken in procession on a wagon throughout the Scythian lands before being buried in huge pits with their golden treasures and a number of sacrificed attendants. After a year 50 attendants and 50 fine horses were sacrificed and displayed on wheels supported by stakes around the funerary mound.

No excavated nomad burials have revealed remains of this gruesome arrangement, but there is plenty of evidence of sacrifices, of both people and horses. A huge barrow at Arzan in southern Siberia contained the burials of 23 individuals besides the man and woman at the centre, and 160 sacrificed horses. Even the relatively modest burial of a woman recently found on the Ukok plateau in the Altai mountains was accompanied by six horses.

DEEP FREEZE

The Altai mountains have many nomad burial mounds and these have been plundered by treasure-seekers almost from the moment when the mourners left. In 1924 a Russian archaeologist, Sergei Rudenko, led a reconnaissance expedition to the Pazyryk region, where he found a number of promising mounds. In 1927 he began excavations here and in 1947 returned to the region to excavate further mounds.

The task Rudenko's team faced was extraordinarily difficult. During the severe winters in this region, the ground becomes frozen to a considerable depth. The nomads had dug their grave shafts during the summer, but after they filled in the graves water had accumulated within them. The following winter this had frozen, sealing the graves in a permanent block of ice. Now the archaeologists were faced with the problem of unfreezing them. Nineteenth-century archaeologists had experimented with lighting fires on the graves. Rudenko's team tried a different approach: they poured buckets of boiling water over the ground. The unpleasantness of working in the resultant sea of icy mud can be imagined!

Robbers had dug into the mounds within a few decades of the burials being made, so all were disturbed. They must have carried off many precious objects of gold and silver, but they left behind a great wealth of other treasures. Because the tombs had remained frozen a great many organic artefacts were preserved – an extremely unusual situation.

TEXTILES AND TATTOOS

In one grave was found the mummified body of a man aged about 60, who had been furnished with a false beard made of human hair. His limbs and torso had been tattooed with designs of animals, including lively horses kicking up their heels and imaginary monsters. In more recent years other tattooed bodies have been found in burials in the Altai mountains and it was clearly a common decoration favoured by both men and women.

This man had been buried in a coffin made from a hollowed-out larch tree-trunk decorated with pieces of leather cut out in the shape of deer. A woman of about 40, her hair in pigtails, was also buried in this tomb. Many of their clothes had survived – soft leather boots for indoor wear, decorated with gold leaf and beads sewn on to the soles; caftans of squirrel skin and sable fur; a shirt of woven hemp with red woollen braid and stockings made of felt.

Like other grave mounds discovered in the region, the burials had been placed inside a chamber constructed of wooden logs set in the bottom of a deep shaft. Sacrificed horses were placed in the shaft around the chamber and these too were furnished with richly decorated textiles, including saddles and other pieces of harness made of wood and leather, woollen saddle cloths and elaborate headdresses with felt decorations.

Another grave yielded the earliest Persian carpet to have survived, showing a line of horsemen and a frieze of elks, set between geometric bands of decoration. The nomads were linked by trade with both east and west, for the grave also contained a fine Chinese silk cloth embroidered with phoenixes. A large felt wall hanging decorated with a repeating design of a goddess on a throne and a moustached warrior on his horse before her was made by the nomads themselves.

Above: *A golden belt buckle from a nomad tomb depicts a tiger fighting with a fabulous beast – a fine example of the vibrant art of the steppes.*

A LUCKY FIND

We can only guess what treasures the graves contained before they were looted by the ancient robbers. Luck gave one team of archaeologists a glimpse of the original magnificence of such tombs when, in 1913, an expedition from the Russian Imperial Archaeological Commission entered its fourth season of excavating a massive Scythian burial mound at Soloha on the River Dnieper. The central chamber on which the team had been working over the previous years had been plundered not long after the burial was made. Before starting work, the director of the excavation, Professor Wesselowsky, had carefully examined the burial mound and had come to the conclusion that it probably also covered a second, less substantial burial chamber placed

to one side. Investigations revealed that he was right and that the robbers had failed to make this deduction, for the chamber proved to be undisturbed.

In the tomb's outer chamber, five horses, decked in gold and bronze finery, were laid in a row, with their groom beside them. Beyond these was a guard armed with bow and arrows. Another soldier, with a sword and clad in a coat of mail, lay at the king's feet. All around the king lay his weapons and splendid armour, including a bronze helmet, a coat of mail

---

Below: *A wall hanging of coloured felt found at Pazyryk depicts a warrior riding a saddled and bridled horse, in front of a goddess seated on an elaborate chair.*

---

and a sword in a wonderful gold sheath. A great gold torc was around his neck and gold bracelets on his arms. Five magnificent silver vases stood beside him, decorated with scenes of Scythians hunting, picked out in gilt, while a vast gold dish was concealed in a niche at the king's head along with a wooden bow and arrow case covered with a beautiful silver and plaster scene depicting a battle.

THE ROYALS OF RYZHANOVKA

In 1996, another completely unlooted tomb was discovered, beneath a 9-metre (30-foot) high tumulus at Ryzhanovka, south of Kiev. The mound had been investigated previously in 1887, when the burial chamber of a princess was discovered. She lay arrayed in her finery of gold jewellery, including a headdress decorated with a gold band depicting dancing

Maenads (wine-frenzied women, devotees of the god Dionysus) and two rings made from Greek coins. She was furnished with a bronze situla, two silver cups, a wine amphora, bronze vessels and a number of Greek pots, as well as a mirror and a spindle. Some of her grave goods suggest that she was a priestess. Remains of the sacrificed body of her maid, a young girl, lay at the foot of the stair leading down into the burial chamber.

The excavators did not realize it, but they stopped their excavation only inches away from the main burial chamber in which a Scythian prince, perhaps the husband or father of this lady, was buried. Earlier, attempted looters had also just missed the burial chamber, which lies at the bottom of a shaft, 2.5 metres (8 feet) below ground level. The decapitated body of a horse and a sacrificed servant armed with a bow were placed in the shaft. On one side of the chamber, curtained off, lay the prince on a substantial wooden platform, a gold torc with lion's-head terminals around his neck, at his side his bow and many arrows and in his hand a gold-hilted sword in a silver sheath. Tiny fragments of surviving cloth show he was dressed in red trousers and headdress and a cream jacket. Damage to his skull suggests that he died after falling from his horse. On the ground nearby was a heap of female clothing: a headdress decorated with gold plaques, a veil with 34 gold medallions depicting the Gorgon Medusa, and 140 gold appliqués from a dress. These perhaps represent the prince's wife, who, unusually, was not sacrificed to accompany him.

Two bronze cauldrons containing mutton and horse meat, set on a hearth, four huge amphorae holding 118 litres (26 gallons) of wine, two trays of mutton ribs with a serving knife, a bowl of beans flavoured with wild garlic, two silver cups for serving fermented mare's milk (*koumiss*) and many Greek pots lay in other parts of the chamber, providing a lavish funerary feast. A magnificent silver vessel bore a relief of griffins devouring a bull and a deer.

Top: *Recovered from a royal grave, these two neck ornaments, of contrasting form but with similarly elaborate decoration, well illustrate the goldworking skills of the Scythians.*

Bottom: *These cut-out plaques, probably decorations that were sewn on clothing or harness, are sensitive portraits of the horses that were the carefully tended treasures of their Scythian owners.*

INDUS CIVILIZATION

A FORGOTTEN PEOPLE

The nineteenth century was a great age of discovery in West Asia and by the early twentieth century the riches of Assyria and Babylonia, and of their third-millennium predecessors the Akkadians and Sumerians, were well known. In India, however, no civilization was known prior to the first millennium BC and the region was thought to be a backwater.

But in 1924, when Woolley was beginning to reveal the marvels of Ur, Sir John Marshall, Director-General of the Archaeological Survey of India, announced the remarkable discovery of an unsuspected civilization in the Indus valley, contemporary with that of Mesopotamia. It soon became apparent that the two had traded with each other, senior partners in a mercantile network that linked all the countries bordering the Persian Gulf.

These two great powers could not have been more different. Mesopotamia had long been a region of warring city states, eventually united in 2350 BC when King Sargon of Agade conquered his rival rulers. The Indus civilization seems to have always been a land of peace, united into a single state from the time of its rapid emergence around 2600–2500 BC. Sumerian and Akkadian cities were composed of unplanned residential areas that sprang up around the temples that had dominated urban life from the earliest times. Palaces housed the elite, both priests and royalty, and the latter were buried with lavish offerings. In the Indus region, in contrast, the cities had planned residential areas with streets orientated north–south and east–west but there were few structures that can clearly be identified as public buildings. The Great Bath at Mohenjo Daro is the closest thing to an identifiable religious structure and there are no obvious temples; nor are there palaces or royal graves. Even the personal possessions of the Indus people give little clue to social hierarchy: most city dwellers seemed to have had similar fine pottery and stone or metal tools. Figurines depicting Indus people showed that women wore bangles, elaborate headdresses and necklaces of beads. Many pieces of jewellery were also found, in houses or in graves: bangles of shell or stone and thousands of beads of many materials – shell, copper, pottery and many attractive gemstones, including agate and carnelian.

Occasionally hoards have been found of more precious materials and more "expensive" jewellery – pieces that had taken

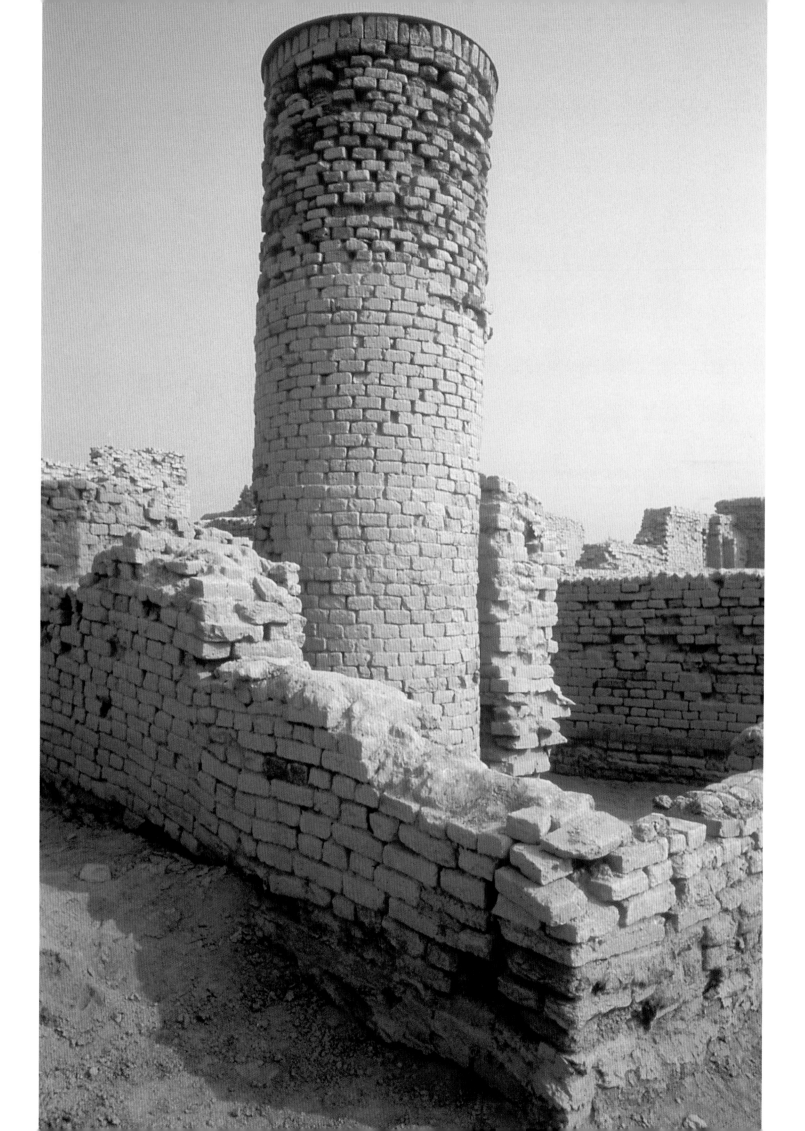

a long time and much skill to make. Two were uncovered in the east of the Harappan realms: an early hoard at Kunal containing gold and silver objects, including two silver tiaras; the other from the period of Indus decline, found at Mandi in Uttar Pradesh and made up of two bronze bowls filled with jewellery manufactured from sheet gold and silver – necklaces of gold and agate beads and tubular gold and silver bangles and anklets. The Mandi hoard was found by chance by a villager, sparking a gold rush among the locals, degenerating into fights. The police stepped in, followed by government archaeologists. The site was properly excavated and the villagers were encouraged to hand over the objects they had taken, by impressing upon them the historical significance of the find, the honour it brought to their village and the appropriate recompense they would receive.

SURPRISE AT ALLAHDINO

The American archaeologist Walter Fairservis specialized in studying the Indus civilization. In the 1970s he worked on a tiny but important Indus settlement near Karachi, known as Allahdino, where he uncovered the remains of a house, workshops and storerooms, as well as stone-built drains. Indus houses were generally constructed around a courtyard, often had an upper storey and were usually provided with a fine bathroom with excellent drains.

The 1976 season of excavation at Allahdino began with the workmen clearing soil that had accumulated on the site's surface since the end of the previous year's work. Suddenly Fairservis stopped his workmen and sent them away – it was his wife's birthday, he told them, and he had decided to give them a holiday. In fact Fairservis's eagle eye had spotted gold and he was taking no chances. While the workmen moved off, his assistant, Elizabeth Walters, carried on her work, calmly cleaning round a small pot that was beginning to show up – the spot where Fairservis had seen the gold. When they were alone the pair removed the pot and its contents. The excavation driver, Tahir Hussain Khan, could be relied on, so Fairservis had him drive them back to their hotel. Safely ensconced in Karachi's Hotel Metropole, Fairservis and Walters examined their find.

THE PUZZLING HOARD

Within the pot they found a hoard of Indus jewellery. There were silver rings made of coiled wire that may have been worn on fingers or toes. Pieces of gold were stored to be made into jewellery in the future and there were several thin bands of gold that might have been headbands. Numerous silver beads made up three strings, held apart by spacer beads. Eight large silver discs were part of another necklace, along with a half-moon-shaped centrepiece. The most impressive object was a massive belt made of beads, similar to those worn by the women depicted in many Indus figurines. Bronze spacer beads held together six strings of carnelian beads, each one 6–10 centimetres (2½–4 inches) long. These beads were superb works of craftsmanship, requiring a specially hard and fine drill to make the central perforation down their length and each may have taken a week or 10 days to drill. It would also have taken days to make the bead from the original lump of stone. So the 36-bead belt represented about a year and a half's work for a skilled craftsman.

The pot therefore contained a substantial treasure at the time it was hidden. It was presumably the property of the principal family in Allahdino, local landowners or major government officials. What threat caused them to hide their treasure and what prevented them from retrieving it, we shall never know.

GOLDWORK FROM THE MYSTERIOUS MEGALITHS OF SOUTHERN INDIA

SIMILAR TO EUROPEAN STRUCTURES

Megalithic monuments – large structures built of massive stones – are among the most impressive and most prominent remains of the prehistoric past in western Europe. Men sent out from Britain in the early nineteenth century to work in southern India were amazed to discover similar megalithic monuments scattered about the landscape. Some were low mounds enclosed by circles made of massive boulders. Within the mound, and often partly exposed by erosion, there was frequently a cist, a rectangular stone box built of dressed slabs or uncut boulders. The most impressive were massive cromlechs, free-standing structures built of enormous undressed rocks.

The similarities with European megaliths were striking. Was there a connection, despite the great distances involved and the general absence of such monuments in the intervening lands? What were the megaliths built for and was the reason the same in both areas? Many antiquarians connected the European megaliths with the Celts and their priests, the Druids. They suggested that the megaliths might be temples with altars upon which human sacrifices were made. Some antiquarians in India adopted the same theory.

When local southern Indians were asked about the megaliths, they produced unsatisfactory answers. The structures dated back to a time when people lived for hundreds of years, they said. When they became really elderly, they were quite unpleasant to have around, so their relatives built megaliths in which to shut them up, giving them plenty to eat and drink but keeping them out of the home. Alternatively, they said that the megaliths were the homes of ancient pygmies of superhuman strength or of the monkey-people who helped Rama, hero of the Hindu epic poem the "Ramayana".

Some antiquarians took these stories at face value. They excavated some of the megaliths and recorded seriously that there was no evidence that the skeletons they found inside had been those of either pygmies or monkeys. Nor did the megaliths seem to be houses. They certainly contained some domestic objects, such as pottery and tools, but lacked normal features of houses such as hearths, proper doors and furniture.

IRON-AGE GRAVES

Judging by the number of bones found in those that were excavated, it seemed very likely that these magnificent structures were graves. More recent investigations have proved this suggestion to be right in most cases – although there are still some mysterious megaliths that were not graves, such as the standing stones erected alone or in lines. Some individuals

Opposite: *A brick well now towers above the walls of Mohenjo-daro's houses.*

were buried lying on their back or side; others were cremated and their remains collected in an urn placed in the grave. In many cases the graves contained the collected remains of a number of people – skulls and long bones in particular, sometimes neatly sorted by type and stacked in heaps.

The majority of these megalithic graves contained grave goods – attractive black-and-red pottery was very common and often the deceased were wearing beads. Most of the tools and weapons – knives, daggers, chisels, axes, swords and the like – were made of iron, for unlike the European megaliths, those of India have turned out to be of Iron Age date, from around 700 BC until the early centuries AD. Similar grave goods have been found in other kinds of graves that clearly belong to the same period, such as burials in urns of various sizes, some surrounded by a small stone circle, others packed close together in urn fields. The most unusual are burials placed in curious terracotta sarcophagi in the shape of bathtubs standing on multiple pairs of legs.

HORSE-RIDERS AND PRINCES

Although most of the offerings in these burials are of ordinary, everyday objects, some are more elaborate. The people in the most northerly group of graves, in Maharashtra, were horse-riders and were buried with the horse harness they had used, such as stirrups and bits. Sometimes the horses were also sacrificed to accompany them. These graves often contained copper or bronze decorations for horses, bronze bells and bronze dishes, bowls and lids decorated with figures of animals.

Similar bronzes were found in a few graves further south, at Adichanallur in southern Tamil Nadu, where an enormous urn cemetery was discovered. Some of the urns also contained diadems made of sheets of beaten gold. Gold or silver beads were found occasionally in graves elsewhere in the south.

But the most spectacular burial was uncovered in the French toehold in southern India, Pondicherry district.

A massive stone circle at Souttoukeny surrounded a large cist grave in which a "bathtub" sarcophagus had been placed, along with the bodies of a man and a woman. A splendid sword accompanied the burials, along with magnificent and elaborate gold jewellery showing superb craftsmanship. This included earrings in the shape of a flower with radiating petals and pendants in the form of lotus flowers dangling on gold chains. There were also gold bangles and many beads of gold and silver. Surely this was the burial of a prince and princess. Was she sacrificed to accompany him into death? *Sati* (wife immolation) was an Indian practice of later times and perhaps we see it here.

Above: *The earrings found in the grave at Souttoukeny were made by inserting many small elongated gold cones into a gold disc. Equally elaborate were the floral pendants.*

INDO-GREEKS AND KUSHANS

BACTRIA AND GANDHARA – LANDS OF THE NORTH-WEST

In 533 BC the first Persian emperor, Cyrus the Great, overran north-west India. This gold-rich area became the twentieth satrapy (province) of the empire – and its richest, providing 360 talents of gold dust in tribute. The Gandhara region saw many changes of master in the centuries that followed. Alexander the Great held the north-west briefly after conquering the Persian Empire, but in the chaos and civil war that followed his death, Chandragupta Maurya (reigned 321–297 BC) incorporated Gandhara into his expanding Indian empire, which reached its greatest extent under his grandson, Ashoka (reigned 268–232 BC), c. 260 BC. When the Mauryan Empire declined, the north-west came under the rule of petty Greek kingdoms that had grown up in Bactria from colonies founded by Alexander the Great. The Indo-Greeks in turn were succeeded as rulers of the area by Central Asian nomads, the Shakas (Scythians) and later the Kushans, who controlled the region until it fell in AD 460 to the merciless invasion of the Huns.

CITY OF MONKS AND MERCHANTS

Taxila, the capital city of Gandhara, developed over the years into a major centre of trade, art, learning, industry and religion. It moved at least three times, the Mauryan city on the Bhir Mound being superseded by a planned Indo-Greek city, Sirkap, and later a Kushan foundation in Central Asian style, Sirsukh, replaced Sirkap. The crossroads of routes leading from the west into Central Asia and India, cosmopolitan Taxila was open to influences from many cultures. While the Mauryans ruled the region, Buddhism became established here, and many fine monasteries were built in the valley. Wealthy merchants and princes made rich offerings in the Buddhist shrines – the Kushans were particularly generous patrons.

A fine hybrid art style developed under the Indo-Greek rulers, Indian motifs and themes from both Buddhism and folk religion being combined with Classical realism. Western religions also flourished under the Indo-Greeks and their successors: shrines erected in Taxila included a probable Zoroastrian fire temple and legend has it that the early Christian missionary, St Thomas, converted one of the Shaka rulers, Gondophares, to Christianity.

From Taxila merchants and missionaries set out along the dangerous and difficult Silk Road to China through Central Asia, a route that developed from the late second century BC and which prospered particularly under the Kushans who controlled the western portion of the regions through which it ran. Wealth flowed into and through the city. Gold, silver and gems were used to make exquisite jewellery and reliquaries for holding holy remains of the Buddha and of Buddhist saints, while imported luxuries included

TODAY'S UNFOUND TREASURES

GENGHIS KHAN

Temujin was born around 1167, the son of a Mongol clan leader. When he was nine his father was poisoned and his clan dispersed. Over the subsequent years, however, Temujin steadily built up a following, gradually uniting all the Mongol tribes, and in 1206 was awarded the title Genghis (Chingghis) Khan, or "Universal Ruler". From 1217 he led the Mongols in a ruthless attempt at world domination, conquering most of China and the lands from Korea in the east to the Black Sea in the west, murdering and plundering the riches of defeated cities. More than merely a conqueror, however, Genghis Khan organized his hordes into effective and enduring khanates. He also adopted writing and other civilized arts from the neighbouring Uighurs. Genghis died on August 18, 1227 on campaign in China, and by his wish his warriors carried his body into the heart of the steppe, killing any person they encountered in order that no outsider should learn the secret of the great khan's final resting place. Numerous horsemen trampled the surrounding ground to hide the grave. Rumoured to lie near near a mountain called Burkhan Khaldun, this has never been rediscovered.

Above: *This painting of Genghis Khan on his throne is one of many scenes from his life depicted in the fourteenth-century Persian chronicle* Jami' al-tawarikh *by Rashid al-Din Hamadani.*

elaborately decorated tableware and Classical statuary from Alexandria and the Roman world and silks from China.

Taxila's wealth made it a target for invaders. Defensive walls were erected around many of the monasteries to protect the monks and their treasures against the frequent attacks on the valley. Despite this, many were killed as the discovery of groups of skeletons attests. Sometimes the people of the city received enough warning to give them time to hide their treasures. However, when they fell at the hands of the intruders, the secret of their hidden wealth died with them – to be rediscovered by the archaeologists who excavated the houses and monasteries of the city almost 2,000 years later.

Gold and silver coins, silver dishes, gold and silver bracelets, earrings and necklaces, small Buddhist stone sculptures, soapstone toilet trays for mixing cosmetics, gold figurines of Indian goddesses, ivory combs and many other personal treasures were recovered from the successive cities and religious foundations at Taxila.

ROYAL TREASURE-HOUSE OR CUSTOMS SHED?

Ivories were also foremost among the treasures discovered from the town of Kapisha (modern Begram), which lay to the north-west of Taxila, near the western end of the Silk Road. In 1938 a Belgian archaeological team excavating the town came across a bricked-up room which they opened, revealing a wealth of treasures from east, west and south. Chinese lacquer vessels lay alongside goblets of Roman alabaster and painted glass, one depicting the famous Pharos lighthouse at Alexandria. Bronze statuettes were also imports from the Mediterranean, and these included figures that had been used as weights on a steelyard balance. Decorative plaques depicting Buddhist scenes were among the beautifully carved ivories from India found in the Begram treasure. A statue of a goddess personifying the holy River Ganges was one of many ivory pieces that had once formed elements of carved furniture. Pieces of ivory with finely inscribed decoration in the Parthian style were also found.

Left: *The treasures in Begram's storeroom were accumulated from many different sources. This blue glass bottle, decorated with gilded glass trails, was made in the Graeco-Roman world.*

The objects in the Begram hoard had been made at different times from the first century BC until the mid-third century AD. Since the town was a major trade entrepôt, some people have suggested that the storeroom contained customs tolls collected from merchants journeying through the area. More probably, however, these treasures were accumulated by successive Indo-Greek and Kushan kings of the ancient state of Kapisha and were hidden here when the city was threatened. The building in which they were stored was destroyed in AD 241 when the town was invaded by the Sassanian King Shapur I (reigned 241–272), and their owners never returned to dig their treasures from the ruins.

Right: *Small naturalistic carvings of animals, such as this panther, were among the decorations fashioned in ivory that were discovered at Begram.*

Below: *In this decorative ivory plaque from Begram a woman and her baby stand below a torana (the gateway to a Buddhist stupa), while other women are grouped within horseshoe arches typical of rock-cut temples.*

GOLDEN BURIALS

The lands along the River Oxus (Amu Darya) had enjoyed considerable prosperity in the Bronze Age and in later times, under Indo-Greek and Kushan rulers, they were involved in the lucrative Silk Road trade network. The riches that could be accumulated by noble families in this region are shown by a chance discovery at Tillya Tepe, a small mound on the Oxus in southern Bactria.

The Russian archaeologist Victor Sarianidi was excavating a Bronze Age settlement on this site in the late 1980s when he suddenly came upon six burials of the Kushan period (early centuries AD) that had been cut down into the earlier deposits. He and his team worked against the clock to excavate these six graves, which were stuffed with treasures, determined to recover all there was to find before treasure-seekers moved in to plunder the site.

The six individuals buried here, a man and five women, were placed first in a simple wooden coffin and this was wrapped in a shroud decorated with discs of gold and silver. Like the nomad inhumations of the steppe, these burials were placed in a deep shaft and covered by a wooden roof. Despite the relative simplicity of the graves, they contained a remarkably rich set of grave goods – some 20,000 items in all. The greater part consisted of clothing and jewellery worn by the deceased, made of gold and semi-precious stones – headdresses decorated with hundreds of pendant discs, rings, necklaces, earrings and the like as well as weapons decorated with gold and ivory and mirrors from distant China. The lively decoration on many of the pieces shows the many influences at work in Kushan society at the time – traditional themes from West Asian art going back millennia; motifs and styles introduced by the Hellenistic Greeks; and ideas brought in by steppe nomads, including the nomadic Kushan forebears of the settled people of this region.

PLUNDERED HOARD

In 1880 three merchants were journeying across Afghanistan when they were set upon by bandits and robbed. Their servant escaped and reached the local British political officer, a Captain Burton, who at once set out, catching the bandits around midnight and making them hand over a large proportion of what they had stolen. This included a number of fine gold pieces from a hoard that had apparently been discovered on the banks of the Oxus at Takht-i Kuwad. Burton purchased one piece from the merchants, a gold bracelet with terminals in the form of griffins. Originally this had been inlaid with precious stones. In both shape and style, this bracelet was similar to examples known from the Persian Empire.

This hoard is said to have comprised about 1,500 coins and 150 other objects, all of gold or silver. As the pieces belong to various different periods, it is likely that the hoard was made up of offerings accumulated through time in a temple treasury. Other

Opposite: *Elaborate golden diadems decorated with pendant discs were among the rich ornaments found with the six individuals buried in the mound at Tillya Tepe.*

Below opposite: *A sheet gold plaque from the Oxus treasure shows a Zoroastrian priest with rods used in religious rites.*

Right: *This massive gold bracelet from the Oxus treasure is a companion to the piece purchased by Captain Burton.*

Below: *A golden chariot carrying two men and drawn by four horses formed part of the hoard found in 1880 on the banks of the River Oxus (Amu Darya).*

pieces from the period of the Persian Empire included a magnificent repoussé sheet gold plaque depicting a priest clad in tightly fitting trousers, a short-sleeved tunic and a hood. A number of gold signet rings included some that were Persian in style and others that were Greek. One of the most elaborate pieces was a gold model of a chariot drawn by four horses. Within it stood the charioteer, his hands on the reins, a gold torc at his neck and wearing a simple tunic, while at his side on a bench sat a more sumptuously dressed figure wearing a long, decorated robe.

TREASURES FOUND AND LOST

Recent years have seen the discovery of more treasures from Afghanistan's past. A striking example is the silver plaque found in the city of Ai Khanoum, the furthest east of all the cities founded by Alexander the Great. This plaque, decorated in low relief, depicts the gilded figure of the goddess Cybele riding in a gilded chariot, drawn by lions with golden manes across gilded ground. Behind her walks a priest holding a parasol, before her is a priest making a sacrifice on an altar and beside her a winged figure representing Victory.

In 1947, a villager drawing water in the small Afghan village of Mir Zakah found a gold coin in her bucket. Investigations, first by the villagers and then by archaeologists, revealed a hoard of more than 10,000 coins. The excavators believed they had thoroughly investigated the site. However, in 1992 torrential rain caused erosion, exposing another coin, leading to the discovery of an enormous hoard: 550,000 gold, silver and bronze coins, along with other precious objects – which was immediately seized by the Afghan warlords. After passing through many other hands, in many countries, the finest pieces were sold at auction, despite an international outcry. This did succeed, however, in discouraging museums around the world from purchasing the rest of the hoard, offered originally at $20 million, then reduced to $5 million and still unsold.

Although many of Afghanistan's treasures have been looted or sold abroad over the centuries, many others, including all the objects from Tillya Tepe, found a proper home in the National Museum in Kabul. During the Soviet occupation of Afghanistan and the factional wars between rival warlords that followed the Soviet withdrawal, some of the museum's collections were moved to a succession of places of safety. The museum, however, was wrecked by shells and most of its remaining contents destroyed or looted, leaving a tragic void in Afghan cultural

heritage. When the Taliban came to power, their fanatical views led them to destroy other treasures of the Afghan past, most famously in 2001 when they dynamited the gigantic rock-cut sculptures of the Buddha at Bamiyan, to the utter horror of the rest of the world. Less well publicized was their deliberate destruction of many collections of material from the National Museum.

After the Taliban was overthrown, there was great pessimism: surely anything that had survived the destruction and looting would have been secretly sold off, captured by the warlords or taken home by the Russians. But, with remarkable courage, those museum personnel who had known where the museum's treasures had been secreted had told no one, despite very real threats. In 2003, six locked boxes were found in the safety of the Central

Bank vaults beneath the president's palace, where they had been moved when the National Museum was damaged during the Soviet occupation. These were formally opened in the presence of the Afghan Minister of Culture. Amazingly they were found to contain the entire 20,000-piece treasure from Tillya Tepe.

Opposite: *These objects were looted from Ai Khanoum: decades of warfare have made it difficult to prevent the illegal trade in Afghan antiquities.*

Above: *Four-fifths of the formerly magnificent collections in the Kabul Museum have been stolen or destroyed: this plaque, depicting the goddess Cybele, is one of the few pieces to survive.*

THE CAVE OF 1,000 BUDDHAS

A CHINESE ADVENTURER

The Silk Road link between east and west was opened up by the Chinese in the years after 128 BC, when General Zhang Qian returned from a perilous mission. He had been sent out 11 years earlier, by the Han emperor Wu Di, to make contact with the Yuezhi nomads, enemies of the Xiongnu nomads who were causing considerable trouble to the Han Empire. After being captured by the Xiongnu and held prisoner for 10 years, Zhang Qian escaped and reached the borders of India. Further misadventures followed, but he eventually managed to return home. Although Zhang Qian failed in his mission to win military Yuezhi support, he brought back a great deal of useful information about the west and opportunities for trade which Wu Di was swift to act upon. He and his successors established military outposts in oasis towns along the routes skirting the fearsome icy wastes of the Taklamakan desert and opened up trade with the west. For many centuries caravans travelled along this route, carrying Chinese silk and lacquer, furs imported from the steppe nomads, glass and alabaster wares and statuary from the Mediterranean, spices and cotton textiles from India, incense from Arabia and the fabulous "horses that sweat blood" from Ferghana on the Silk Road itself.

Buddhist missionaries also travelled the Silk Road from west to east, taking Buddhism to China, Korea and Japan, where it rapidly won adherents. Buddhist shrines and monasteries were established in many of the oasis towns along the Silk Road, often decorated with impressive sculptures and paintings. By the fifth century AD Chinese pilgrims were travelling west to study and worship in the Buddhist centres and shrines of India and Sri Lanka and to obtain copies of sacred manuscripts. One, Xuan Zang, who undertook this difficult and hazardous journey in the seventh century AD, left a vivid account of his travels.

INTO CENTRAL ASIA'S ICY WASTES

Xuan Zang's writings were a constant and inspiring companion to Sir Aurel Stein, a scholar who intrepidly explored the Silk Road and its towns in the early years of the twentieth century. And, by good fortune, they also provided the key that unlocked the door to Stein's greatest discovery.

Stein, accompanied by his Chinese secretary, Jiang Siye, his little dog Dash and a small team of native helpers, visited and investigated a number of ruined oasis towns along the Silk Road. Here he found the remains of fruit trees, an indication that their inhabitants had maintained efficient irrigation systems many hundreds of years earlier. He excavated houses, uncovering rubbish that revealed a fascinating picture

of life – discarded clothing, a mousetrap, musical instruments and documents which include the homesick musings of Chinese officials doing garrison duty in lonely outposts like Dunhuang.

While he was working on these sites, Stein heard rumours that interesting manuscripts had been found at Dunhuang. He therefore paid a visit to this former town and religious centre. Here he found rocks riddled with artificial caves in which Buddhist monks had created monastic cells and shrines, often beautifully painted.

TRICKY NEGOTIATIONS

The Daoist monk who took care of the complex was absent at the time of Stein's first brief reconnaissance visit, but a Tibetan monk was able to show him a manuscript from the supposed hoard. This had apparently been discovered by accident during repairwork a few years earlier. The monk, anxious for the safety of the precious manuscripts, had sealed them behind a wooden door.

A few weeks later Stein returned to Dunhuang. A meeting with the Daoist

---

Above: *The valley of Dunhuang was riddled with caves excavated into the laterite cliffs. These were used as Buddhist shrines and as dwellings for monks over many centuries.*

guardian, Wang Daoshi, quickly convinced him that extreme care would be needed in handling this timorous and indecisive character. Stein sent his secretary Jiang to open negotiations, promising to make a substantial donation to the shrine if he himself were allowed to look at the manuscript collection. Wang seemed interested though uncertain and likely to shy off at any minute. At this point Xuan Zang came to the rescue. Stein asked to be shown around the shrine, of which Wang, who had restored it personally, was very proud. As they looked about, Stein began to talk about Xuan Zang. Immediately Wang lit up. Not only was he familiar with the story of Xuan Zang's travels but he had even commissioned a set of pictures illustrating his life on the cave temple wall. One scene showed Xuan Zang crossing a river with the precious collection of Buddhist manuscripts he had obtained in India. This provided an opening that Stein did not let slip, and gradually he coaxed Wang to allow him to follow this eminent example.

On the first night, Wang brought out some manuscripts with great secrecy and allowed Jiang to examine them. The following day he opened up the hidden recess and allowed Stein to examine some of the texts. And eventually he agreed to Stein removing some of the hoard, on condition that nothing should be said of this publicly until Stein had left Chinese soil.

PRICELESS MANUSCRIPTS

The hidden cache was a find of exceptional importance. It contained a huge number of perfectly preserved manuscripts on wood, bark, silk and other materials. There were Buddhist and other sacred texts, official documents, poetry, books on geography, philosophy and many other subjects, dating from between the fifth and eleventh centuries AD and written in a number of different languages. One was the earliest printed work to survive – a copy of the "Diamond Sutra" text, dating from AD 868. In addition, the cache contained many beautiful silk painted banners. These, which were in themselves a treasure without price, had probably been hidden when the area was threatened by barbarian hordes in 1135.

Wang permitted Stein to remove 24 cases of manuscripts in 1907. These eventually reached the British Museum, where they kept an army of scholars busy for decades. The following year Stein's friend and colleague Paul Pelliot also visited the "Cave of 1,000 Buddhas" and was permitted to take away 15,000 more manuscripts.

However, news of the find had now trickled out and the authorities began to take an interest. They ordered that the remaining manuscripts be sent to Peking, and in compensation made a large payment to the shrine. The money never reached the shrine – it was diverted into many pockets on the way instead – and the manuscripts similarly dwindled away on their journey, only a small proportion reaching Peking. Fortunately, Wang had kept back some of the texts, carefully hidden away, and when Stein paid a final visit in 1914 he was able to give him a further 600 manuscripts.

Below: *The numerous cave shrines at Dunhuang were richly decorated with stucco sculptures and paintings in tempera, depicting the Buddha and his followers, processions of Buddhist saints and scenes illustrating parables from former lives of the Buddha.*

TOMB OF THE FIRST CHINESE EMPEROR

AN EFFICIENT TYRANT

Wars between rival Chinese states had been a way of life for centuries when Prince Zheng ascended the throne of the Qin state in 246 BC, aged just 13. One of the first things that he did was to begin work on his tomb, which was to be of unprecedented splendour. Qin had been gradually winning the fight since 316, conquering its rivals or taking them over by diplomacy, and the new king continued its expansion. Between 230 and 221 BC, Qin's armies defeated the remaining six rival states and Zheng became ruler of the first united Chinese state.

Shi Huangdi, First Emperor, as Zheng now styled himself, was a man of extreme contrasts and later opinions of him are very mixed. Aided by his able first minister, Li Si, and his chief eunuch, Zhao Gao, he reorganized China's administration, reformed and codified the laws, standardized the script, coinage, weights and measures and even axle lengths on chariots, improved agriculture and created an efficient network of roads and canals for transport and irrigation. He also extended the empire and provided it with effective defences against the hostile barbarians on its northern fringes by joining the walls that rival states had erected on their borders, to form the first Great Wall, a massive earthen rampart.

But his advances were paid for in great suffering. Thousands of peasants died while undertaking compulsory labour to construct the Great Wall – many of their skeletons lie crushed beneath its foundations. The emperor dealt ruthlessly with opposition, both actual and potential. He ordered the burning of all books on history, philosophy and other subjects that could give people the opportunity to compare his reign unfavourably with former times and to develop rebellious thoughts, and he put to death 460 scholars who might similarly have fomented rebellion. Harsh punishments were laid down for any who might dare rebel. His wars and massive building programmes were achieved by taxing the peasants unmercifully and by excessive forced labour and conscription, causing the economic and social fabric of the state to crumble.

PREY TO FEAR AND SUPERSTITION

Not surprisingly, there were many who wished to see Shi Huangdi dead. One plot nearly succeeded. Jing Ke, a scholar and warrior, was granted an audience with the emperor to present him with the head of a slain opposing general and a map of the kingdom of Yan. Hidden inside the rolled-up map was a poisoned dagger and when Jing Ke was within range he snatched this out and grabbed the emperor by the sleeve. Before the assailant's blow could land, however, Shi Huangdi had torn himself away, ripping off the sleeve, and had darted behind a pillar.

Opposite: *A later painting of Shi Huangdi burning books and executing scholars.*

Below: *The tree-clad slopes of this burial mound hide the tomb of the First Chinese emperor, while in the surrounding plain lie the many pits containing his funerary treasures, including the terracotta army.*

While the emperor struggled to draw his long sword, the court physician hit Jing Ke with his medicine bag. Within seconds Shi Huangdi freed his sword and set upon Jing Ke, stabbing him eight times and killing him.

The emperor lived in daily fear of his life and devised elaborate precautions to protect himself. He had many palaces throughout his realms, furnished with everything he could need, including concubines, and he travelled constantly, often incognito, so that no assassin could predict his whereabouts from day to day. Constantly seeking a way to prolong his existence, he sent out expeditions in search of the Elixir of Life and employed scholars, quacks and magicians to devise a life-preserving potion. One scholar caused him extreme fury by fleeing while in his service, claiming that the emperor was unworthy of having his life extended.

Shi Huangdi's obsession worked to the advantage of his trusted Li Si and Zhao Gao. When the emperor died suddenly in 210 BC, they hid the news and continued the royal progress as if nothing had happened, disguising the smell of his rotting corpse by placing his chariot near a cart of decaying fish. This gave them time to arrange the death of the crown prince and other impediments in their path to power, which they seized in the name of the emperor's youngest and weakest son. But their success was short-lived. Within four years the massive revolts that followed the emperor's death had swept them from power and a peasant called Liu Bang had seized the throne as first emperor of the Han dynasty, which was to rule China for more than 400 years.

THE EMPEROR'S TOMB

For 36 years an army of 700,000 conscripted labourers had been working to construct Shi Huangdi's final resting place at Mount Li. Details of the tomb were recorded by the Han historian Sima Qian. A vast complex was built above ground, with palaces and pavilions set within massive walls with splendid guard towers. In its centre was erected a mound more than 100 metres (330 feet) high, covering the chamber in which the emperor was to be buried. The chamber itself was a model of the world – the ceiling showed the pattern of the heavens with stars picked out in precious stones,

Right: *Ranks of terracotta warriors guard the emperor's tomb.*

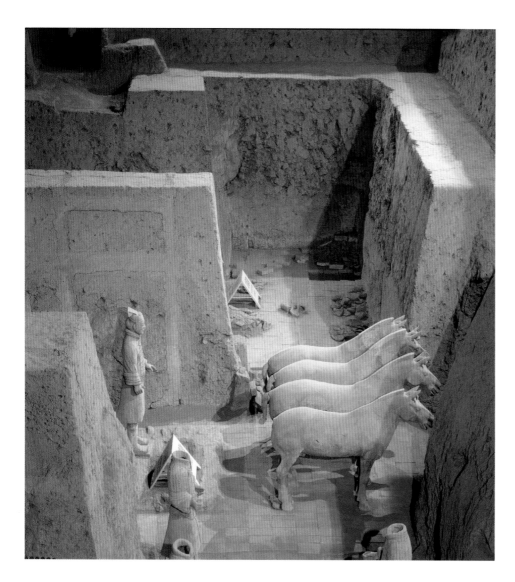

and charioteers – although the chariots, being of wood, have decayed away. The figures were made in separate pieces – legs, arms, hands, heads – in moulds. After each figure was assembled from these pieces, a thin layer of clay was spread over it and details were carved into this, representing individual uniforms, hairstyles and particularly faces. Some people believe that the soldiers of the emperor's living army sat for their portraits to be faithfully reproduced on the terracotta figures, for they are all different and amazingly lifelike.

LOOTED OR INTACT?

The terracotta army has survived for 2,000 years but it is unarmed. When they were lined up in their wooden chambers, the soldiers were richly furnished with fine weapons. But within four years, the living armies of revolt had swept through. Soldiers entered the chambers and seized the weapons to aid them in overthrowing the Qin regime of tyranny, burning the wooden chambers as they left and destroying the palaces and other buildings of the funerary complex. And what of the emperor's tomb with its fabulous treasures? Sima Qian is enigmatic on the subject – some believe he says that the army also looted the tomb, while others maintain it is still intact. Archaeologists have still to find out: no one has yet taken on the massive task of excavating the burial chamber. However, soil analyses have already shown part of Sima Qian's claims to be true: these detected a great quantity of mercury within the mound – presumably the rivers and ocean of which Sima Qian wrote. Geophysical surveys indicate that the emperor's tomb lies a staggering 50 metres (165 feet) below ground.

A ROYAL LANDSCAPE

The excavators have not stopped work in the tomb complex, however. It is now known to be much larger and more varied than originally supposed. The grounds – a complete artificial landscape known as the Funerary Garden (Lishan Lingyuan) – extend for 57 square kilometres (22 square miles). Within the walled enclosures lies the huge mound covering the emperor's burial chamber, planted with trees and

while the floor was laid out with models of palaces, temples and other important buildings. The courses of the Yangzi and Yellow Rivers were cut into the floor and filled with mercury, which by some cunning mechanical means was made to flow perpetually into a miniature mercury ocean.

In the centre was the massive sarcophagus of cast copper in which the emperor was to be buried. All manner of treasures were to be placed with him. To prevent the impious disturbing his eternal peace, many booby traps were installed, including crossbows that would fire automatically if the tomb was broken into. When the emperor's body had been laid in the tomb, the jade entrance doors were sealed, trapping inside the pallbearers who had passed the booby traps and therefore knew too much.

Others of the emperor's goods and treasures were buried in pits around the funerary complex. These included bronze model chariots, the emperor's horses and the animals from his menagerie.

ETERNAL GUARDIANS OF THE EMPEROR

Sima Qian did not describe everything, however. In 1974 some peasants drilling for water discovered an underground chamber filled with terracotta statues. Archaeologists were called in to investigate – and have been working there ever since. Their excavations have revealed an amazing funerary offering – an entire army, more than 8,000 strong. Whereas earlier custom had been to sacrifice servants to accompany the royal dead into eternity, by the time of emperor Shi Huangdi models were being substituted for real people.

Four pits had been dug by the emperor's workforce. One was not completed by the time of his unexpected death and remains empty. Of the other three, one is quite small and represents the army's headquarters, housing life-size statues of the chief officers. The other two contain serried ranks of thousands of life-sized terracotta soldiers, drawn up in battle order and eager to fight. There are spearmen and archers, horses

Above: *In the smallest pit were 68 officers: an elite guard was arranged on either side of the four-horse command chariot, while behind it were grouped four senior officers who were identified by ribbons.*

bushes to disguise it as a natural hill. The pits containing the terracotta army lie east of the enclosures. Near the funerary mound, within the enclosures, are a number of sacrificial pits filled with grave goods, including many beautiful bronze vessels. Immediately to the west of the mound is a pit containing two beautiful half-life-sized bronze chariots, each complete with a bronze charioteer and four bronze horses. One was a light war chariot and its driver was suitably armed with a sword and a crossbow. It had a large parasol over it to keep off the sun and rain. The other was a roofed carriage for comfortable travel.

Also near the mound were many buildings: shrines devoted to the worship of the divine emperor and houses for the staff who tended the shrines and maintained the gardens and funerary complex. Daily rituals here involved making offerings of food and drink to the emperor's spirit, so the staff included cooks. There were probably around 180 pits of various types within the Funerary Garden.

Some contain more terracotta figures. In one were 12 officials, standing dutifully with their hands in their sleeves, small caps tied on their heads with strings fastened under their chins. At least 20 horse skeletons were also placed in the pit. Another two pits contained at least 100 horse skeletons, again with terracotta figures in attendance. Fourteen small pits each contained a terracotta figure of a kneeling servant. Outside the enclosures was another pit containing horse skeletons, with servants in attendance feeding them millet and oats, offering them water, shoeing them and engaging in other stable duties.

Eighteen other pits contained the creatures from the emperor's menagerie, mainly deer and various birds. Another was full of suits of ceremonial or imitation armour – mail shirts, each made of hundreds of small rectangular limestone plaques stitched together with metal, and matching helmets. One suit of armour was designed not for a person but for a horse, a unique find in this period. These outfits were too heavy to have been worn in battle: each mailshirt weighed around 18 kilograms (40 pounds).

Particularly interesting was a pit containing at least 11 muscular terrracotta figures, clad only in a kilt, in unusual positions: some with their hands clasped in front of them, others stretching up their arms and sometimes standing on tiptoe. These were probably acrobats, wrestlers and other entertainers to amuse the emperor.

Far outside the enclosures, part of the funerary complex was converted into an artificial marsh, an F-shaped pit accessed by a ramp, through which a water channel ran between wooden banks. This was filled with bronze models of water birds – ducks, swans and cranes – swimming or standing in lifelike poses. In another part of the pit were terracotta models of men: from their clothing and attitudes, they have been interpreted as musicians, perhaps providing entertainment for a royal picnic.

Below: *No one knows if, as in this reconstruction, the rebel armies managed to penetrate the interior of the emperor's tomb.*

SPLENDOURS OF ANCIENT CHINESE TOMBS

GRAVE OF THE WARRIOR QUEEN

A thousand years before Shi Huangdi, during the period when the Shang dynasty ruled the major Chinese state on the Yellow River, it was still the custom to sacrifice real people to accompany royalty to the grave. The most spectacular burial found from this period was that of Fu Hao, consort of the great Shang king, Wu Ding (1324–1266 BC).

Wu Ding was an unusual man. In an age when women were expected to confine themselves to household management and the bearing and raising of children, he entrusted 20 of his wives with the task of organizing many of the major concerns of his kingdom – farming, stock-breeding and fishing, for example. To Fu Hao he gave command of his troops in many of the wars that he waged. She raised large armies, led many successful campaigns against neighbouring tribes and conducted important religious ceremonies. She also managed large estates of her own and bore children to the emperor.

When she died, she was buried in a deep shaft grave in the royal cemetery of Xiotun near the Shang capital, Anyang. Sixteen sacrificed servants were buried in niches cut in the walls of the shaft and on the roof of the wooden grave chamber constructed at the bottom of the shaft. A number of dogs were also sacrificed.

Within the wooden chamber were placed about 2,000 funerary offerings. These included more than 1,600 bronze objects, mainly ritual vessels, showing remarkable skill in their manufacture. Precious materials had been used for many other objects, particularly jade, used to make around 600 beautiful carved animals and birds. One of the most striking objects was a tall drinking vessel of rare ivory inlaid with turquoise. Within a wooden coffin lay the queen herself. She wore jade ornaments, bone and jade hairpins and combs, and a number of figurines made of jade were placed with her. There were also more than 6,000 valuable cowrie shells, imported from South East Asia and used as money. And of course, since she was a warrior queen, she was buried with her weapons – axes, daggers and archery equipment, including a beautiful jade thumb guard.

JADE FOR ETERNITY

For the ancient Chinese, jade had a special significance. It represented the immortal beings of the other world and was thought to have life-giving properties. Jade amulets were worn to prolong life and jade was placed with the dead to preserve their souls in eternity and to help them overcome the grim perils of the afterlife, where demons and evil spirits abounded and bureaucrats of the Celestial Deity waited with records of their earthly deeds and misdeeds.

Prince Liu Sheng was the son of Jingdi, one of the early emperors of the Han dynasty who had seized the imperial throne in 206 BC. Liu Sheng was appointed ruler of the kingdom of Zhongshan in northern China, one of the ancient states that now formed part of the Han Empire. He and his wife, Dou Wan, were determined that they should enjoy eternal life. They had magnificent tombs constructed at Mancheng, not in the normal style of wooden underground chambers but cut straight into the hillside 50 metres (165 feet) deep, drawing permanence for themselves from the enduring qualities of the stone.

The tombs were laid out as if they were palaces for life. On either side of the entrance were long, narrow stables and storerooms.

Four magnificent chariots, complete with splendid horses, were installed in the stable block of Liu Sheng's tomb and two more placed in the passage. On the right side, a great quantity of food and wine was stored along with other domestic objects. The passage opened out into a central chamber in which stood a wooden hall with a tiled roof. Two tents were set up here in which the dead prince could hold banquets and conduct religious rites. His private apartment lay behind, built within the rock-cut cave out of closely fitting stone slabs and sealed by a white marble door. Stone figures of servants waited to do the prince's bidding.

Dou Wan's tomb was similarly laid out and furnished. The couple's private chambers were filled with their prized possessions, ready for their use. Bronze wine vessels inlaid with gold and silver were among their treasures – one in Liu Sheng's tomb bore an inscription encouraging him to eat and grow fat, that he might live long in good health. Silver and gold acupuncture needles were present, to treat any ailments. Exquisite gilded bronze ornaments included a pair of leopards in Liu Sheng's tomb.

The prince and his consort occupied the centre of these chambers, enclosed within a wooden coffin and lying on a white marble bed. Each was encased from head to foot in a suit of the preserving jade. Craftsmen had worked for as long as 10 years to produce the suits, laboriously piecing them together from more than 2,500 shaped plaques of jade. The plaques were fastened with gold wire at each corner – that used in Dou Wan's suit weighed 680 grams (24 ounces) in all. The suits were constructed in pieces to make it easy to put them on when death came upon the prince (in 113 BC) and princess – feet, legs, body front and back, sleeves, gloves, helmet and face mask.

Sealed within their jade suits, Liu Sheng and Dou Wan hoped their bodies would last for ever. To make doubly sure, they also had the tombs sealed – rubble was piled against the sealed door and the openings filled with iron. But it was all in vain – in 1968, when the tombs were accidentally discovered, all that remained of the jade prince and princess themselves were a handful of dust and a broken tooth.

Above: *This elaborately decorated bronze, one of the huge number buried with Fu Hao, is a ding, or rectangular food vessel. The Chinese used piece moulds to cast such bronzes.*

Below: *These two exquisite gilded bronze leopards were used as weights to hold down the edges of the funeral pall in Liu Sheng's tomb. Lesser individuals had jade pigs as weights.*

LADY DAI

In contrast, the body of a lady who died some 50 years earlier was miraculously preserved with much less effort. She was the wife of the Marquis of Dai, a Han nobleman in the kingdom of Changsha. Wrapped in 20 layers of brocade, her body was laid to rest inside a nest of lacquered coffins placed in a wooden chamber which was carefully sealed within layers of charcoal and clay. As this arrangement meant that her tomb was airtight, her body survived so well that when she was discovered her skin was still supple, her long black hair carefully arranged and it proved possible to conduct an autopsy on her. The cause of her death? Lady Dai had been fond of her food and was rather overweight; she also suffered from gallstones and lumbago. Shortly after eating a musk melon she had a heart attack which carried her off at the age of about 50.

The funerary mound at Mawangdui that covers her tomb is one of many in the area, most of which have been plundered. The vast size of this mound had daunted grave robbers, however, and it was not until a hospital began to be constructed on the site that the mound was disturbed, revealing the grave shafts of three burials. When these were excavated in 1974 they proved to contain the bodies of Li Cang, Marquis of Dai, who died in 186 BC, his wife and one of their sons. The inventory of grave goods that always accompanied burials, for the use of the other world's officials, showed that the son had died in 168 BC. Lady Dai outlived both of them, for she was buried last.

A great household of 162 model servants accompanied Lady Dai, carved from peachwood, painted or dressed in silk. Some were attendants but others were entertainers – dancers and musicians with their instruments: pipes, zithers and mouth organs. Music was important to the ancient Chinese as a means of communicating with the spirit world. Real instruments were also included among the grave offerings. The tomb was packed with other valuables belonging to the lady – bales of silk cloth, rich clothing, including silk slippers and colourful robes, bronze mirrors and tin bells. She was very well supplied with food of all kinds and with herbal remedies for heart disease.

A huge array of lacquerware was also stacked in several compartments of her tomb. Lacquer was extremely expensive, costing ten times as much as bronze, so it was only wealthy and important people who took it with them into the grave. Lady Dai had containers and ladles for serving food, dishes, cups and bowls, spoons and chopsticks for eating and drinking, boxes, trays, and many other household objects of the beautiful lacquerware, finely decorated in black. Some of the bowls bore an inscription inviting the user to drink wine from them. One lacquer box contained a vanity set including combs and brushes, powder, a cosmetic mirror and a hairpiece.

Lady Dai's coffins were also of lacquered wood, some plain and some decorated. A silk banner covered the innermost coffin, its decoration depicting the lady's journey to the other world. In the bottom register her grieving family is shown offering sacrifices beside her bier, while below lurk the monsters of the underworld. In the centre of the banner she is seen supporting herself on a stick, flanked by phoenixes waiting to escort her to the celestial realms depicted in the upper register.

The other tombs were filled with equally remarkable offerings. The young man had a library of some 30 books, written in ink on silk or on strips of wood. These included treatises on astronomy and medicine, two copies of the Daoist text, *The Way and its Power*, and one of the great Confucian classic, *I Ching* (*Book of Changes*). The men's tombs were furnished with weapons inlaid with gold as well as gameboards, silks and lacquerware. A final treasure was a collection of maps painted on silk.

Above: *Radiography and other sophisticated modern scientific techniques have been used to reveal details of Lady Dai's health and diet, and the cause of her death.*

Below: *Lady Dai's vanity box had two compartments. The lower one contained nine small boxes with cosmetics, comb, brushes and other toilet equipment, while the upper half could hold clothing accessories such as gloves.*

ROYAL TOMBS OF KOREA

THE THREE KINGDOMS

The martial emperor Wu Di greatly expanded the Han Chinese state. Among the areas he conquered was northern Korea, where in 108 BC the Han established four provinces or commanderies. The Koreans proved troublesome subjects and only one province, Lelang, survived for long. Chinese power in Korea finally came to an end in AD 313, a time when native tribes had begun to coalesce into three states, frequently at war with each other. Goguryo in the north was strongly influenced by China. Baekche in the south-west had links with Japan and the lands to the south. Silla in the south-east was separated from Baekche by Gaya, an area of autonomous city states, which it gradually swallowed up by military conquest. Joining forces with the Chinese, Silla then defeated Baekche in AD 663 and Goguryo in 668.

All three kingdoms had a very marked social hierarchy, from poor peasants up to godlike kings. Prosperous agriculture and industries at home and profitable overseas trade brought great wealth to the kingdoms, which found expression in the lavish furnishings of the royal tombs. In Goguryo, the tombs were built of cut stones in the shape of square-based pyramids. The majority were plundered in the past but the fine paintings that decorated their walls still survive, giving a vivid picture of all aspects of life in the Goguryo state. Occasionally the looters missed a few objects, gold and gilded bronze ornaments which give a hint of the richness of the original grave offerings.

In Baekche, tomb robbers were similarly active and many burial mounds also suffered at the hands of the Chinese and Silla conquerors in 663, who burned and looted extensively. By chance, however, the tomb of King Muryong near the one-time Baekche capital, Gongju, survived intact and was discovered by accident during repair work to a neighbouring painted tomb. Built of grey bricks decorated with lotuses, it had an entrance passage leading to a barrel-vaulted chamber. The stone figure of a winged animal guarded the burials. White porcelain from Liang and other Chinese imports filled the tomb, surrounding two lacquered coffins. One contained the burial of Muryong, who died in AD 523, while the other was that of his queen, who outlived him by three years. Of the royal pair nothing survived except two teeth, but their grave goods were magnificent.

Below: *Vast earthen mounds were constructed over cairns of cobbles to protect the elite tombs around the Silla capital at Gyeongju. More than 155 are known here and many exist elsewhere in Silla.*

Both king and queen wore a golden crown, an upright cut-out sheet looking like a tree in flower. Holes in the "trunk" were used to attach the crown to a silk cap. Wooden pillows decorated with gold were provided for their head and feet, and both wore bronze shoes. The king wore a silver belt and a sword with a gilded hilt, and the royal couple were both richly provided with jewellery, including a gold hairpin, silver bracelets, a belt with a silver pendant, gold earrings and jade beads.

SPLENDOURS OF SILLA

Unlike those of their neighbours, the tombs of Silla's royalty, built around Gyeongju, were strongly protected against robbers. The remains of the royal dead were buried in a chamber cut into the ground or built of wood at ground level. The chamber was then completely covered with large cobbles set in clay and a vast earthen mound was erected over it. One of the most impressive mounds, excavated in recent years, contained two royal graves. The southern grave was that of a king, wearing a gilded bronze crown. A sacrificed girl had been thrown down beside the chamber. A separate adjacent chamber was filled with an enormous number of iron weapons and pots as well as four imported glass vessels: a brown and white cup from China, the earliest piece of Chinese glass yet found; a cup from Persia; a striped glass goblet from Alexandria and a jug from Syria. Silla, which exported gold, probably traded with the west by both land and sea.

The northern chamber was much more splendidly furnished, indicating that the lady buried here had ruled in her own right alongside the king – ruling queens are known from Silla history, although this particular queen is not mentioned. She was decked in a magnificent crown of sheet gold. This followed the usual form for Silla gold crowns, being made of a gold band supporting uprights in the shape of stylized trees. Gold spangles and jade gokoks (comma-shaped beads) fastened with gold wire decorated it. The queen also wore a massive golden belt with dangling pendants. This too is a type of ornament found in several of the remarkable Silla royal tombs, of which a number have now been investigated.

Right: *At least 10 magnificent gold crowns have been found in Silla tombs. All are variations on the same theme – a circle of gold supporting sheet gold uprights and dangling gold and jade ornaments.*

TANG AND MING TREASURES

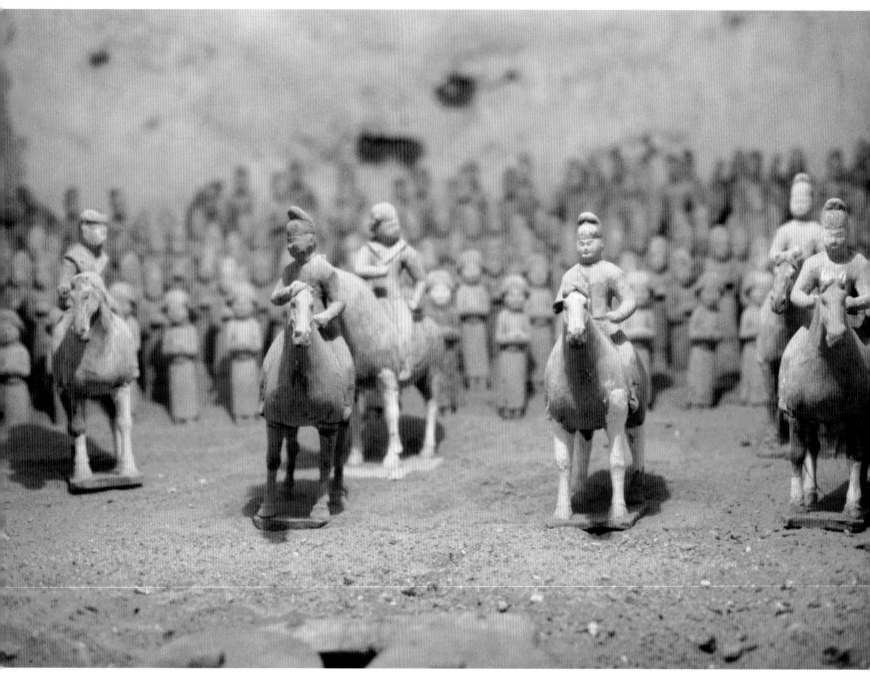

TANG PAINTED TOMBS

The Tang dynasty, who seized the Chinese imperial throne in AD 618, was instrumental in securing Silla's victory over its rivals in Korea in 668, but was unable to consolidate its own position there. Nevertheless, the Tang state controlled a huge empire, its influence extending to the western end of Central Asia and into southern China and Manchuria, bringing it into trading contact with the states of West Asia and South East Asia. Many members of the imperial family were buried in royal cemeteries in the hills north

of the Tang capital, Chang'an. Among these was the funerary precinct of Qianling, tomb of the Emperor Gaozong, who died in AD 683, and his wife Wu Zetian. Their tomb has not been opened but three lesser tombs have been excavated: those of Prince Zhanghuai, Gaozong's sixth son, and his nephew and niece, Prince Yide and Princess Yongtai.

Theirs was a tragic story. Wu Zetian was a concubine who charmed her way into the affections of the young, inexperienced emperor. In order to get rid of the empress, in 655 she murdered her own newborn

daughter and threw the blame on her rival, whom she then supplanted. By her forceful character she utterly dominated Gaozong. After his death, she continued to rule with her younger son as a puppet emperor until 690 when he was deposed; Wu then ensured that she became empress in her own right.

While Wu was an extremely able ruler, she was also completely ruthless. When in 684 an attempt was made to oust her from power, she took the opportunity to eliminate almost the entire imperial family. She forced the crown-prince, Zhanghuai, into exile and then suicide. In 701 she murdered Princess Yongtai, her own granddaughter, for speaking out about Wu's scandalous affair with two dissipated young men. Yongtai, a celebrated beauty, was only 17. Her husband, Wu's nephew, was also murdered. Yongtai's brother Yide was executed in the same year, aged 19, for opposing his grandmother. Only after Empress Wu was forced to abdicate in 705 were they given burial in splendid tombs at Qianling.

Despite some looting, their tombs still held numerous pottery models of attendants, officials, warriors, horsemen and entertainers, along with hundreds of objects of jade, gold, silver and bronze. The burial chambers were approached by corridors whose walls bore beautiful frescoes of scenes from court daily life: active outdoor pursuits, such as polo, recently introduced from Persia and played by both men and women, and hunting with dogs, hawks or cheetahs, and more leisurely activities like walking in the gardens. A mural in Yide's tomb shows the city walls, magnificent towering gates and principal buildings of Chang'an, from which a royal procession of chariots and horsemen is setting out. The range of court personnel is shown in detail, from princes and princesses to maid servants and the eunuchs who exercised very considerable power. Foreign diplomats are also depicted, being greeted by local officials. Other foreigners are represented among the stone statues in the approach to the Qianling tombs, including

Opposite: *These small Tang figurines come from the tomb of the unfortunate princess, Yongtai. In the foreground are lively horsemen, while behind them stand rank upon rank of courtiers.*

Below: *Trade along the Silk Road brought Tang China many imported luxury goods from the West. Particularly important was fine Sassanian silverware, the styles of which influenced Chinese art and craftsmanship.*

a Persian king who took refuge at the Chinese court after he was overthrown. Here also are statues of horses with grooms and imperial guards, imposing lions and pillars carved with winged horses. A stele, whose letters were inlaid with gold, records the magnificent deeds of Emperor Gaozong but another, commemorating Wu, was left blank at her own request, in the hope that later generations would regard her more kindly than her contemporaries and would record her achievements rather than her ill deeds.

CONCEALED IN HASTE
The empire enjoyed its greatest glory under the emperor Xuanzong, who reigned from AD 712 to 756. Love brought about the emperor's downfall. He became enamoured of Yang Guifei, a young woman who had been the consort of one of his sons. In his besotted state, he bestowed positions of power on her relatives. One of the emperor's generals, An-Lushan, fearing for his own position, rebelled in 755 and the emperor was forced to flee his capital. To his anguish and shame, he was also forced by his troops to execute his beautiful paramour.

As the court fled, many nobles and members of the imperial household must have hidden their valuables. Although the Tang dynasty was eventually restored, some did not return to retrieve their treasures. One such abandoned hoard was discovered in 1970 in Hejiacun, a suburb of Chang'an, in a mansion that had belonged to the family of the emperor's cousin, Li Shouli, son of Prince Zhanghuai. Two large pottery jars and a silver vessel between them contained more than 1,000 pieces of treasure, providing a wonderful insight into aristocratic life at the time.

As well as hundreds of Chinese coins, the hoard included a handful of foreign silver coins – Sassanian, Byzantine and Japanese – reflecting the extensive overseas contacts of the Tang. A vase of fine onyx stone was probably imported from the Sassanian Empire and many of the silver vessels, although made in China, recall Sassanian art in their decoration and form. A gold pedestalled bowl reflects the interaction of these traditions, with a background dotted with flowers and leaves in western style, combined with a lotus-flower form and animal designs that are purely Chinese. Peonies were a craze of the court at Chang'an at this time, and a number of the silver bowls bore a scroll decoration of these flowers. Other influences are visible in an extraordinary flask of silver imitating the baggy shape of a leather bottle of the type used by steppe nomads. It was decorated on each side with a gilt figure of a horse with a silver mane, holding a bowl in its mouth: these were a pair of the 400 famous dancing horses beloved of Emperor Xuanzong.

The excellence of Tang craftsmanship is particularly apparent in five parcel-gilt dishes of polished silver, decorated with real or mythical animals, and an exquisite pot of the same materials, depicting parrots among luxuriant foliage. This pot contained uncut precious stones, sapphires, rubies, topaz and chalcedony, topped by a gold leaf on which pranced 12 minute gold dragons. Jewellery and clothing accessories of jade and gold included decorative plaques from a belt, each one depicting a western entertainer.

Jade was also used for a beautiful eight-lobed bowl, an extremely valuable object: gold and silver were far more common for elite vessels. An agate bowl and several other vessels from the hoard were used to grind supposedly medicinal materials, such as gold, cinnabar and sulphur, to make elixirs believed to increase longevity or improve health but often having the opposite effect.

BUDDHIST TREASURES
In 1981 heavy rain caused the partial collapse of the 13-storey pagoda at the heart of the ancient Buddhist Famen monastery. It was decided that a replacement should be built: this presented an opportunity to excavate the foundations of the old pagoda and its wooden predecessor. Beneath these a palatial suite of stone chambers was revealed. This contained the precious relic that the shrine was built to house

and a number of treasures donated later, particularly by the Tang emperors who were great patrons of this monastery.

The relic was reputedly a fingerbone of the Buddha – a rare treasure that made the shrine famous. Periodically it was taken for a few days to be displayed and venerated in the imperial capital. In the shrine it was wrapped in gold-embroidered silk and housed within a nest of five miniature coffins, the inner one of jade, and the others, in sequence, of crystal, sandalwood, silver-gilt and iron, the outer one wrapped in silk. This reliquary was concealed in a niche in the inner chamber wall. The shrine also had three replicas of the fingerbone, also finely housed: these may have been intended as decoys if the shrine was ever looted. One was housed in a miniature silver-gilt coffin inside an exquisite model stupa of gilt bronze, wrapped in silk and placed within a larger stupa of stone. Another was placed inside eight nested reliquary boxes, each fastened with a padlock, the outer one of sandalwood, then one of plain silver, two of parcel-gilt silver, one of marble and jewels, two of gold and the innermost an exquisite tiny gold pagoda – these were commissioned by Empress Wu. The last lay in a miniature silver-gilt coffin within an iron casket, wrapped in layers of textiles and placed within a large stone stupa, also the gift of Empress Wu. Some of the caskets were decorated with Buddhist figures or symbols.

Opposite: *Decorated inside with peonies, this parcel-gilt yu shang, or winged cup, from Hejiacun is a superb product of Tang skill and craftsmanship. Ducks and peony scrolls adorn the exterior.*

Below: *A Sassanian silver carafe decorated with dancers, floral motifs and wildlife. Many Sassanian goods reached China in the Tang period when foreign trade was at its height.*

Among the other treasures were objects used in Buddhist ceremonies, such as censers, a wonderful incense burner and vessels for pouring scented water. Others served more secular purposes, including a parcel-gilt silver tea service, one piece of which was a jar for holding tea or spices, decorated with panels showing scenes from everyday life, including two men playing chess. There were also many dishes and containers of fine Chinese stoneware and gilded Islamic glass, as well as 1,000 silk textiles, now sadly deteriorated.

An extraordinary and beautiful silver-gilt figure of a Bodhisattva, covered with strings of pearls, kneeling on a lotus-flower throne and holding in his arms a tray, was made as a gift for Emperor Yizong in 871 and was designed to hold the finger relic when it was displayed in the capital: this happened for the last time in 873. A beautiful parcel-gilt silver staff made in the palace workshops was carried at the head of the procession of imperial carriages that went from Chang'an to return the relic to the shrine, some 110 kilometres (70 miles) away. More than 100 gold and silver gifts were presented to the shrine by the Tang emperor on this occasion, including the staff and the Bodhisattva figure; he also erected a stele providing an inventory of all the shrine's treasures. The vault was then sealed, and remained so for more than a millennium, until its recent rediscovery.

IMPERIAL CEMETERY

The Ming dynasty was founded in 1368 after a period of civil war in China. Continuing troubles from nomads along the northern border led the Ming emperors to strengthen and rebuild the Great Wall and the third emperor, Yongle, moved the capital to Beijing, closer to the north than the previous capital, Nanjing.

Forty-five kilometres from the new capital, in a valley carefully chosen to meet the requirements of fengshui (geomancy), then a powerful element in Chinese belief, Yongle had a vast funerary complex laid out. A great processional road, the Spirit Way, was constructed, lined on either side by huge stone figures of guardian warriors, mythical beasts, elephants and camels. Passing through a series

Left: *The 13-storey pagoda that towers over the Buddist monastery of Famen. Its partial collapse in 1981 brought about the discovery of precious Buddhist relics and wonderful treasures donated by kings.*

of monumental gates, the Spirit Way led up to the Phoenix and Dragon Gate, set across the road to prevent malevolent spirits (which, it was believed, could fly only in straight lines) from penetrating the sacred necropolis beyond.

Thirteen emperors were laid to rest here. Each was buried within a massive tomb under a gigantic tumulus set at the end of a series of courtyards containing ceremonial buildings. The vast scale of the tombs deterred archaeologists from excavating them until the mid-twentieth century when Dingling ("tomb of Security"), the tomb of Wanli, was investigated.

SPLENDID MAUSOLEUM OF AN UNWORTHY EMPEROR

Wanli was just a boy when he came to the throne in 1572 and for the first 10 years of his reign China prospered under the efficient rule of his minister, Zhang Juzheng. After the latter's death, however, the weak, extravagant, irresponsible emperor began a regime of self-indulgence and neglect of duty that undermined Ming power. The dynasty collapsed in 1644, 24 years after Wanli's death.

Wanli began construction of his tomb in 1584. Employing 600,000 men and costing 227,000 kilograms (8,000,000 ounces) of silver, the huge walled precinct with its four courtyards, administrative buildings and pavilions was completed in 1590. Wanli gave a great banquet within the complex to celebrate.

When archaeologists decided to investigate Wanli's tomb in 1956, they were puzzled where to start. A massive wall surrounded the great tumulus – where was the entrance? Selecting a place in the wall where some of the bricks were loose, they struck lucky, for behind these lay the archway of the outer entrance. A tunnel led from here into the mound. Digging out the earth from this passage and passing through an antechamber, the excavators came to a pair of massive doors of white marble, firmly sealed. When closed, a mechanism caused a stone pillar to fall in place as a bar locking the doors from the inside. The archaeologists determined not to damage the doors, discovered they could be opened by inserting a strong, but flexible metal rod between them to lever the pillar out of the way.

An outer hall led them to another set of doors, which they opened in the same way. They now found themselves within the sacrificial chamber, gazing at three marble

TODAY'S UNFOUND TREASURES

CAPTAIN KIDD'S TREASURE

Captain William Kidd was a Scot, born around 1645, who by 1690 was sailing in American waters with an English letter of marque, an official licence to use his ship as a private man-of-war, capturing the ships of England's enemies. In effect he was a government-sponsored pirate, and in 1695 he received a further government commission, to deal with Indian Ocean pirates who were preying on English shipping. Four years later Kidd seized the *Quedagh Merchant*, a merchant ship operating under a French pass. He did not bring the ship in to a legitimate port and on his return to America he was arrested for piracy. Sent back to England, he was tried and hanged. But was he guilty? Were his acts of piracy forced on him by a mutinous crew, as he claimed, or was this a cover? Had he been a pirate in his younger days? While awaiting execution, he claimed to have buried a substantial treasure, but did not reveal the location. Many spots around the globe are rumoured to be the hiding place. In the 1930s a chest bearing Kidd's name was found, with a treasure map of an unidentified island in the China Sea. A number of similar charts have been discovered.

Right: *An imaginative twentieth-century portrayal of Captain Kidd on Gardiners Island near New York, by Howard Pyle. He is watching carefully as his men bury his treasure.*

thrones, the central one belonging to the emperor and the other two to his empress, Xiaoduan, who died in 1620, the same year as Wanli, and the concubine Xiaojing, mother of his heir, who died in 1611 but was poshumously made an empress and reburied here beside the emperor. All were beautifully decorated, the emperor's with dragons and those of his wives with phoenixes.

At the far end, through another set of marble doors, was the burial chamber itself, in which three coffins were placed, containing the bodies of Wanli and his two empresses. Pieces of jade were placed between the outer and inner coffins, continuing the belief that this would prevent the bodies decaying. Within his nested wooden coffins, Wanli was wrapped in nine layers of blankets, topped by a brocade quilt, within which was his body, richly clad in damask and satin. All three were furnished with elaborate headdresses of gold, silver and other precious materials. That of Xiaojing was made of brilliant blue kingfisher feathers and jewels set on a frame of lacquered bamboo and surmounted by gold figures of dragons and a phoenix. Around and in the coffins were heaped many fine objects of jade, gold, silver and several varieties of porcelain. Silks and brocades were also furnished in abundance. Small personal objects included chopsticks of gold and silver.

Below: *A huge porcelain urn stood before each throne in Wanli's tomb. Filled with sesame oil and furnished with a wick, they were intended to light the tomb through eternity.*

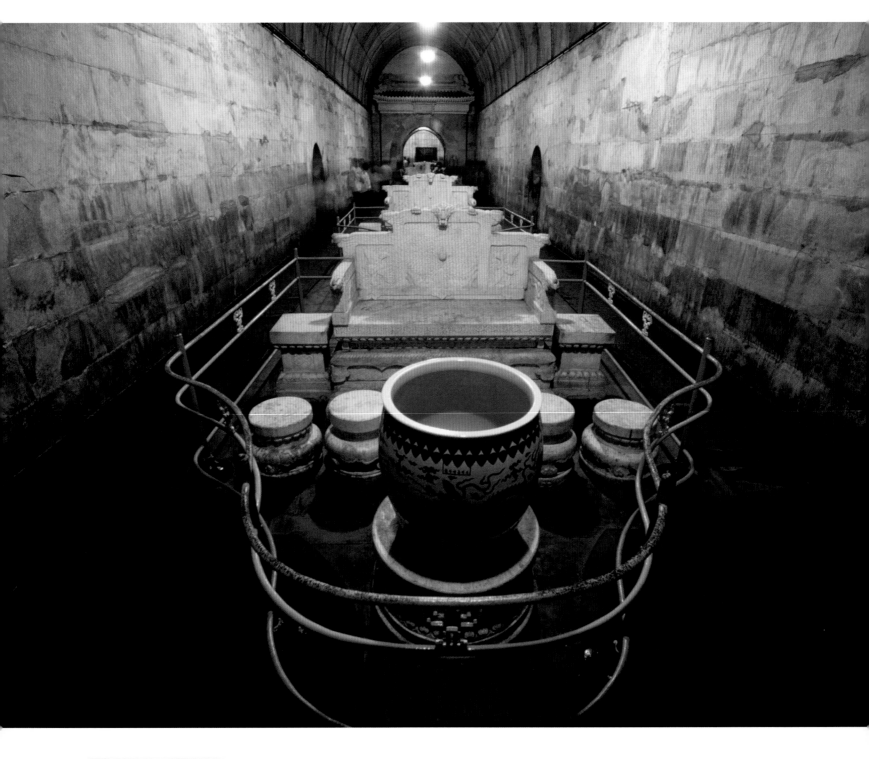

SHIPWRECKS OF THE PORCELAIN AND SPICE TRADE

SHIPWRECKED EARLY TRADERS

In 1998 a unique wreck was found in Indonesian waters. It was discovered by fishermen as a heap of Chinese pottery lying over timbers. Excavations by the marine archaeologist Michael Flecker revealed the well-preserved timbers of a ship and clues that have allowed something of its history to be painstakingly teased out, as well as providing physical evidence of a trade previously known only from written sources.

It was relatively easy to date the ship: it was carrying various different types of Chinese pottery made in the ninth century AD, and one bowl even had an inscription showing it was made in 826. Three radiocarbon dates on organic material confirmed a ninth-century date. This was a period when Indian, Persian and Arab traders were active in eastern waters: Chinese pottery was particularly popular at this time in the states bordering the Gulf.

Above: *This charming Chinese silver-gilt box, perhaps a royal gift, was recovered from the Arab dhow wrecked near Belitung around 826 AD.*

The ship was constructed of timbers sewn together with twine, a technique of shipbuilding used in the Indian Ocean but not in China; it was also used in South East Asia but to build very different vessels. The construction matched written accounts and pictures of ships from the Indian and Islamic world, although no wrecks of such ships survive. Samples of the waterlogged and deteroriated wood were analysed to see where the timbers had come from, a difficult task given their poor condition. However, it proved possible to identify teak, an Indian timber. This did not give conclusive proof of origin, as Indian timber, particularly teak and coconut palm, was exported to the Islamic

world for shipbuilding. Further analyses seem to have clinched the ship's origin – most of her timbers proved to be made of *Afzelia africana*, a tree that is widespread in Africa – the Arabs had established trading towns on the East African coast by around AD 800.

The ship had probably sailed from the great Persian port of Siraf or the equally important Omani port of Sohar, calling in at Quilon or another Indian port (the clue to this was a box made of Indian wood, and it fits written accounts of the trade routes in use at that time). It had probably passed through the Sunda strait between Sumatra and Java into waters controlled by the great maritime empire of Srivijaya, and stopped at a Srivijayan port to renew the twine holding its timbers and the wadding that kept it watertight (the twine and wadding from the wreck appeared to be of South East-Asian origin). It then probably sailed to Ghangzhou (Canton), the main Chinese port for foreign trade, perhaps calling in at other ports on the way. Here its cargo was sold and it was reloaded with Chinese pottery and other things, including lead ingots, a large jar of star anise, cast-iron cauldrons (the West had yet to develop the technology for casting iron) and some valuables: gold and gilt silver bowls and spoons, a gilt silver flask and Chinese mirrors.

The ship began to retrace its outward route but in the South China Sea it unfortunately attempted to pass through the Gelasa strait, perhaps making for a port on Belitung island, and ran aground on an extensive coral reef.

EUROPE AND CHINA, FACE TO FACE

Trade between east and west, bringing silk and spices to Europe and silver to China, had during medieval times been conducted largely along the Silk Road through Central Asia. In the mid-fourteenth century, however, this trade was disrupted by major crises – the spread of bubonic plague, which decimated the population of China, Europe and the Central Asian trading cities, followed immediately by the creation of the short-lived hostile empire of Tamerlane (Timur-leng) in Iran and western Central Asia. The Ottoman conquest of the eastern Mediterranean in the fourteenth and fifteenth centuries brought to a close the flourishing trade through these regions.

The nations of Atlantic Europe began in the fifteenth century to look for other ways to gain access to the riches of the Orient, intrepidly exploring the unknown seas and lands to both their east and west. In 1497–8 the Portuguese navigator Vasco da Gama succeeded in sailing round the Cape of Good Hope and reaching India, and by 1555 the Portuguese had established trading stations throughout the east, on the coasts of India, southern China and the islands of the East Indies, as well as Africa. Throughout the sixteenth century they monopolized the spice trade, allowing other nationals to trade only under licence from them. By 1600, however, they were facing competition from the Dutch and English and domestic troubles led to the decline of their international importance.

The Dutch and English now battled for control of the east, the Dutch rapidly gaining dominance in the East Indies and Sri Lanka (Ceylon) while the English established the "factories" that marked the beginnings of their trading empire in India. Here they soon faced competition from the French, but France's repeated defeats in European wars prevented her consolidating her toeholds in India. Although the Dutch monopolized trade with the East Indies, England was able to use India as a base from which to trade with China, exchanging Indian silver and opium for Chinese silk, tea and porcelain and acquiring spices and cotton cloth from India itself.

THE PERILS OF THE DEEP

Ships plying the sea routes between Atlantic Europe and the east faced many hazards. Scurvy, caused by lack of vitamin C, decimated crews and it was not until the late eighteenth century that it was prevented by issuing sailors with regular rations of lime juice. Other illnesses were also rife and shipboard accidents common in bad weather. It was not unusual for a ship from the Netherlands to have lost half its crew by the time it put in at the Cape of Good Hope, the midpoint of its journey to the East Indies.

Storms and rough seas presented a constant and unpredictable risk. The determination of the ship's location was still largely dependent on dead reckoning from the position of the midday sun and bad weather could quickly put out the captain's calculations, allowing the ship to run on to known reefs and rocks. In addition, often the maritime regions through which the ships sailed were poorly known and inadequately charted. A southern continent was for centuries believed to exist, on the grounds that this gave symmetry to the world, but it was not until the early seventeenth century that Europeans first set eyes on the shores of Australia and its outline was not fully established until Cook's expeditions in the 1760s and 1770s. Even what had been discovered and charted could be distorted – captains whose ships ran aground through carelessness were not above charting dangerous shores and rocks in the wrong place, to cover up their mistakes in navigation.

And there were human dangers too. Nations at war considered it perfectly proper to seize one another's merchant ships and cargoes. The VOC (Vereenigde Oost-Indische Compagnie, or Dutch East India Company) ship *Witte Leeuw*, for example, was wrecked in a sea battle with the Portuguese off Africa (see page 97). European traders could get caught up in local hostilities between native princelings and might have their ships confiscated or sunk. Pirates abounded, both European buccaneers on the high seas and indigenous pirates in East Indian waters and the China Seas. Nevertheless, there were fortunes to be made from successful voyages and the trade generally prospered.

THE GELDERMALSEN

Batavia (modern Jakarta) was the centre of Dutch trade in the east. From here, agents of the VOC shipped spices from the East Indies and porcelain from China. The spices were paid for with gold, silver and manufactured goods brought out from Europe. Gold was cheaper in China than elsewhere in the east, so ships carrying porcelain from China often also brought back gold to be used in East Indies trade.

By the eighteenth century, tea, which was in great demand in Europe, had become one of China's most valuable exports. English ships loaded tea in Chinese ports and sailed home directly, whereas Dutch shipments of tea, porcelain and gold were taken first to Batavia, where the gold was unloaded for local use. This meant that tea shipped by the English arrived sooner and was fresher. So the Dutch made a new arrangement. Instead of calling at Batavia, their ships were to take the direct route home, unloading the gold on to waiting smaller ships when they passed through the Sunda Straits.

On December 18, 1751, the VOC ship *Geldermalsen* began its journey along this route from Guangzhou (Canton) in China, where it had been loaded with a valuable cargo of 311 tonnes (306 tons) of tea, along with 147 gold bars each worth about 365 Dutch guilders and about 235,000 pieces of porcelain, mostly mass-produced wares that were popular with the Dutch middle classes.

Various hazards lay along the route and on the sixteenth day the captain, Jan Morel, was expecting to sight a dangerous reef. Assured by his boatswain, Christoffel Van Dijk, that they had already passed it, the captain altered his course to sail south. Van Dijk was mistaken, however, and as dusk fell, some three hours later, the ship crashed on to the reef.

All was chaos and confusion. The crew succeeded in refloating the ship but it was badly holed and as night came on it began to sink. Someone attempted to salvage the gold bars, but they were lost in the sea. Men piled into the *Geldermalsen*'s two boats but, when only 32 were aboard, the boats came adrift, leaving the remaining two-thirds of the crew to drown. The survivors reached Batavia 10 days later but the VOC did not salvage the lost ship.

THE "NANKING CARGO"

For more than two centuries the *Geldermalsen* lay undisturbed. In the early 1980s a salvage diver, Mike Hatcher, was working on a Chinese junk wrecked on the Admiral Stellingwerf Reef, east of the Indonesian island of Bintan, and located a VOC wreck nearby. From 1985 Hatcher and his partner Max De Rham turned their attention to this wreck, from which they recovered a large quantity of porcelain packed in wooden crates. Most of this consisted of dinner services and tea sets, along with a number of figurines, all made to VOC specifications. In the centre of the wreck the salvors found the private baggage of the wealthy passengers and company officials, including finer pieces of porcelain that they had hoped to trade on their own account. In the last days of the salvage operation, exploration outside the wreck revealed the lost gold bars – or at least, 126 of them. Auctioned at Christie's in 1986 as the "Nanking Cargo" – for the ship's identity was not at first established – the material salvaged from the *Geldermalsen* fetched a record price. It is curious to reflect that the porcelain now so highly prized was only 5 per cent of the value of what the ship was carrying, while its precious cargo of tea would now be worth relatively little even if it had survived 200 years in the sea.

THE LOST JUNK

In the early days of their trade with the east, the VOC merchants in Batavia had been supplied with Chinese goods by the Chinese themselves, who had for centuries plied the eastern waters in their junks, among the most seaworthy ships of the time. One such ship, sailing for Batavia around 1690, met an unfortunate accident, for reasons we shall never know, and was burnt down to the waterline.

In the 1980s, a Vietnamese fisherman made an unusual catch in a favourite fishing spot – a concreted mass containing Chinese porcelain. Eventually the flow of fine pieces from this site (which became known as the Vung Tau Wreck) brought it to the notice of the authorities and Vietnam's official salvage company took over, aided by a Swedish

Right: *A Chinese junk wrecked off Vietnam around 1690 was rediscovered in the 1980s. Its cargo included a rich collection of porcelain vessels destined for the Dutch domestic market.*

salvage company based in Singapore. Seven fine Ming bronze cannons were recovered from the wreck, decorated with reliefs. The ship had been carrying a mixed cargo for it would have called in at many places on its journey from Xiamen in China down the coasts of Vietnam, Malaysia and Sumatra to its final destination of Batavia. Trade goods for local consumption included bamboo combs for removing headlice, floor tiles and everyday pottery. For its European customers in Batavia it had been carrying more than 28,000 pieces of porcelain.

Chinese porcelain became extremely popular in Europe in the late seventeenth century. The VOC merchants closely matched demand by commissioning large quantities of porcelain from the kilns at Fowliang (Jingdezhen), to patterns sent out from the Netherlands. Many of the pieces in the Vung Tau cargo show how closely the porcelain matched western requirements – vases depicting Dutch houses, for example.

Below: *Some of the gold ingots salvaged near the wreck of the* Geldermalsen *were cast in the shape of a Chinese lady's shoe. Each weighed around 370 grams (13 ounces).*

THE SHINAN WRECK

For many centuries before the arrival of European traders, China had been active in overseas trade. Under the outward-looking Song dynasty, which ruled from the eleventh to the thirteenth century, they traded with Japan, where Chinese porcelain and celadon pottery were in great demand, with Korea, itself a major producer of fine pottery, and with other lands as far away as East Africa. Between 1405 and 1433, under the Ming dynasty, the great Chinese admiral Zheng He sailed with a fleet of more than 200 ships throughout the East Asian seas and further west, consolidating links with East Africa, Arabia and India and bringing back many exotic goods, including a giraffe, and the king of Sri Lanka.

In 1975 fishermen trawling between two islands off the south-west Korean coast discovered Chinese pottery in their nets. Some of their number, recognizing that they must have disturbed an ancient wreck, alerted the authorities, who paid the fishermen the value of their finds and mounted a major rescue operation. The location was particularly difficult to work in, owing to the swirling mud and icy waters, but the wreck proved well worth the effort. According to one of the wooden

cargo tags, the ship, a Chinese vessel, had left its home port of Ningbo (near Shanghai) in 1323, loaded with fine green celadon and white porcelain, bound for Hakata (Fukuoka) in Japan; on its way it had called in at a Korean port where it had taken on some locally made celadon. Continuing its journey, it had met with some unknown disaster, perhaps a storm, and had sunk. The muddy seabed had soon swallowed it up, preserving its timbers. Its excavators were able to recover virtually the whole vessel intact, and it has now been reconstructed in the Korean National Maritime Museum at Mokp'o.

The cargo too was intact – 28.4 tonnes (28 tons) of Chinese copper coins and numerous other metal objects, a large quantity of sandalwood and 20,000 pieces of pottery, packed in peppercorns to cushion them, inside the wooden cases that still bear the Chinese inscription "great luck". However, it was the archaeologists, not the merchants, whose great luck it became.

DESTRUCTION BY COMMERCIAL FISHING

The value of prompt investigation of wrecks after their discovery is illustrated by what happened to a vessel known as the Desaru wreck. This ship, built in China and armed with two Scottish-made short-range cannons for protection against pirates, went down sometime after 1840 off the south-east coast of the Malay peninsula. Its cargo was Chinese ceramics, mainly blue-and-white pottery, including more than 50,000 pottery spoons, along with brown stoneware, particularly jars and teapots, all destined for the South East-Asian market. After it sank, the ship became covered by a thick deposit of mud and very little protruded above the sea floor.

Recently the area began to be exploited by Thai fishermen using trawlers. In

May 2001 the crew of one such vessel inadvertently discovered the Desaru ship: they twice snagged their nets on a seabottom obstruction and found sherds in their trawl net. Nanhai Marine Archaeology, a salvage company that works closely with the Malaysian government, investigated the site, mapping the timbers and recovering the cargo. After their first season, summer and autumn 2001, the team returned in spring 2002 to find that further trawling in this area had churned up and destroyed much of the surviving structure of the ship, despite the presence

of a marker buoy. The trawlers involved had also suffered for their foolishness, for among the ship's timbers were fragments of torn trawl nets and a steel chain. Another vessel, the Longquan ship, which sank around AD 1400, suffered a similar fate from trawlers, her entire upper portion being shaved off.

Above: *Great care had to be taken while lifting the cases of porcelain from the* Geldermalsen.

REDISCOVERING THE WRECKS OF MODERN TREASURE SHIPS

THE *ADMIRAL NAKHIMOV*

Ownership of wrecks can be a vexed question. Sometimes it is possible to settle this amicably. For example, in 1972 the Dutch government transferred to the Australian government its rights to VOC ships wrecked off Australia. Frequently, however, disputed ownership can bring about serious problems and even diplomatic troubles between nations. Such was the case of the *Admiral Nakhimov*.

In 1904 the Japanese took exception to Russia's activities in the Far East. These had been building up over several decades and included the construction of Russia's Pacific port of Vladivostok, the linking of this with Moscow by building the Trans-Siberian railway, Russia's treaty relations with China and finally its annexation of Manchuria in 1900. The Japanese therefore broke off diplomatic relations and on February 10

declared war. The Russian authorities were not averse to a war at this time, hoping to distract the attention of the swelling ranks of dissidents from the serious domestic problems that led ultimately to the Russian Revolution in 1917.

As an attempt to rouse patriotic feelings by winning easy glory the Russo-Japanese War was a complete failure, for the Russians were heavily defeated. After war was declared, they moved their Baltic fleet of 38 ships to Vladivostok. Among the fleet was the cruiser *Admiral Nakhimov*, apparently carrying a cargo of $53 million in gold as well as 30 platinum bars. Reaching Japanese territorial waters at Tsushima Island, the fleet was attacked by the Japanese and soundly beaten. In the battle the *Admiral Nakhimov* was hit by a torpedo and severely damaged. Attempts to save it failed, so its commander, Rear-Admiral Nebogatoff, ordered that its sea-valves be opened to ensure it sank quickly.

DISPUTED OWNERSHIP

Several attempts were made by the Japanese to salvage the great treasure between 1938 and 1956. One team dived to the wreck

and cut into it using small charges of explosives. Eventually they abandoned their operations due to lack of funds. A new attempt was made in 1980 and this time the Russians made a fuss. They filed a claim to the ownership of the wreck, which they said had been sunk by its commander, not by the enemy. The question of ownership hinges upon this point, for if the Japanese had captured or sunk the ship, international law says that it would have become a legitimate war prize and therefore Japanese property. Since it was a Japanese torpedo that caused the damage that led to the *Admiral Nakhimov*'s sinking by her commander, the issue was not clear-cut. Nevertheless, the Japanese went ahead and started the salvage attempt, allegedly raising the first ingot in September 1981 and recovering gold and platinum worth more than £1,000 million.

WAR GOLD

After Germany invaded Russia in 1941, Britain and the USA agreed to supply Russia with military equipment such as tanks and aircraft. These were conveyed by sea through the Arctic Ocean, from Reykjavik in Iceland

Previous page: *The Battle of Tsushima Strait was a resounding victory for the Japanese, who captured or destroyed almost all the Russian fleet, at the cost of only three vessels of their own.*

TODAY'S UNFOUND TREASURES

BALAMBANGAN

In 1763 the fortunes of war and diplomacy enabled the British East India Company to establish a base on the island of Balambangan off the north coast of Borneo, a welcome opportunity for Britain to re-enter the East Indies sea trade long monopolized by the Dutch. The position of chief at the new station went to John Herbert, who set out in June 1771 and survived the hazards of the voyage, arriving in December 1773. Official trade proved less successful than had been hoped, since neither British merchants nor Chinese traders showed sufficient interest or faith in

the new settlement. Herbert began a successful undercover trade in opium on his own account. He also dabbled in local politics, antagonizing the Sultan of Sulu, the region in which Balambangan lay. On March 4, 1775 a band of Sulus and other locals attacked the station, sacking it and setting it on fire. Herbert and many of his men escaped, but abandoned the Company's assets – gold ingots and thousands of silver coins – as well as their personal wealth. Many people believe that they had time to conceal these riches before they fled and that they still lie hidden somewhere on Balambangan.

Above: *John Herbert.*

to the Russian port of Murmansk. The journey through the Arctic seas was not an easy one, but British convoys successfully supplied the Russians until early 1942. At this point the Germans, who had occupied Norway, began to attack the convoys in earnest, causing considerable losses. Despite this onslaught, the vital supplies continued to be sent.

In April 1942 the cruiser *HMS Edinburgh* escorted a convoy of 33 merchant ships, minesweepers and destroyers to Murmansk. Some ships were lost or damaged en route but the majority arrived safely. On April 28 the *Edinburgh* set off on its return journey, escorting 13 merchantmen and carrying a valuable cargo – 5.1 tonnes (5 tons) of Russian gold, then worth £45 million, which was stowed in the bomb rooms. Unfortunately, the convoy was spotted by German reconnaissance planes and on April 30 was attacked by German destroyers and submarines.

The *Edinburgh* was hit in two places by torpedoes fired by the German submarines. Although the British cruiser managed to sink one of its attackers, the destroyer *Hermann Schoemann*, it was seriously maimed and the captain, Hugh Faulkner, gave the order to abandon ship. Once aboard the minesweeper *Harrier*, he gave orders for the *Edinburgh* to be torpedoed and sunk, to prevent its cargo falling into enemy hands.

SALVAGE FROM THE ICY WATERS

The *Edinburgh* now lay in 244 metres (800 feet) of freezing Arctic water. A salvage company, Risdon-Beazley, gave serious consideration to its recovery in 1954, but the difficulties seemed insuperable. By 1980, however, many technical advances in reconnaissance and diving technology had taken place and the salvage of the *Edinburgh* no longer seemed impossible, although this was still a daunting task. Several companies put forward bids to undertake its recovery and the contract was awarded to Jessop Marine Recoveries Ltd, who undertook to cut into the wreck – a more fitting way to deal with the ship, which had been designated an official war grave in 1957, than other proposals to use explosives to penetrate the wreck.

Negotiations between Jessop and the British and Russian governments resulted in a formal agreement that the proceeds of the recovery should be split in the proportions 45 per cent to the salvors, who undertook all the labour and expense of the recovery,

two-thirds of the remaining 55 per cent to the owners of the gold, the Russians, and the rest to the British, who had undertaken the risk of carrying it in 1942.

The first task was to locate the wreck precisely. A survey ship, the *Dammator*, used sidescanning sonar to search the area in which the naval action had taken place and detected a large wreck. Was it the *Edinburgh* or the German destroyer that it had sunk? A remote-controlled robot was used to investigate the wreck, which proved to be the *Edinburgh*. Next a fully equipped salvage vessel was brought in.

The task was not an easy one. Not only were the divers working in Arctic conditions – they wore special suits heated with hot water which occasionally scalded them – but they were also attempting to salvage the gold from a room in which active bombs were also stored. Their heroic efforts resulted in the recovery of 431 gold bars, but the remaining 34 had to be abandoned when bad weather closed in.

A RICH FREIGHT

The US provided an essential lifeline for the Allies during the war, sending a regular supply of essentials across the Atlantic in freighters popularly known as the Liberty Ships. In 1944 one such freighter, the *John Barry*, was loaded with drill pipes, military vehicles and refinery equipment for the new Saudi oil refinery at Dhahran. Also loaded, discreetly and unobtrusively, were boxes containing three million Saudi silver riyals, struck in America on behalf of the Saudi government. The *John Barry* travelled through the Red Sea to Aden in the comparative safety of a convoy, but from there it was on its own so it steered an erratic course to confuse potential attackers. But on the August 28, off Oman the ship had the misfortune to cross the path of a German submarine, U-859, travelling out to Malaya. A torpedo from the submarine damaged the *John Barry* and caused the crew to abandon ship; a second cut the ship in half and it immediately sank.

Statements, perhaps misunderstood, suggested that it had been carrying silver bullion worth $26 million at that time. Due to the depth at which it was lying, 2,591 metres (8,500 feet), no immediate attempt was made to salvage it but in 1989, under the auspices of businessman Sheikh Ahmed Farid al-Aulaqi, the expertise of a number of different salvage specialists was pooled. The wreck was located using side-scan radar and its identity checked using a

Above: *Despite the immense difficulties of the salvage, Keith Jessop and his team raised the first gold bars from the* Edinburgh *on September 21, 1981, to their great excitement and satisfaction.*

ROV (remote-operated vehicle). A French company, IFREMER, skilled in conducting very controlled deep-sea explosions, was employed to blow open the hold but had little success, due to the quantity of debris and the depth of the wreck. IFREMER was therefore commissioned to design and build an intelligent grab capable of working at more than eight times the depth at which such a device had previously been used with success. In 1994, the mammoth but sophisticated device, equipped with video, was deployed and the Saudi riyals were raised, to pour in a shower onto the deck of the salvage ship. Of the silver bullion reputed to be on board, however, there was no trace, and it seems likely that it had never existed.

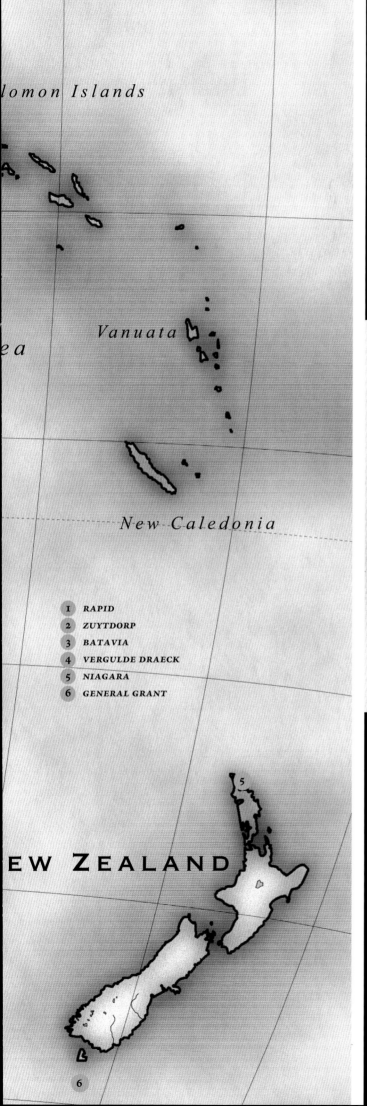

Solomon Islands

ea

Vanuata

New Caledonia

1 RAPID
2 ZUYTDORP
3 BATAVIA
4 VERGULDE DRAECK
5 NIAGARA
6 GENERAL GRANT

NEW ZEALAND

5

6

AUSTRALIA & THE PACIFIC

Above: *Though they have sailed the Pacific for only four centuries, many European ships have been wrecked there.*

THE *BATAVIA*

In 1602 the newly independent United Provinces of the Netherlands entered the lucrative international trade in East Indies spices, such as cinnamon, nutmeg and pepper, with the foundation of the Vereenigde Oost-Indische Compagnie (VOC), the Dutch East India Company.

WRECK OF HOPES

Dutch navigational and military skill, combined with ruthlessness, soon brought the VOC marked success in the cut-throat competition with its Portuguese rivals, who had long held a virtual monopoly in this trade, and with the English, who were also newly entering the market. In 1619 the VOC established a fortified base for this trade at Batavia (modern Jakarta) on Java and, when the company launched the first of its new, larger trading ships in 1628, it named the vessel after this prospering trading station.

The *Batavia* set sail gloriously on October 29 in consort with seven other vessels, but already all was not well. Its captain, Adriaen Jacobsz, a coarse and violent individual though a good seaman, had quarrelled in the past with the Commander of the whole convoy, Francisco Pelsaert, and ill feeling between them flared up repeatedly. Soon a terrible storm scattered the convoy and the *Batavia* reached the Cape of Good Hope in company with only two other ships, from which further misfortunes soon separated it. Pelsaert was in poor health, keeping to his cabin for much of the voyage, and discipline on the ship became lax. One of the passengers, a beautiful married woman called Lucretia van den Mylen, sailing to *Batavia* to join her husband, was assaulted.

The ship was following a sea route pioneered a few years earlier by Hendrik de Brouwer: this ran east from the Cape of Good Hope as far as the recently discovered and little-known coast of Australia before turning to sail north to Java. Seamen were aware that treacherous rocks and coral reefs lay along the shores of Australia, but their location had barely begun to be charted. Jacobsz and his crew therefore kept a close lookout for these hazards. On the morning of June 4, 1629, however, they believed from their calculations that they were still well to the west of Australia's shores and were not troubled by what seemed to be the moon's reflection on the sea – but which was in reality surf from low breakers. Suddenly the ship shook violently and ground against some obstruction – it had struck on Morning Reef, one of the northern group of islands in the Houtman Albolhos, an archipelago so low-lying that it was virtually invisible.

It soon became clear that there was no chance of refloating the ship. In panic, the passengers fought for a place in the longboat while unruly members of the crew broke open the liquor store and got deliriously drunk. Those who could took refuge on tiny Beacon Island near the site of the wreck – an island that was to acquire the sinister nickname "Batavia's Graveyard". Some food and water was salvaged from the wreck before it broke up and sank but it was obvious this would not last long. Pelsaert and Jacobsz, with about 40 others, set off in the ship's boat in search of water. Finding none on the islands to the north or on the coast of mainland Australia, they carried on, desperately hoping that they would reach the town of Batavia. On June 27 they sighted land – the island of Nusa Kambangan in Java, where to their relief they were able to moisten their parched throats with fresh water. They finally reached Batavia, ill and exhausted, on July 7. On July 15, Pelsaert set out again on another VOC vessel, the *Zaandam*, to attempt to rescue the people he had left and the VOC's treasure.

Left: *The* Batavia *was the first of the new type of East Indies trading ship designed by the VOC, which they began to build in 1626.*

CORNELISZ THE MONSTER

On Beacon Island things had been going from bad to worse. The ship's supercargo, Jeronimus Cornelisz, the most senior man remaining there, seized control and set about reducing the number of survivors in order to eke out the remaining provisions. First he enlisted the support of 36 disreputable and conscienceless soldiers and members of the crew, who took an oath to obey him. He then got rid of most of the loyal soldiers by sending them off in the longboat, without their weapons, under the command of Wiebbe Hayes, to search for water. The remaining soldiers he dispatched on rafts with his own followers, who systematically drowned them. He induced 45 of the survivors to transfer to Seal Island, an inhospitable ribbon of coral, where he left them to die of starvation. Other survivors he murdered individually, sparing some of the women to become concubines. He himself seized the hapless Lucretia van den Mylen.

Against all odds, however, Wiebbe Hayes and his men had found both food and water, on the substantial West Wallabi Island further

---

Above: *A diver photographs the hull of the* Batavia *lying on the seabed. Meticulous recording ensures that every scrap of information about the seventeenth-century ship is collected, building an invaluable picture of the vessel and its cargo.*

to the west. They signalled their discovery with beacon fires – at first, to their surprise, no one came, but eventually they were joined by a handful of resourceful individuals who had managed to escape Cornelisz. Hearing the grim news of the murders, Hayes set about fortifying and defending his position. None too soon, for Cornelisz and his followers had determined to wipe them out, on the principle that dead men tell no tales. Battle was joined on July 27, Hayes and his party raining stones on their attackers. Several men were killed, Cornelisz was captured and the mutineers withdrew.

They renewed their attack on September 17, but were again beaten off. By a miraculous coincidence, the *Zaandam*, its progress having been slowed by bad weather, now appeared off West Wallabi

and Hayes managed to reach the ship first, bringing news of the dreadful situation. The mutineers now also arrived, in the guise of peaceful survivors, secretly intending to seize the ship, but being forewarned, the crew of the *Zaandam* quickly overpowered them. Sailing on to Beacon Island, the ship rescued the few pitiful survivors of the mutineers' murderous activities – 125 had perished at their hands. Skilled divers from Gujarat were put to work on the wreck, from which they salvaged the bulk of the precious cargo. Pelsaert conducted an investigation, with torture, of Cornelisz and his henchmen – each blamed the others but enough evidence was gathered to convict and execute Cornelisz and six of the ringleaders. Almost all of the others were executed when the *Zaandam* returned to Batavia.

THE LOST WRECK

Much of the *Batavia*'s valuable cargo was taken off in the first days after it struck the reef. Divers from the *Zaandam* recovered most of the rest after it sank, including three casks of cochineal, a red dye valued almost as highly as silver, and many of the money chests. The *Batavia* had been carrying 12 of these, containing in total 250,000 silver guilders, and 10 were recovered. One other chest lay pinned down by a cannon while the twelfth had been opened, its contents scattered by the drunken sailors shortly after the *Batavia* was wrecked. The ship had also been carrying a silver dinner service belonging to Pelsaert and this too was not recovered by the *Zaandam* divers. Pelsaert died the following year, and within a few years

TODAY'S UNFOUND TREASURES

THE PISCO CHURCH PLATE

The priests of Pisco church in coastal Peru jealously guarded a great treasure of gold candlesticks, gold ingots and jewels whose existence only they knew of – until, in 1849, a runaway priest foolishly mentioned it to a villain, Diego Alvarez. Alvarez and three accomplices convinced the Pisco priests that the treasure was in imminent danger of being seized by a band led by the runaway cleric. The credulous priests therefore entrusted Alvarez with the task of conveying the treasure to safety. Once it was in his grasp, he lost no time in sailing off with it. He and his fellow pirates crossed the Pacific to the Tuamatos islands in French Polynesia, where they concealed the treasure before sailing on to Australia. Here misfortune struck them: three died and the fourth, Killorain, was imprisoned for 20 years. On his deathbed, however, he revealed the location of the Pisco treasure to Charles Edward Howe. After 17 frustrating years of searching, Howe is believed to have found a chest of jewels, but could not recover the rest of the treasure, which Killorain had said was hidden in a deep murky pool. Subsequent attempts to drain the pool and recover the gold have failed.

Right: *The Pisco church, whose credulous, unworldly priests allowed themselves to be duped out of their treasure by unscupulous villains.*

the VOC abandoned hope of recovering anything more from the wreck.

Knowledge of the western Australian coast and its hazards became better and more detailed as the centuries passed, but the vague grasp of its geography in earlier times had led people to believe that the *Batavia* had been wrecked on the southern group of islands in the Houtman Albrolhos archipelago, which they named the Pelsaert Group. Searches around these islands, of course, failed to reveal the wreck of the *Batavia*, although they did yield that of another VOC ship, the *Zeewiijk*, wrecked there in 1727 and largely salvaged by its survivors.

Opposite: *These tastefully decorated silver vessels were among the luxury goods that the VOC hoped to sell in India to the Mogul emperor and wealthy courtiers.*

One scholar, however, the historian Henrietta Drake-Brockman, was convinced that the search was being undertaken in the wrong place. Having exhaustively studied both Pelsaert's journal and other contemporary accounts of the wreck and its aftermath, she argued that the northern group of islands had been the scene of the disaster. In 1960, however, a small investigation around the Wallabi Islands by the journalist Hugh Edwards and the underwater photographer Maurie Hammond yielded no trace of the *Batavia* and her crew, so Drake-Brockman's theory was still unproven.

In 1963 the group that had explored the *Zeewiijk* turned their attention to the northern islands, where Drake-Brockman's work had convinced them that the wreck should lie. Max Cramer, a member of the group who lived nearby in Geraldton, on the mainland, began a systematic search on the islands for traces of the survivors of the

wreck. A lobster fisherman on Beacon Island, Dave Johnson, showed Cramer and his colleagues a skeleton that had been discovered locally, which they saw, with excitement, had a broken neck and a musket shot in the ribs. Was it one of Cornelisz's victims? Undoubtedly so, for as soon as Johnson learned that they were searching for traces of the *Batavia*, he was able to show them the wreck itself – he had noticed it three years earlier but hadn't realized that it was of any interest except as a source of scrap metal.

THE *BATAVIA* YIELDS ITS SECRETS

With considerable effort and great ingenuity, Cramer, his brother and another diver, Greg Allen, recovered a cannon from the site. The date and VOC seal engraved on it left no doubt that the *Batavia* had been found. A full-scale expedition was mounted, with army and navy support, and detailed investigation

of the wreck began. More cannon were raised, along with many everyday objects such as earthenware jars that had originally held spirits. Some coins were also found. Hugh Edwards and others became involved too, exploring the islands and uncovering the remains of the camps where Wiebbe Hayes and his companions had lived and fought off the mutineers' attacks. In the wake of the great public interest generated by the discovery of the *Batavia*, in 1964 the Australian government passed a law to give protection to this and other historic wrecks. Later laws strengthened this protection. Nowadays the public are encouraged to visit and explore these wrecks but are forbidden to damage them or remove objects from them.

Who owns wrecks? In principle a ship continues to be the property of its original owners and their heirs, so the *Batavia* and other VOC ships wrecked off Australia belonged to the Netherlands. In 1972 the Dutch government transferred its rights over these ships to the Australian government. Scientific documentation and excavation on the wreck and on Beacon Island have continued over the years, with the Western Australia Maritime Museum beginning a major investigation in 1973. More skeletons

have been uncovered on Beacon Island, although many more still lie hidden beneath its sandy soil. Much of the *Batavia* had disintegrated during its long sojourn on the seabed but a large section of the hull survived and divers and conservators were able to lift this in sections and reassemble it in the museum.

They also built a structure that had been planned almost 400 years earlier. The trading station at Batavia had been founded only a decade before the ship's ill-fated voyage and was still under construction. The *Batavia* was carrying the carved and dressed stones to erect a monumental portico in the "Waterpoort", the gateway to the fortified citadel of the town. These stones were recovered from the wreck undamaged and erected in the museum. Here too are others of the *Batavia*'s treasures: silver tableware that Pelsaert had hoped to trade with eastern potentates, more than 7,000 coins from the two unsalvaged chests, cannons and anchors, as well as many small personal objects such as pewter spoons.

And now the *Batavia* again sails the seas. In the early 1980s a Dutch shipwright, Willem Vos, decided to

build a replica of a seventeenth-century trading ship. The idea took off and in 1985 a foundation was established, based at Lelystad in the Netherlands, to construct a replica of the *Batavia*, using traditional techniques and materials (but employing modern tools and equipment). Historical information about the constructional details of VOC ships and of European seventeenth-century vessels in general were complemented by the findings of the Australian archaeologists investigating the wreck, so that the replica could be as faithful a reconstruction of the *Batavia* as possible. The mammoth task was completed in 1995, In 1999 the new *Batavia* began her voyage to Australia.

Above: *This engraving of the massacre on Beacon Island illustrated Pelsaert's account of the tragic fate of the* Batavia *and those aboard her. It was published in 1647, after his death.*

Left: *This splendid Dutch replica of the* Batavia *was taken to Australia by barge in 1999 and was moored in Sydney during the 2000 Olympics. Since 2001 she has been on display in Lelystad.*

OTHER DUTCH TREASURE SHIPS

A DESPERATE PLIGHT

Despite the hazards, most VOC ships sailing along the Brouwer route to Batavia arrived safely. The next major loss was the *Vergulde Draeck* (*Golden Dragon*), which set sail from Texel in the Netherlands on October 4, 1655 with a crew of 193 men under Captain Pieter Albertsz, and three women passengers. All went well at first and the ship arrived safely at the Cape of Good Hope the following March. Pursuing its journey eastwards, blown by the Roaring Forties and making good progress, it suddenly struck a submerged reef off the western Australian coast on April 28, 1656, and at once sank.

There was no time to salvage anything from the ship and those who had the misfortune to be below decks at the time were drowned. Albertsz and 74 others struggled ashore. A few provisions were washed up from the wreck and one of the ship's boats survived. The situation was desperate and the captain decided to send the pilot and six volunteers off in the longboat to seek help. Five weeks later the seven exhausted, starving men landed in Batavia.

Despite the unfavourable season – winter with its violent storms was just beginning – two ships were dispatched to rescue the survivors and the cargo, trade goods worth around 100,000 florins and eight chests containing silver coins worth 78,600 florins. The ships were soon blown apart and neither could find any trace of the wreck, despite searching for several months; one ship lost 11 of its crew; and they abandoned the search and returned to Batavia. Two ships were then sent from the Cape of Good Hope but were also unsuccessful; and so was a final expedition in 1658. Traces of wreckage from the ship still lay on the shore, but of the ship's company there was no trace at all.

REDISCOVERY

In 1931 a boy discovered 40 seventeenth-century Dutch silver coins in the sand dunes of Cape Leschenault but it was not until 1963 that the wreck itself was discovered. Divers over the reef found various objects, including ballast bricks, an elephant tusk, silver coins and a cannon bearing the VOC monogram. These they presented to the Western Australia Maritime Museum, whose staff were able to identify them as coming from the *Vergulde Draeck*. Over the years, divers from the museum have worked on

the wreck site, documenting and excavating the surviving remains.

This was a difficult task. On sinking, the ship had broken up very rapidly and its fragments were scattered widely over the reef. They became heavily encrusted and most remains became indistinguishable from the reef on which they had come to rest. Only the ship's cannon and anchors could easily be made out, marking the site of the wreck. Some portions of the ship, including the captain's cabin with the treasure chests, sank into deeper water. The ravages of nature were exacerbated by the activities of treasure-hunters after the discovery was publicized in 1963 – several used dynamite to blow up portions of the reef and wreck, in an attempt to get through the encrustation.

Despite these problems, however, the museum's divers have been able to recover more than half of the coins and other items from the cargo. Eight boxes of iron bars, welded together by concretions, proved particularly difficult to excavate and raise. Among the other finds were the remains of wooden barrels, associated bones showing them originally to have contained the ship's provisions of salt beef, pork and other meat.

LOST WITHOUT TRACE

The *Zuytdorp*, built in 1701, was one of the VOC fleet regularly sailing between the Netherlands and Batavia. On July 27, 1711 it set sail on its third such voyage, in company with another VOC ship, the *Belvliet*. Between them they were carrying a treasure of gold and silver bars and silver coins, including all those minted in 1711 in the Middleburg Mint. Both ships spent some time in the Dutch provisioning station of Cape Town on the Cape of Good Hope, enlisting sailors to replace those lost to scurvy on the first leg of the journey – 112 of the *Zuytdorp*'s 286-strong crew had perished. The *Zuytdorp* succeeded first in making up its crew and set sail again without its sister ship on April 22, 1712, in company with the *Kockenge*, another VOC ship.

During the journey the vessels became separated. The *Kockenge* reached Batavia safely on July 4, but the *Zuytdorp* had vanished. The mystery endured for more than 200 years.

Above: *Excavation of the northern part of the* Vergulde Draeck *in 1983 yielded many interesting finds, including this astrolabe.*

TELLTALE TIMBERS

In 1927 pieces of ship's timbers and eighteenth-century coins were found washed up at the base of a cliff some 64 kilometres (40 miles) north of the Murchison River. Could these be the remains of the long-lost *Zuytdorp*? Desultory investigations over the years were transformed into serious research when in 1954 the geologist Dr Phillip Playford heard of the discoveries. From 1958, he and a few colleagues explored the area both on the shore and on the cliffs above. They found a thick, ashy deposit on the cliff top, the remains of a huge fire – probably a signal fire lit by the wretched survivors of the wreck in the forlorn hope that it would be spotted by their companion vessel, the *Kockenge*. The team also discovered other objects salvaged from the ship by the survivors – glass bottles, the hoops from provision barrels and broken clay pipes.

Many coins that had come to rest among the rocks at the foot of the cliff turned out to be 1711 Middleburg silver pieces – precisely the cargo known to have been travelling in the *Zuytdorp* – so there could be no doubt of the identity of the vessel that had been wrecked here. Investigating the ship and recovering its cargo, however, was a prodigious task, for dangerous currents made diving over the wreck difficult and hazardous. A team of experts in many relevant fields became involved in salvage operations after the site became the responsibility of the Western Australia Maritime Museum in 1964. They have succeeded in recovering not only much of the silver bullion – which formed a "carpet of silver" in the stern region of the wreck – but also cannon, the ship's bell and other objects. They have mapped the wreck too, using a variety of sophisticated techniques including aerial photography. Playford continued to study the remains on land, aided by many experts.

The question that they were particularly interested in answering was: where had the survivors gone? The area lacks drinking water and is situated in inhospitable terrain, so the shipwrecked mariners could not have lasted long here alone. But there was no sign of their dead bodies. Could the local Aboriginal groups have taken pity on them and helped them to survive? Some clues suggest that they did – records show that Aborigines cared for several later European castaways and a few Dutch artefacts have been discovered in Aboriginal camps in the area. It is therefore possible that the *Zuytdorp*'s crew had inadvertently become the first European settlers on the Australian continent.

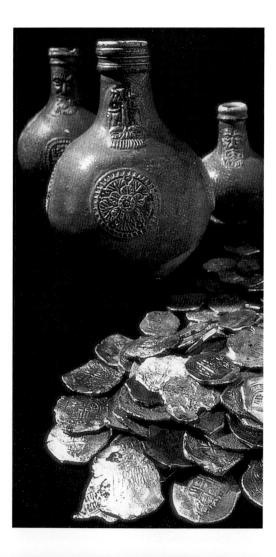

Right: *Pottery "Beardman" jugs and silver coins were among the objects recovered from the* Vergulde Draeck.

TODAY'S UNFOUND TREASURES

STOLEN GOLD

Andrew Robertson was a Scottish sailor who, by 1826, had settled in Callao, Peru. The port was regularly visited by prosperous ships, including the *Peruvian*, which on one occasion was carrying two million piastres in gold. Robertson could not resist the temptation. With 12 hand-picked men, he seized the ship. Determined to share the treasure with as few people as possible, he chose two villains, Williams and George, and together they cast adrift all but four of the crew. They then anchored off Agrihan, a small Melanesian island in the Marianas group, where they are believed to have hidden the gold. Setting sail again for Hawaii, the three overpowered the remaining crew members, scuttled the *Peruvian* and went ashore pretending to have been shipwrecked. After a prudent interval, Robertson and Williams (George had "disappeared") found a skipper, Thompson, to convey them to the Marianas. On the way, Williams "accidentally" drowned. Robertson attempted to dispose of Thompson in the same way, but he was picked up by a Spanish frigate commanded by Señor Medinilla, the governor of the Marianas. Medinilla soon captured Robertson and persuaded him to lead them to the treasure. As they landed on Agrihan, Robertson fell or threw himself into the water and was drowned. The secret of the treasure's location died with him.

Above: *Gold coins.*

WRECK OF THE *RAPID*

AMERICAN TRADERS

In the early nineteenth century Americans also began to take part in the trade with China. Given the distances involved, the vessels used had to be large to carry goods in economic quantities and fast so as to undertake the journey in a reasonable and competitive time. The *Rapid*, built in 1807 near Boston, proved its worth on its maiden voyage in 1809. On September 28, 1810 she set out from Boston again, carrying 280,000 Spanish dollars with which to purchase the desired Chinese goods.

All went well at first. The ship called at the Cape of Good Hope and then set off across the Indian Ocean, aiming to turn north when the coast of Australia was sighted. But on the ninety-eighth day it drove on to the Point Cloates reef off Western Australia. Matters were made worse when a storm developed.

After some soul-searching the captain decided that there was no chance of saving the ship and gave the order to scuttle it. This would leave no trace of it above the water to attract the unwanted attentions of salvors; but neither would there be anything for the crew to spot again, so it was vital to memorize the spot where it went down after being set on fire by the crew. Taking to the ship's boats, the captain and crew of 22 successfully made the long and difficult journey to Java, from where they were able to return to Philadelphia. In 1813 the insurers

sent out another ship, which relocated the wreck and raised most of the silver.

FOUND AGAIN

In 1978 four divers were nearing the end of their free-diving and spearfishing trip out on the Ningaloo Reef. Missing a fish, one of their number, Frank Paxman, was amazed to see before him part of an unknown wreck. Archaeologists from the Western Australia Maritime Museum were alerted to the find. Scouring the records they found a short announcement in an 1811 newspaper, the clue they needed to identify this as the *Rapid*. Between 1979 and 1982, divers from the museum worked on the wreck. They made detailed observations on the vessel itself and recorded the crew's personal possessions, abandoned when the ship went down. From these the archaeologists were able to build up a picture of the American-China trade vessels and life on board them, something that had previously been known only from literature. The divers also succeeded in raising 20,000 silver dollars that had been missed when the wreck was originally salvaged.

Top: *Divers from the Western Australian Maritime Museum excavate and record details of the* Rapid*'s hull.*

Above: *The original salvors of the* Rapid *missed thousands of silver dollars, recovered recently, along with the ship's bell.*

AUSTRALIAN GOLD RUSH

GOLD FOR THE TAKING

In the 1840s gold was discovered in California and the excitement this event generated reached even Australia. Many abandoned their lives there and boarded ships for the gold fields of America. One of them was Edward Hammond Hargraves, who soon returned to Australia, where he taught others the techniques used in panning gold. Now all that was needed was the gold itself. Hargraves or others with whom he was working eventually found gold at Bathurst, New South Wales, in 1851. Immediately a human tide began to flow in this direction and the same year other sources were found at Ballarat and Bendigo in Victoria. All were easy to work, requiring only simple equipment. Tens of thousands of people poured into the gold areas, hoping to make their fortune, and many came away satisfied, with a certain amount of gold.

In March 1866 the *General Grant* was due to sail from Melbourne to Liverpool. It was carrying a regular load of wool, hides, zinc, timber and bark, as well as two sturdy chests containing about 71 kilograms (2,500 ounces) of gold. Among the 56 passengers were quite a few who were returning home with the small fortune they had made in the gold rush, so the total quantity of gold on board is likely to have been considerable.

GONE DOWN

The captain, Henry Loughlin, set a course for Cape Horn. This route took advantage of prevailing westerly winds, which gave good speed, but it was not at that time well charted. Progress was good, and Loughlin noted that the ship had passed New Zealand and the Auckland Islands. Then the weather turned nasty. The wind dropped, slowing the ship, and fog prevented the captain from taking the daily observations necessary to chart the vessel's position. When the fog began to lift, after two days, everyone on board was horrified to see land looming up ahead of them. Worse still, the absence of any wind made it impossible to control the ship and the current pulled her mercilessly toward sheer rocks on the west coast of Auckland Island. It was later discovered that the Auckland Islands had been misplaced on the existing charts.

The ship struck the rocks with great force and the rudder was smashed. Further damage rapidly took place as it was scraped along the rocks like cheese on a grater. A break opened up in the rocks – a cavern, into which the ship was pushed and jammed by the current. The masts struck the cave roof, bringing down lumps of rock that smashed into the ship, followed by the masts themselves. The pounding of the sea swell

Below: *Gold prospectors digging at Sheep Station Point on the Turon river.*

continued to batter the ship and it was clear that it would soon sink.

Three small boats were available to take the shipwrecked passengers and crew to safety – far too little space for the 83 people who had been on board the *General Grant*. The longboat was soon crowded with 40 people; the sea picked it up and capsized it, drowning all but three of those who were aboard. Many individuals clung to the gold that was to have made their fortune and were dragged down into the depths of the sea by it. The unfortunate women were hampered by their petticoats, which quickly became waterlogged and heavy, and only one woman, Mrs Jewell the steward's wife, reached safety.

Only 15 of the passengers and crew managed to leave the ship in the boats. Captain Loughlin was not among them, but went down with his ship. The survivors set to, rowing back the way they had come, along the coast of Auckland Island, the large main island of the group. They spent a miserable night on a bleak islet and it was only after a further gruelling day at sea that they found a place where they could safely land, in the inlet now called Port Ross.

FIRE FOR LIFE

A natural leader emerged, a man called James Teer. Twenty years of hard living had given him many practical skills and the knowledge needed for survival in rough conditions. The priority was to light a fire to keep everyone warm and dry. Someone produced matches but these were all damp except one. Miraculously, they succeeded in lighting a fire with this and were careful to keep the fire burning throughout their sojourn on the island.

Fortunately, they had rescued a few provisions from the ship and gradually they discovered the food that the cluster of islands could provide. There was no lack of fresh water. Pigs, goats and rabbits introduced to the islands by previous visiting ships had flourished, though it took the castaways a

long time to devise a method of catching the pigs. There were fish, mussels and limpets, birds and their eggs and plenty of seals. The castaways discovered huts from a short-lived, abandoned settlement and patched them up; they also found various useful pieces of equipment, including an axe. They used grass for bedding and, by trial and error, discovered how to make clothes for themselves and sails for the boats from seal skins. In the old settlement they found a few potatoes growing: they saved these for seed, which they replanted the following year. At first they suffered bouts of dysentery and other illnesses though these grew fewer through time. Nevertheless, one of the older members of the party died.

After nine months on the islands, four men decided to attempt to escape and get help. Stocked with provisions and fortified by the good wishes of the others, they set off in one of the boats. Lacking any navigational equipment, their chances of reaching New Zealand were slim and indeed they were never heard of again. The castaways also sent off miniature boats and inflated pig's bladders with messages, hoping someone would read them and bring help.

On October 19, 1867, they saw a ship. They tried in every way to attract its attention but it sailed on. But on November 21 another sail appeared, close to land. The castaways launched their boat and succeeded in reaching the *Amherst*, a whaling brig. With great thankfulness in their hearts, the 10 survivors were taken on board, after 18 months on the island. By extraordinary coincidence, a few days later they met a cutter, the *Fanny*, which was coming to look for them, having discovered one of their message boats.

LOST FOREVER

James Teer was the first to return in search of the lost gold. As a survivor, he had a clear idea of the appearance of the wreck site. He chartered a steam tug and criss-crossed the area where he had last seen the ship. No luck.

In 1870 another survivor, David Ashworth, was offered the opportunity to accompany an expedition to search for the wreck. After reaching the general locality, three crew members stayed with the ship while the captain, Ashworth and six other members of the crew took a whaleboat to explore the cavern where the *General Grant* had gone down. The three waited for days but the whaleboat and its crew were never seen again.

Another survivor of the shipwreck, Cornelius Drew, made a separate attempt to locate the ship in 1876, but again without success. Many other expeditions were made over the years by hopeful people but none met with any better luck, although artefacts from other wrecks were discovered in the vicinity: some may even be from the *General Grant* itself, but there is no conclusive proof. One recent attempt was made by divers experienced in salvage work. They were able to examine the whole of the interior of the underwater cavern and could find no trace at all of the *General Grant*. They suggested that it might have stayed in one piece and floated out of the cavern after sinking, rather than immediately breaking up. If so, it may have finished up anywhere.

Opposite: *A vivid contemporary news image of the wrecking of the* General Grant.

Right: *David Ashworth.*

THE *NIAGARA*

In 1940, the liner *Niagara* was travelling from Australia to Canada carrying passengers but also 590 gold ingots, around 8 tonnes (8 tons), to pay for the essential supplies of munitions that the US was sending across the Atlantic to Britain. On July 19 it set out from Auckland harbour but soon ran into a minefield, secretly laid by Germans who were aware that the harbour held naval vessels. It exploded: all those aboard had time to take to the boats, but the gold was lost. It was, of course, important to salvage the gold, but the ship lay at a great depth and there was the potential complication of further unexploded mines.

United Salvage Proprietary Ltd and an experienced and adventurous diver, John

Edward "Johnno" Johnstone, were hired by the Bank of England to attempt the operation and Johnno roped in his younger brother, William, a member of the Australian Royal Navy. In order to work at the extreme depth, over 122 metres (400 feet), at which the wreck lay, a special observation diving bell, big enough for two, was built, designed to have a constant supply of oxygen so that the men could breathe normally and with a telephone so they could communicate with the surface.

The first priority was to locate the wreck. Even this was a daunting task: the wartime demands on shipping meant that the only ship available for the salvage was a small and ancient coastal steamer;

the weather was frequently too bad to work; conditions underwater were cloudy so visibility was poor and there were the mines — one nudged the ship as the reconnaissance proceeded and another became entangled with the salvage ship's mooring cable.

Soon after the wreck was located, there was nearly a fatal accident. While Johnno was down in the observation bell, one of the salvage ship's mooring cables gave way, dragging the bell along the wreck and narrowly missing severing its suspension cable. Weeks were then spent getting the ship into exactly the right position over the wreck, secured to six massive buoys. Months of controlled explosions followed, each small charge contributing to the hole being nibbled through the decks to gain access to the strong room. Some wreckage required a larger charge, which shook the salvage ship above, loosening rivets and making it leak.

Finally they reached the strong room, but the difficulties were not over yet. First they had to remove the door – which unfortunately fell in on top of the gold. The salvors deployed a large grab: it was a difficult and delicate operation to get this into the right position to go through the hole into the strong room, directed by Johnno in the observation bell. But eventually they succeeded – and the grab got its teeth into a box. When this was raised, it was found to contain two shiny ingots of gold – the first of many. A further six weeks' successful work yielded some 555 ingots – but by the end each one was more difficult and slow to retrieve than the one before, as debris fell into the emptying strongroom, so it was decided to abandon the last 35 ingots.

The Johnstones salvaged 30 of these in 1953 – but five still remain. In 2007 Keith Gordon, an enthusiastic historian of the *Niagara* and its salvage, made his own contribution to that history by raising the *Niagara*'s bell, telegraph cable and steam whistle and other interesting artefacts from the ship.

Opposite: *The* Niagara's *telegraph equipment, lying on the seabed.*

Above: *The eeriely peaceful timber-framed windows of the* Niagara's *superstructure. In contrast, divers say the wrecked strongroom is a scene of devastation, making it impossible to find the remaining five gold bars.*

Right: *The experienced Australian deep-sea diver, Craig Howell, proudly holds the bridge bell that he salvaged from the wreck of the* Niagara. *The depth of the wreck makes diving on her difficult.*

ARCTIC
OCEAN

GREE

ALASKA

*Gulf
of
Alaska*

CANADA

*Hudson
Bay*

1   **BROTHER JONATHAN**
2   **LITTLE BIGHORN**
3   **GALVESTON ISLAND**
4   **TENOCHTITLAN**
5   **MONTE ALBAN**
6   **CHICHEN ITZA**
7   **GASPARILLA ISLAND**
8   **ATOCHA AND SANTA MARGARITA**
9   **NOTRE DAME DE DELIVERANCE**
10   **MOLASSES REEF**
11   **GUADELUPE AND CONDE DE TOLOSA**
12   **CENTRAL AMERICA**
13   **QUEEN ANNE'S REVENGE**
14   **SS REPUBLIC**
15   **WHYDAH**
16   **OAK ISLAND**
17   **TITANIC**

UNITED

STATES

*Gulf of
Mexico*

MEXICO

*Gulf of
Campeche*

PACIFIC

OCEAN

BELIZE

GUATEMALA   HONDU

EL SALVADOR   NIC

COSTA

brador
Sea

Newfoundland

17

Nova Scotia

16

15

14

NORTH
ATLANTIC
OCEAN

13

Saragaso
Sea

BAHAMAS

10

11

HAITI

DOMINICAN
REPUBLIC

AMAICA

ribbean Sea

NORTH AMERICA

Above: *A nineteenth-century painting of the seventeenth-century annual Spanish treasure fleet assembling off Havana before sailing home.*

GOLD FROM MONTE ALBAN

The Oaxaca Valley in highland Mexico, home of the Zapotec people, was one of the early centres of civilization in the Americas. Around 500 BC the Zapotecs constructed a massive hilltop capital at Monte Albán, with temples and palaces. On its slopes they built houses and excavated tombs in which they buried their dead with beautiful pottery. But, by AD 750, the glory of their civilization was passed and the Zapotecs moved away.

OAXACA'S GLORY

By 1350 the Oaxaca Valley had been infiltrated by the Mixtecs, people from small kingdoms to the west. The Mixtecs were exceptional craftsmen, who made very attractive pottery in many colours, jewellery of many different materials, elaborate and beautiful mosaics of turquoise and superb goldwork. Metallurgy had come late to Mesoamerica: around AD 800 the techniques for working gold, silver and copper had been introduced to the region from South America, where they had a long and distinguished history. The Mixtecs were among the finest workers in these materials and their products were eagerly sought by their neighbours, including, eventually, the Aztecs.

AN AMAZING TOMB

In the 1930s the Mexican archaeologist Alfonso Caso decided to investigate the site of Monte Albán. He suspected that various objects of jade and gold acquired by museums had come from looted tombs in this ancient city, and he wanted to find out more about them and their makers. In 1932, therefore, with his wife, several assistants and a team of workmen, he began to uncover the magnificent architecture of Monte Albán's hilltop centre, long hidden by earth and vegetation. Working beyond the citadel, he and his team also found the remains of nine tombs, six of them unlooted. Tomb 7 proved extremely exciting.

A shell trumpet and some jewellery of jade placed on the roof of the tomb alerted the team to its presence. They made a small hole in the roof and carefully climbed in. Immediately before them they found a skull, with a beautiful goblet of rock

Right: *The glowing reputation of the Mixtec goldsmiths is borne out by this magnificent gold breastplate depicting a skeletal deity crowned by a serpent headdress.*

crystal: a work of extraordinary virtuosity in this exceptionally hard material. Working their way around projecting blocks in the walls of the tomb, so as not to disturb the buried remains, they glimpsed an amazing array of offerings laid out in several chambers, alongside piles of bones. The whole floor was covered with small pieces of turquoise that had once formed part of elaborate mosaic masks, as well as the scattered beads from necklaces of pearls and gold. The archaeologists carefully measured the extent of the tomb, to allow them to locate the outer door from the ground outside.

Returning to the outer world, they uncovered the doorway, buried to its lintel in soil. It was now six o'clock in the evening, but knowing what was in the tomb they felt they could not stop. It was 3 a.m. before they had cleared the door and could open the tomb. One of the first sights that greeted them was a superb golden diadem with a golden plume. On this first night the excavators found no fewer than 36 pieces of goldwork, including a great breastplate in the form of a human head and shoulders, surmounted by a magnificent helmet, made in one piece by the sophisticated lost-wax casting process. When morning dawned on the exhausted but exhilarated team, Caso took the valuable finds and drove them to Oaxaca City for safe keeping, while the others guarded the tomb.

For a whole week the team slaved away for 14 hours a day to uncover the riches of this amazing tomb. They found that it had originally been carved by the ancient Zapotecs. On coming to Monte Albán the Mixtecs cleared out the tomb, leaving behind only a few pots, and reused it for the elaborate burial of one of their nobility. Nine people were interred there, eight of them servants to accompany their lordly master – or mistress, for it proved impossible to say with certainty whether the tomb's owner was a man or a woman. The bodies were wrapped in cloth and placed in the tomb in a seated position. When the cloth rotted, the bundles disintegrated, scattering the bones and the finery with which they were adorned: necklaces, earrings, bracelets and other jewellery of every precious material known to the Mixtecs: gold, silver, jade, rock crystal, turquoise, coral and jet. With them were vessels also made of fine materials, including beautiful onyx vases. The most exciting finds were jaguar bones carved with wonderful Mixtec depictions of gods and people.

Below: *Temple pyramids dominate the hilltop Zapotec centre of Monte Albán. On the west lies the Palace of the Danzantes, in which were found slabs depicting the contorted bodies of sacrificed enemies.*

THE MAYA SACRED WELL OF CHICHÉN ITZÁ

WELL OF SACRIFICE

Edward Herbert Thompson was fascinated by the ancient Maya, whose traditions had been recorded by the Spanish missionary Diego de Landa in the sixteenth century and whose ruins in the Yucatán (in Mesoamerica) had been explored and beautifully described by the explorers John Lloyd Stephens and Frederick Catherwood in the early nineteenth century so he was thrilled when he secured a consular post in the region. In 1885 he first set foot in the city of Chichén Itzá and walked along the remains of the Maya ceremonial road to its sacred well, the Cenote of Sacrifice.

In this region the Maya relied for their water mainly on sinkholes in the limestone (in Spanish, *cenote*), which gave access to underground water. A particularly massive example, 62 metres (200 feet) in diameter, its sheer cliffs rising far above the water level, must have first attracted settlers to Chichén Itzá. This cenote was considered a sacred place as early as the fifth century AD, when people began to throw offerings into it. It became particularly important when the Toltec from highland Mexico took over at Chichén Itzá, and was still a holy place, attracting pilgrims from far and near, well after the Spanish conquest of the region. Diego de Landa recorded that human victims were hurled into its waters, along with all the objects that pilgrims held most precious.

PENETRATING THE WATERS

Intrigued by this account and those of other Spanish observers, Thompson wanted to investigate the well. But how? He spent years making preparations and plans, including buying the land and learning how to dive. In 1904 he returned to the cenote to begin his investigations. For three years he and his men operated a winch which he had devised; this scooped up material from beneath the waters, lifted it to the top of the well and deposited it on a platform that they had constructed. At first their finds were disappointing: lots of mud, rocks, dead vegetation, fallen wood and sometimes whole trees, and the occasional bones of an unfortunate animal that had fallen in. Was this to be all? Thompson began to suffer sleepless nights from worry, for many of his friends had invested in his enterprise.

But one day things began to change. The dredge brought up some lumps of a curious substance that turned out to be copal incense, used by the Maya. Then artefacts

began to come up: knives of obsidian (volcanic glass), pottery and jewellery. But these finds were still very few and the bulk of the material that emerged was still stones and vegetation. Thompson decided that he would have to adopt more direct methods.

In 1909 he engaged the services of a Greek sponge diver and together they entered the well. Each was kitted out in diving gear, including a huge copper helmet, a heavy lead necklace, waterproof canvas suit and iron-soled shoes. An airhose led up to the surface, where a team of workmen operated pumps to keep Thompson and his assistant supplied with air. The two divers took a lamp to help them in their search, but this proved useless because waterweed and mud made the water in the well so murky that the beam could not penetrate it. Therefore they resigned themselves to working by feel.

They had an exciting time. Every so often pieces of rock would become detached from the wall of the cenote high above their heads and come crashing down through the water – fortunately creating waves that pushed the two men to one side. They also began bringing up magnificent objects: copper

---

Above: *The powerful airlift directed by the National Geographic's divers sucked up water mixed with sediments and poured it out on to a gigantic sieve, where objects could be spotted and recovered.*

Opposite: *Many attempts have been made to explore the murky waters of the Cenote of Sacrifice at Chichén Itzá, where for centuries the Maya offered precious objects.*

bells, jade carvings and gold discs decorated with scenes, probably from Maya and Toltec history. Human bones were also recovered, demonstrating the truth of de Landa's stories. Often the objects had been deliberately broken, presumably for ritual reasons, before being thrown into the well.

RENEWED INVESTIGATIONS

When Thompson decided to call it a day, he reckoned that he had left about nine-tenths of the well unexplored. Others took up the challenge as time went on. A group of aqualung divers tried in 1954 but were put off by the poor visibility. In 1960 *National Geographic* magazine and a team of Mexican investigators began a more systematic exploration of this difficult site. They worked with an airlift, a tool often employed by underwater archaeologists, but this proved less than perfect in the conditions of the cenote. Objects from the sediments tended to get sucked up and broken, and the sediments themselves could not be excavated in a controlled manner that would have given some idea of the cenote's stratigraphy.

A more ambitious attempt was made in 1967, when water was removed to a depth of 4 metres (13 feet). This made it possible to excavate a part of the sediments as if they were exposed on dry land, a method calculated to retrieve the maximum amount of information about the order in which objects had been dropped into the well. It turned out that there had been two main periods when the cenote received many offerings. The earlier period included many gold and jade objects brought from far and near, along with household pottery and other domestic objects. The second period took place after Chichén Itzá had ceased to be the dominant city of the region. In this poorer period, it seems, the people who made offerings here looted earlier tombs to provide splendid objects of jade to add to their humbler offerings of wooden figurines, copper bells and pottery.

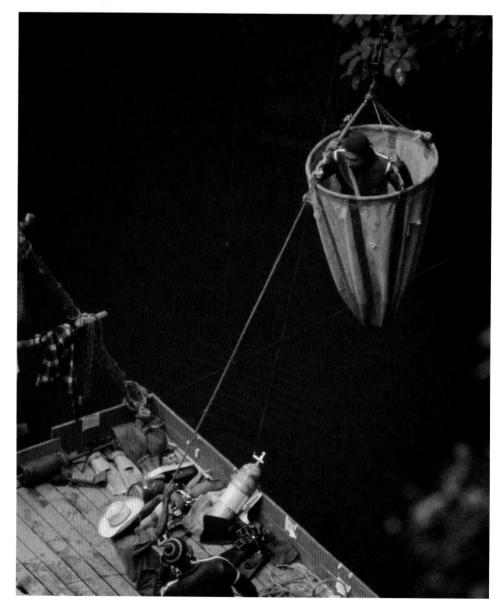

Top right: *Jade, exceptionally hard as well as beautiful, was highly prized by the Maya who used it to make ornaments like this pectoral. Many of the precious offerings thrown into the cenote were made of jade.*

Right: *The intrepid divers were lowered into the cenote in a canvas bucket suspended from a crane high above on the mouth of the well, using a block and tackle.*

SPANIARDS IN THE AMERICAS

UNKNOWN RICHES

The Italian explorer Christopher Columbus (1451–1506) discovered the New World for the Spanish crown in 1492 and there was no lack of young Spaniards ready to seek their fortunes in this land of unknown riches. None was more ambitious than Hernán Cortés, a nobleman from Estremadura in Spain, who went out to the island of Hispaniola in the West Indies in 1504. There, he eventually rose to command an expedition sent in February 1519 by Diego Velázquez, the governor of Cuba, to explore the Mesoamerican mainland.

The country in which Cortés's expedition landed was part of the vast dominions of the Aztecs. News of the strange white-skinned Spaniards in their curious ships had been brought to the Aztec ruler, Montezuma (Motecuhzoma II), in the previous year when an expedition explored the Veracruz region. Learning of the arrival of Cortés in his empire, Montezuma sent gifts to honour this emissary of a foreign power: a gold dish and one of silver; four ritual outfits, including jewellery of turquoise, jade and gold; and a quantity of food.

Soon Velázquez sent a message recalling Cortés to Cuba. Cortés, however, had his own ideas. His appetite whetted by the richness of the diplomatic gifts, he decided to march inland with his small force of 400–500 men. Having dispatched his

---

Below: *In this scene depicted in the Lienzo de Tlaxcala manuscript, the Spaniards and their Tlaxcalan allies are killing nobles of the western Mesoamerican state of Michoacan for refusing to yield their treasures.*

---

largest ship to bear gifts to the Spanish king, Charles V, in order to validate his authority, he burned his other ships and set off for the fabulous city of Tenochtitlán.

The Aztec Empire included many disaffected conquered areas that groaned under the burden of taxation. Other regions enclosed by the empire remained independent but with the status of official enemies. With them the Aztecs engaged in their ritual "Flowery Wars", set-piece battles in which the object was to seize captives for the frequent human sacrifices required by the Aztecs' religion. Foremost among these peoples were the Tlaxcalans. The Spaniards at first waged war on the Tlaxcalans, but it was not long before the two sides joined forces against the Aztecs.

TENOCHTITLAN

On November 8 the army came in sight of the great Aztec city of Tenochtitlán. Constructed on an island in Lake Texcoco in the Valley of Mexico, the city was linked to the lake shores by three causeways, while surrounding the dry land of its centre were vast suburbs of chinampas, floating gardens with houses built within them. Cortés and his men entered the city and were met by a royal procession carrying a palanquin in which rode Montezuma. They were greeted hospitably and lodged in one of the emperor's palaces. Here by chance they discovered a door into his treasure chamber, which contained riches beyond their wildest dreams.

The Spaniards resolved to lay their hands on the hoard; but how? Cortés decided that the way to secure their safety and freedom of action was to control the emperor, and he soon managed to trap Montezuma, who now became a Spanish prisoner. Dividing the treasure, Cortés allocated shares to Charles V and Governor Velázquez as well as to himself. He issued one-fifth of the treasure to be divided among his army and locked up the rest securely.

At this juncture Cortés received news that Velázquez had sent another expedition, under Panfilo de Narváez, to bring him to heel. Leaving Pedro de Alvarado to guard Montezuma, he set off post-haste to the coast to deal with this new problem.

DISASTER

Cortés had been moving with circumspection and diplomatic skill but Alvarado was a man of a very different character. During Cortés's absence an important Aztec feast was held and Alvarado seized this opportunity to massacre some 600 Aztecs, most of them important nobles. When Cortés returned in June 1520, having defeated Narváez, he found the city in uproar and Alvarado under siege. Soon Montezuma was dead, apparently the victim of a stone thrown by one of his subjects, and the Spanish found themselves in a desperate situation.

Opposite: *This turquoise and shell mosaic mask representing the god Quetzalcoatl was one of the few Aztec treasures that reached Europe as the result of Cortés's expedition.*

Below: *By the mid sixteenth century the Spanish were beginning to create coinage for local use by the colonies. This silver coin of 1556 was one of the first to be struck in Mexico.*

Seizing what gold and treasures they could carry, they attempted to flee the city by night. The Aztecs had cut the causeways, and now attacked the Spaniards from canoes. Many Spaniards were killed or drowned and almost all the treasure was lost in the lake as men struggled to cross the damaged causeways.

Spanish fortunes were now at their lowest ebb, but, amazingly, Cortés managed to retrieve the situation. He and his allies defeated a vastly superior Aztec army at Otumba in July and by the spring of 1521 they and their allies were strong enough to besiege Tenochtitlán.

Piece by piece the city fell and on August 13 the new Aztec emperor was captured. The Spaniards' native allies sacked the city with unspeakable ferocity, and the Spaniards began the attempt to retrieve the lost treasure from the lake around the causeways. They dived in the area, searching the bottom with their feet, but there was little to be found. In the months since they had lost it the Aztec gold had been located and spirited away by its owners.

About one twenty-fifth of the treasure was retrieved. Cortés packed this on to a ship and dispatched it to Charles V. But the ship was intercepted on its way by a French privateer and all its treasure was seized.

STILL HUNTING

The Spanish had been seeking gold in the New World and they had found it, although they had lost it again. They were convinced that there was more to be seized if they knew where to look. Some went south and found it, destroying the empire of the Incas and hounding the peoples of the neighbouring gold-rich lands. Others turned their eyes to the north. An expedition under Narváez was sent from Spain to conquer Florida but was shipwrecked on the coast in 1528. Alvar Núñez Cabeza de Vaca and three companions survived. For eight years they wandered across this unknown terrain, helped by some native groups, enslaved by others. Their travels took them almost to the west coast, from which they managed to make their way south to Mexico City, the new Spanish foundation

built on top of Tenochtitlán. They brought back rumours of the supposedly fabulously wealthy Seven Cities of Cibolla, said to lie some distance to the north of the areas through which they had travelled. Many explorers set out in hope of locating these mythical cities, but they were doomed to failure. The cities of which they had heard were probably the prosperous settlements of the Pueblo people in the American South-west – but of gold they had none.

Above: *Hawikuh, a large Zuni pueblo, was the first native North American town to be conquered by Coronada. The Spaniards were impressed by its houses, but frustrated by its lack of riches.*

Right: *A map of Coronada's futile expedition to find the Seven Cities of Cibolla, whose fabulous wealth and very existence proved merely to be figments of overheated Spanish imagination and greed.*

KARTE
zu CORONADOS EXPEDITION nach
CIBOLA und QUIVIRA

SPANISH GOLD ARGOSIES

Above: *Wooden statues and gold chains salvaged from the* Santa Margarita, *which was wrecked in 1622.*

SPANISH GOLD

Old coins occasionally turned up on Florida's beaches and in 1949 Kip Wagner joined a group diving in search of their source: a site offshore where one of the group thought he had located a shipwreck. By the end of that summer they were $12,000 out of pocket and had found nothing. Disillusioned, the group split up, but Wagner was smitten with the treasure-hunting bug and knew that he couldn't stop until he had located the elusive wreck.

His interest was reinforced when he took a walk along the beach after a hurricane and found a silver coin. He was sure that it must have been washed out from a sunken ship somewhere in the neighbourhood, but he realized he needed to know more. What ships were known to have gone down in the area and where exactly? Did any of them tie in with his coin, which was dated 1714? Wagner and his friend Doc Kelso began to scour the records in libraries near and far, looking for ships that had sunk around that time. Gradually they built up a picture of the possibilities.

One seemed too good to be true. After their conquest of Mexico and Peru, the Spanish began to exploit the rich deposits of gold and silver of these lands, annually sending the treasure back to Spain in a fleet of strongly armed galleons and merchant ships. In 1715 this fleet had the misfortune to be caught by a hurricane and 10 of its 11 ships, carrying a fabulous quantity of gold and silver, had been wrecked somewhere off Florida. But where? Some authorities thought they had gone down off the Florida Keys, others suggested Cape Canaveral. Then Doc Kelso had a stroke of luck: he found a book written only 60 years after the fleet sank. Not only did this state that the fleet had been lost off the Sebastian River, not far from the homes of Wagner and Kelso, but it also had a map marking the shipwreck site.

TODAY'S UNFOUND TREASURES

GASPARILLA ISLAND

According to legend, José Gaspar's promising career as Spain's youngest admiral in the 1780s was cut short when he was accused of stealing royal jewels. Fleeing, he gained possession of a ship and took to privateering. By about 1800 he had captured more than fifty ships sailing in Atlantic waters, including those of his compatriots. He now established a new base in the Gulf of Mexico, on a tiny island which he called Gasparilla after himself. Here, he and his followers built a number of settlements and concealed their ill-gotten gains in the ground. Gaspar now branched out: in addition to looting ships of their goods and treasures, he started holding the female passengers to ransom. But when the US government acquired Florida, it determined to clear the remaining pirates from the area. By 1821 Gaspar's position was threatened by the arrival of government forces in the nearby Florida Keys and he and his confederates decided to quit Gasparilla. They packed their treasures into ships and many sailed away. Gaspar, however, stayed to capture one last ship – but his intended victim proved to be well-armed and Gaspar's ship was sunk and he himself drowned. What treasures remain on the island and the lost ship is unknown.

Above: *An aerial view of the islands of the Florida Keys. This is a particularly treacherous area of sea, where many a ship from the Spanish flotas met its end.*

THE CLUES ACCUMULATE

The next breakthrough came when Wagner and Kelso obtained a microfilm of Spanish archive material on the disaster. Written in archaic Spanish, the documents took them more than a year to decipher. These gave details of each ship's cargo and of the salvage operations at the time, in which less than half the treasure was recovered. The salvage had taken four years, during which the Spanish authorities and the divers they employed had repeatedly been forced to fend off attacks by pirates and English privateers. The expedition team constructed a fortified camp on the shore to protect themselves and the treasure during the operation.

After a long search, Wagner stumbled upon this camp, on a sandy bluff above the beach. Swimming out from the area overlooked by the camp he eventually spotted a heap of cannon lying on the seabed alongside an anchor. Although he realized that to investigate these wrecks required more sophisticated equipment than he could muster, looking to the future he obtained a lease from the Florida state authorities allowing him to salvage material from wrecks along an 80-kilometre (50-mile) stretch of coast and giving him exclusive rights to salvage this and another wreck he had located.

REAL EIGHT

By 1960 Wagner, Kelso and a group of other treasure seekers had formed a team that included experienced divers. They bought a boat and started diving on one of the wrecks. It was hard work; the site was covered with heavy ballast which had to be shifted before the wreck could be explored further, but eventually their patience was rewarded when they found a number of silver bars, part of the cargo that the Spaniards had failed to salvage.

Now that they had begun to succeed, they decided to put the whole project on a firm legal footing. They formed a company that they called the Real Eight Corporation, from the name of the Spanish coins, *reales*, that the fleet had carried, and they began investigating the second wreck. On their first day out over it, they found a

Right: *A heap of silver coins, concreted with shell during their centuries underwater, lies beneath a beautiful gold rosary, the property of one of the ill-fated passengers of the 1622 Spanish treasure fleet.*

mass of coins fused together: a promising beginning which led to the discovery of a fortune in gold coins. But although this wreck was in some ways easier to investigate, they were frequently hampered by bad weather, sharks and the seabed deposits, which kept moving, sometimes exposing remains and at other times burying them deeply.

In 1963 Real Eight joined forces with Mel Fisher, another experienced diver and treasure-hunter, and his colleagues of Treasure Salvors Inc. They had their difficulties, including legal battles with unauthorized divers on the wrecks on which they held leases, and periods when they worked hard but found nothing or their equipment broke down. But they had many triumphant moments, like the day when one of their number found an exquisite gold pendant on the beach; shaped like a dragon, it incorporated a whistle, a toothpick and an ear-cleaning spoon.

THE FLEET OF 1622

In 1966 Mel Fisher's team decided to move elsewhere, beginning a five-year search for an earlier Spanish treasure fleet. Just like the doomed Spanish fleet of 1715, the ships that sailed for Spain in 1622 were seriously delayed, departing in September way behind schedule and well into the dangerous hurricane season. One day out from Havana, they ran into a force-10 gale and eight of the 28 ships went down over an 80-kilometre (50-mile) stretch off the Florida Keys, including three heavily laden with treasure, *Nuestra Señora de Atocha*, *Nuestra Señora de Rosario* and *Santa Margarita*. Others succeeded in returning to Havana. The sinking of the treasure ships was a major loss and salvage attempts were put in train at once. The *Rosario* was discovered aground on the Dry Tortugas; its crew was rescued and most of its treasure recovered. The *Atocha* was also found in deep water off the Marquesas Keys, but divers could not get

into it to recover anything. Of the *Santa Margarita* there was no trace. A further salvage expedition was mounted in 1626, using a special diving bell invented by the head of the expedition, Francisco Núñez Melián. By this time the remains of the *Atocha* had disappeared. The *Santa Margarita* was at last located and a considerable amount of silver salvaged from its cargo. However, much still remained, inaccessible to the Spanish salvors.

Fisher and his associates employed every means at their disposal: searching the Florida Keys with a range of reconnaissance devices and scouring the archives for clues. The latter enabled them to narrow the area of their search to the Marquesas Keys and in 1971 they met success, discovering a wreck.

The public scramble for underwater treasure that followed Real Eight's discovery of the 1715 wrecks led the Florida state authorities to introduce legislation designed to give some protection to historic wrecks.

Salvage permits now involved a partitioning of the finds between the state and the salvors and attention had to be paid to recovering and recording the important historical details of a salvaged ship's structure and contents that would provide all sorts of valuable information on the ship, its cargo and passengers, information that was sadly lacking from earlier salvage operations.

At first it proved difficult to identify this wreck. The official cargo of gold and silver carried by the Spanish plate fleet was marked with official stamps and attracted a 20 per cent tax. There were harsh penalties for carrying contraband treasure in order to evade this tax, but the opportunity was too tempting and most ships carried a huge illegal cargo belonging to the passengers and crew. This ship was no exception and the first finds from it included unmarked gold bars which gave no clues to the ship's identity. As more objects were salvaged, however, some silver ingots marked with an official number were found and their details matched those given in the official manifest of the cargo of the *Atocha*.

In 1980 Fisher discovered the *Santa Margarita* nearby. Although the ship had broken up after striking the reef, the salvage team discovered a substantial chunk of its timbers preserved on the seabed. This was excavated and raised. Like the *Atocha*, the *Santa Margarita* contained a large quantity of contraband material. Much of this was carried as gold chains, which could easily have been broken up and sold once the owner reached home – though of course these unfortunates never did: about 550 people lost their lives when the eight ships sank in 1622.

Opposite: *The Spanish treasure fleet of 1622, made up of ships bearing goods from various ports in Central and South America, came together in the summer at Havana before setting sail for Spain.*

Above right: *Raising a heavy cannon from a wreck requires teamwork, lifting equipment and careful manoeuvring. Here, a cannon from the Spanish galleon* Atocha *is brought to the surface by her salvage team.*

Right: *Figures stamped on these gold bars recovered from the* Santa Margarita *in the Marquesas Keys were part of the official recording system introduced by the Spanish government in the seventeenth century to prevent smuggling.*

FLORIDA KEYS AGAIN

A similar disaster took place in 1733. Yet again a Spanish plate fleet was the victim of a hurricane: all of its 22 ships were damaged and most sank or broke up on the reefs, only one managing to return to Havana. Here a rescue and salvage team was quickly assembled, bringing immediate assistance to the survivors and over the following years recovering a great deal of the cargo from the wrecked vessels – more, in fact, than the ships were officially recorded as carrying, for, like other fleets, these ships had been loaded with contraband as well as officially recorded goods. But by no means all that had been lost was recovered,

One of the wrecked ships, the flagship *El Rubi Segundo*, was rediscovered in 1930 by a fisherman, and in the years since then many

treasure-seekers have investigated the area, locating nine more wrecks. Because of the efficient original salvage operation, little treasure was still left in these wreck sites, but the surviving remains from them are of great historical value. Some treasure-hunters in the area have adopted a responsible attitude, recording their finds, but many more, unfortunately, have not, virtually destroying the wrecks they investigated. One such wreck, the *San Pedro*, was officially designated an Underwater Archaeological Preserve to protect it.

Above: *Spanish coins recovered from the wreck of the* Conde de Tolosa, *some of them minted only a few years before the ship went down.*

MERCURY

The ships in which the Spanish treasure fleet brought home the gold and silver of the Americas fulfilled an equally vital role on their journey out. For the colonists who had settled in Spain's American possessions, they brought a whole range of luxury objects from home, and for the mining companies they brought vital supplies of mercury, essential for processing ore to extract silver. Adventurous people who intended to settle in New Spain also took passage on the ships of the outward-bound plate fleet.

But many of those who embarked on the journey to the New World in 1724 were destined never to arrive. Packed on board two ships, the *Nuestra Señora de Guadalupe* and the *Conde de Tolosa*, were some 1,200 people. They crossed the Atlantic safely, touching at Puerto Rico to take on supplies, but as they sailed on they ran into a hurricane off Samana Bay on Hispaniola. The *Guadalupe* ran aground on a sandbank but did not immediately sink, and most of its passengers made it ashore. Initially, the *Tolosa* seemed better off, managing to anchor at the mouth of the bay; but the storm tore it

---

Below left: *Precious items salvaged from the* Conde de Tolosa *included around 1,000 pearls, some of which are seen here with gold and jewels that are also from the wreck.*

Below right: *The inscription "Mater Salvatoris" – Mother of the Saviour – identifies the figure on this medallion from the doomed 1724 treasure fleet as the Virgin Mary, whose protection the wearer had sought against the perils of the sea.*

---

adrift and drove it in, smashing it against rocks within the bay. Of the 600 aboard, fewer than 40 survived. Seven did so by a miracle: they climbed the ship's mainmast and spent more than a month clinging to life in the maintops, sustained by food and water from the wrecked ship and menaced by sharks that prevented them from swimming ashore.

The survivors from the *Guadalupe* were 320 kilometres (200 miles) from Santo Domingo, the nearest Spanish settlement. On the gruelling overland journey many died. When the rest reached the settlement, boats were sent to rescue anyone still alive at the wreck site, and to attempt, without success, to salvage the valuable cargo of mercury from the ships.

In 1976 another attempt was made. A company called Caribe Salvage contracted with the Dominican government to look for the wrecks of these two vessels, the proceeds to be divided equally between the state and the salvage company. Although they did not

recover the mercury, the salvors found many beautiful objects. The Spanish authorities prohibited the carriage of non-Spanish goods, but there were plenty aboard. These included a fine brass clock made in London; the excavators had only to clean it and replace a few steel parts for it to run again perfectly, despite its centuries under the sea. There were also exquisite goblets and decanters of engraved glass, and beautiful pieces of gold jewellery of exceptional workmanship. Many of these pieces told a personal story, such as the gold cross of a Knight of Santiago or the bracelet inscribed with the name of Doña Antonia Franco, both the property of passengers on the ship. We can begin to glimpse their lives by piecing together such evidence from the wrecks.

NOTRE DAME DE DELIVERANCE

Some ships from the Spanish argosies were investigated before there were any laws governing salvage of cultural property, but gradually such laws have been passed, reviewed and improved. Nowadays ships within national waters are generally well protected. Would-be salvors usually have to work under licence and must include proper archaeological investigation and recording within their recovery programme, although the quality of this archaeological work is still very variable. In international waters, however, the legal situation is much less clearly defined and many important wrecks are therefore exposed to unregulated plundering that deprives the world of the historical information that they encapsulate. Until the 1980s such wrecks were protected by being inaccessible, but following the development of sophisticated equipment for deep-sea reconnaissance and deep-sea excavation using remotely controlled machinery these wrecks have become vulnerable.

A wreck found 64 kilometres (40 miles) off Florida's Key West has been testing the laws on wreck ownership. On the basis of its location and of a few objects recovered from the wreck, including bottles, a crucifix and silver coins, it was identified by a salvage company, Sub-Sea Research, as probably the *Notre Dame de Deliverance*, an eighteenth-century French vessel. They therefore obtained a US protection order to "arrest" the wreck, giving them the right to protect it against any other would-be salvors, and a further order allowing them to explore and assess the wreck by non-invasive means. However, ownership of the wreck was immediately claimed by the Spanish government, since at the time of its sinking the ship was on lease to the Spanish government, who owned the cargo it was carrying. There were Spanish soldiers on board and the trip was made in a time of war, potentially making this a war-grave site, protected by international law. The French may also feel they have a claim, since the vessel was the property of the French West Indies Company and the crew were French, although this company ceased to exist long ago.

The manifest of the *Notre Dame de Deliverance* recorded that it was carrying 17 chests of gold bullion, six chests of gems, 15,000 gold coins, more than a million silver pieces of eight, nearly 40 kilograms (88 pounds) of raw silver and silver ore, and various other objects, including 153 gold snuff boxes. The ship set sail from Cuba on October 31, 1755, in company with seven or eight smaller vessels, all armed. During the night the fleet was hit by a hurricane. Most of the ships limped on to find safe anchorage in the Marquesas Keys, but *Notre Dame de Deliverance* sank. The survivors from the wreck may have been eaten by the cannibal inhabitants of the nearest land in Florida, the Calusa tribe. The slaughter and consumption of some 400 Frenchmen on Mantaca Key (also known as "Slaughter Key") sometime before 1775 is apparently recorded history. In retaliation, two years' later the French sent a punitive expedition to the area and slaughtered more than 3,000 people.

TODAY'S UNFOUND TREASURES

GOLD AT LITTLE BIGHORN

Transporting gold through hostile territory was never easy but in June 1876 the situation was desperate. The discovery of gold in the Black Hills of Dakota, a Sioux sacred site, had attracted swarms of white prospectors, bringing already tense relations with the native inhabitants to flashpoint and culminating in the massacre of General Custer and his troops at Little Bighorn. Gil Longworth was conveying £30,000 of raw gold from the Montana gold fields to Bismarck, North Dakota. The country was alive with hostile Sioux, and Longworth and his two companions began to fear for their safety. To their relief, when they reached the Bighorn River, some 32 kilometres (20 miles) from its confluence with the Yellowstone River, they encountered an army transport boat, the *Far West*. They persuaded its captain, Grant Marsh, to take the gold on to Bismarck, thankfully turning homeward, but they didn't get far before they were killed by Indians. Marsh regretted his decision almost at once: the gold might exacerbate an already difficult situation. He therefore buried it for safe keeping. For years it was too dangerous to retrieve the gold. Eventually Marsh tried to contact the freight company for whom Longworth had worked, but it had gone out of business. Marsh and his crew did not return to retrieve the gold, so theoretically it is still there.

Above: *In 1876 this beautiful spot was the scene of a desperate fight between US troops and Sioux and Cheyenne warriors during the now famous Battle of Little Bighorn.*

THE "MONEY PIT"

MYSTERIOUS PIT

In 1795 Daniel McGinnis was exploring Oak Island, just across the bay from Chester, Nova Scotia, when he spotted a tree with rope marks – from a pulley? – over a shallow hollow in the ground. He immediately thought of buried treasure. The next day he returned with some friends and started digging. It turned out to be a tremendously deep pit. As they went down they uncovered a number of platforms of oak logs, some sealed with ship's putty. Discouraged, they abandoned their investigation – but returned in 1804 and dug down to 30 metres (100 feet). Probing through the next layer of putty and wood, they thought they could feel treasure chests packed with coins, but by the next day the shaft had filled with water and only the top 10 metres (33 feet) remained clear. The supposed treasure chests seemed also to have fallen from their platform, washed by the water to the depths below. The lads could do no more.

But the pit was not forgotten. Many further attempts have been made to penetrate the mysteries of the shaft, which quickly acquired the name the "Money Pit". No one could tell if there was treasure below but the pit seemed too elaborate not to be concealing something extremely valuable.

As investigations multiplied, the area became completely churned up, with shafts sunk alongside the Money Pit in an attempt to reach its lower levels. These have revealed details of its elaborate construction. The shaft, which is at least 65 metres (212 feet) deep, drops down into a large cavern. The skilful engineers who constructed it dammed the sea from entering the area while they were working. They dug several tunnels into the shaft from the sea, and placed a number of platforms in the shaft. When they had completed their work, they released the sea from its dam. The platforms were arranged so that as soon as certain of them were removed, the sea water would be sucked into the tunnels and fill the shaft – an excellent booby trap. In order to penetrate the depths where the supposed treasure might lie, the sea would have to be dammed again, a task requiring both skill and knowledge of the tunnels' layout.

Vast sums, totalling millions of pounds, have been spent on investigating the Money Pit, and six people have lost their lives. But with modern technology it has proved possible to penetrate some of its mysteries.

A stone bearing the date 1704 has been found nearby, though whether this relates to the Money Pit is uncertain. The cavern at the base of the shaft was photographed in 1971, using a video camera, and this seemed to show three chests, along with a well-preserved severed hand. Divers were lowered 72 metres (235 feet) into the cave but did not report anything.

WHOSE TREASURE?

If the pit does conceal treasure, what is it? A number of people have suggested that Captain Kidd's mysterious island (see page 169) bears an uncanny resemblance to Oak Island, although the name "China Sea" on the chart seems to go against this theory. "Blackbeard" (Edward Teach), who died in 1718, also claimed to have left vast treasures (see page 217) and he is another who is tentatively linked with the Money Pit.

The people of Chester claimed to have seen mysterious lights and fires on Oak Island in 1763. Could these have been lit by the builders of the gigantic booby trap? Another suggestion links the Money Pit with a party of Royal Engineers operating during the American War of Independence, hiding threatened supplies of government money. Or could it have been the men of a disabled Spanish galleon who had concealed their treasure there rather than risk sailing the ocean with it? If the supposed treasure is ever recovered, its date and nature should provide some of the answers. Until then we can only speculate. It seems unlikely that the end-result will justify the expense of the investigations that have taken place nor the devastation that these have wrought on this part of the island, but the attempts have at least satisfied a great craving for adventure.

Above: *The Restall family, two of whom died on Oak Island.*

PIRATES

Until recently pirates were known only from documents, but this has all been changed by the recent discovery of not one but two pirate ships.

Barry Clifford searched for years for the wreck of the *Whydah*; finds of cannon and coins of the appropriate date several times raised false hopes. But when in 1985 he recovered a ship's bell inscribed "The Whydah Galley – 1716" he knew he had at last succeeded. The ship's identity is further supported by the very varied range of objects recovered from the wreck site, including cannon, grenades and other ordnance; Akan goldwork from West Africa and coins from many different countries, the most recent dated 1716, the year before the *Whydah* went down. However, there are probably other wrecks of the period in the same area, so not all the material recovered need come from the *Whydah*.

Since 1985 Clifford has continued to investigate the area off Wellfleet, Massachusetts, near Cape Cod, where the *Whydah* went down, thoroughly breaking up and scattering its cargo over a wide area. It was not until 1998 that Clifford found a hull section that could have come from the ship itself. But he has found plenty of other things – thousands of silver coins, gold dust, many armaments, gold jewellery and even a leather shoe and silk stocking with a pirate's leg-bone still inside.

The *Whydah* belonged to Black Sam Bellamy, an English sailor turned pirate who was active off the American coast in the early eighteenth century. This was an area with rich pickings, with Spanish ships carrying New World gold and silver and ships of other nations also carrying valuable cargoes. The *Whydah* had started its career in this mercantile milieu, as a slaver operating out of London, bartering weapons and manufactured goods on the West African coast for gold, ivory and, especially, slaves. The slaves were carried to the Americas where they could be sold and the proceeds spent on sugar and other local produce to take back to Britain. But in February 1717 the ship was intercepted by two pirate vessels. The captain, Lawrence Prince, surrendered almost without a fight; the pirate captain, Sam Bellamy, transferred into the *Whydah*, recruited some of its crew and turned Prince and the rest loose in his old ship, the *Sultana*.

For the next two months Bellamy and his pirates menaced the west coast of America, capturing and plundering other ships, but on April 26 they were caught by a violent storm off Cape Cod. The *Whydah* was driven on to a sandbar off the Massachusetts shore where it rapidly broke up. When the locals rose the next morning they found the beach littered with dead bodies and all manner of treasures, which they lost no time in collecting. When an agent of the governor, Cyprian Southack, arrived from Boston some days later, they were still at it but there was little of value left to retrieve. Southack carefully made a map of the wreck site, buried 102 bodies and

Below: *Treasures from the wreck of the* Whydah. *The survivor Thomas Davis claimed* Whydah *was carrying 180 bags of gold and silver coins.*

squeezed a small amount of the plundered treasure out of the locals, who had a bad reputation for looting shipwrecks and perhaps even encouraging ships to run aground.

It was Southack's map that Clifford used in his search for the wreck; it showed where the ship had gone down, though not where its disintegrating remains and scattered contents had ended up. For this Clifford employed a range of survey equipment. Information on the ship's contents was provided in the deposition of Thomas Davis, carpenter, one of only two survivors of the wreck, who was tried as a pirate but acquitted because he successfully claimed that he had been forced into piracy when he was captured along with the ship. Davis revealed that the *Whydah* had held the remaining spoils from 53 raided ships, including 4½ tonnes (5 tons) of gold, silver and jewels. Clifford's finds from the wreck site have added further information. For example, a surprising quantity of items, such as fancy buttons, cufflinks and buckles, as well as jewellery such as rings, suggests that the stereotypical picture of filthy, ragged pirates was wide of the mark – many of these pirates were clearly vain of their appearance.

Many grenades were found – hollow iron balls filled with gunpowder, plugged to keep

Above: *This charming metal teapot, recovered from the wreck site of the* Whydah, *sheds light on a more domestic side to pirate life.*

the gunpowder in and set off by lighting an embedded wick. Although the *Whydah* carried cannon with which to threaten its victims, the pirates were clearly unwilling to inflict serious structural damage on the ships they attacked in case they sank without yielding their valuables. Instead the pirates preferred to get in close, throwing grenades, shooting with muskets and spraying with small shot to cause casualties among the defenders. As soon as they could, the pirates would grapple their ship alongside their victim and pour on board to engage in hand-to-hand combat, trusting in their own ferocity to overcome their opponents.

Sam Bellamy described himself as a "free prince" and his treatment of the *Whydah*'s original crew suggests that he was a pirate for profit, adventure and independence. On one ship he captured was a small boy, John King, then probably around 8 years old, who was so enthralled by Bellamy's personal charisma and exciting life that he voluntarily joined the pirate crew.

BLACKBEARD

Edward Teach (or Thatch), known as Blackbeard, was a very different man who deliberately cultivated an aura of terror around himself. He began his career as a privateer, employed by the British government to sink or capture French and Spanish shipping during the War of the Spanish Succession. When the war ended in 1714, Blackbeard continued his activities on his own account, becoming a pirate and using North Carolina's Outer Banks as a safe haven. By 1717 he captained a pirate flotilla of four vessels, with around 300 men under his command.

In November off Martinique they captured a large French slave ship, *La Concorde*, which Blackbeard adopted as his flagship, renaming it the *Queen Anne's Revenge*. Only six months' later, however, the ship ran aground at Beaufort Inlet; another smaller ship, the *Adventure*, was also lost attempting to assist it. With selected crew members Blackbeard made off in a smaller ship to Bath Town in North Carolina, where he took advantage of a temporary amnesty to wring a pardon from the governor. There is some suggestion that he deliberately sank the *Queen Anne's Revenge* so as to break up the ship's company, making it easier for him to take advantage of the amnesty.

He did not, however, desist from his piratical activities. The governor of another state, Virginia, eventually called in the navy, who ran Blackbeard to earth in Okracoke Inlet in North Carolina and gave battle, defeating and killing him on November 22, 1718. Blackbeard's short but bloody reign of terror was over.

THE *QUEEN ANNE'S REVENGE*

A wreck was discovered in 1996 off Fort Macon, North Carolina, by North Carolina's official marine salvors, Intersal, Inc. Work on the wreck site has been undertaken since 1997 by North Carolina's underwater archaeology team, under the direction of marine archaeologist Mark Wilde-Ramsing. The ship has benefited from very detailed archaeological survey, mapping, recording and research, and some excavation, particularly in 2000 and 2001 after extreme storms exposed some timbers and threatened their destruction. Only around 1 per cent of the objects on the ship have been recovered, including diagnostic artefacts such as cannon, along with objects that were at risk from storm currents and other natural hazards. It is calculated that there are around a million individual objects in the wreck site. Work takes place in the autumn when marine conditions are at their best and the excavation season is often quite short. Many efforts are made to keep the public informed about the work and its results. The material recovered from the wreck sheds a great deal of light on life at sea and on land in the eighteenth century, including the slave trade.

The ship went down in shallow water and has been subjected to both strong currents and damage from ships passing overhead so only a small portion of its structure has survived. Most of the remains found on the wreck site were anchors, cannon, barrel hoops and ballast stones, though many other small objects were also recovered, including navigational instruments and glass bottles.

Is this wreck the *Queen Anne's Revenge*? Many clues indicate that it is. The wreck is located near the eighteenth-century entrance to the Beaufort Inlet, where *Queen Anne's Revenge* is recorded as having gone down and where no other ships of this date are known to have sunk. The material from the wreck is mainly British and includes a large number of cannon, some still loaded. Langrage was present – this was shot made by fastening three lead bolts together so they stuck out in all directions – which was apparently not used by official navies but only pirates, privateers and merchantmen. Datable objects from the wreck were made in the late seventeenth and early eighteenth centuries, and none need have been made after 1718. These features matched expectations for a British pirate vessel of the correct period, while the location of the wreck is very suggestive, as is the evidence that this wreck had run aground and sunk, as the *Queen Anne's Revenge* is recorded as having done.

Most of the valuables on board were taken off by the pirates but a few objects remain, including a small amount of gold dust, a tiny proportion of the 9 kilograms (20 pounds) carried by *La Concorde* when it was captured and renamed. At least 24 cannon have been recovered, and there were also a number of muskets and other small arms, but no swords or daggers were left behind. The ammunition recovered from the wreck included bar shot and langrage, used to damage an enemy's sails, and grenades, lead shot and bags of glass pieces and metal fragments for attacking enemy personnel.

TODAY'S UNFOUND TREASURES

JEAN LAFITTE

The Frenchman Jean Lafitte (c.1780–1826/1854) was one of the last of the pirates, though he himself never accepted that name for his occupation. Arriving in New Orleans in 1809 with his brother Pierre, he set up as owner of a blacksmith's shop, a cover for his catalogue of illegal activities. While Pierre ran the New Orleans end of the business, entertaining the great and powerful, Jean operated from the islands of Barataria off the Mississippi Delta as privateer, slaver, smuggler and receiver of stolen goods on a mammoth scale. Jean enjoyed a brief period as a local hero when he and his followers fought for the USA against the British at the Battle of New Orleans in 1815. But mostly the US government pursued him when it felt strong enough, evicting him from Barataria in 1816 and from his later base on Galveston Island off Texas in 1821. He disappeared from history at this point, but is rumoured to have lived till 1854. Lafitte, whose misdeeds made him fabulously wealthy, is believed to have concealed many caches of treasure, still unrecovered, on Barataria and Galveston Island, as well as on the coast between them.

Above: *Jean Lafitte.*

SHIPS OF THE GOLD RUSH

THE *CENTRAL AMERICA*

When James Marshall spotted gold at Sutter's Mill, California, in January 1848, he set in train the great Gold Rush. Within a year more than 100,000 people had poured into the state: prospectors seeking their fortune and sometimes succeeding overnight, along with shopkeepers, hoteliers, bar-keepers, bankers and prostitutes to provide the services the prospectors might want. Some people came to the gold fields overland, joining wagon trains along the pioneer trails from the east. Those who could afford it preferred to make the journey by sea, braving the elements rather than the hostile Native Americans.

The United States Mail Steamship Company operated a fleet of steamers that linked New York and eastern ports with Aspinwall in Panama. From here a railway carried passengers to and from the west coast, where other steamers regularly plied the sea lanes to San Francisco. The *Central America* operated on the Atlantic route, and in August 1857 the paddle steamer set out from Aspinwall with passengers and mail, and a load of gold from the Californian fields. More passengers joined the ship in Havana, bringing the total number aboard to 575 and the value of gold being carried to $2,189,000.

Although at first the journey was pleasant, on September 10 a storm began to brew up, developing into a hurricane that swamped the unstable *Central America*. Despite the crew's heroic efforts, the ship went down on the September 12, 322 kilometres (200 miles) off the coast of South Carolina. Several

Below: *Gold bars sparkle on the seabed around the wreck of the* Central America. *She went down in 1857, carrying the wealth of many prospectors who had struck lucky in the California Gold Rush.*

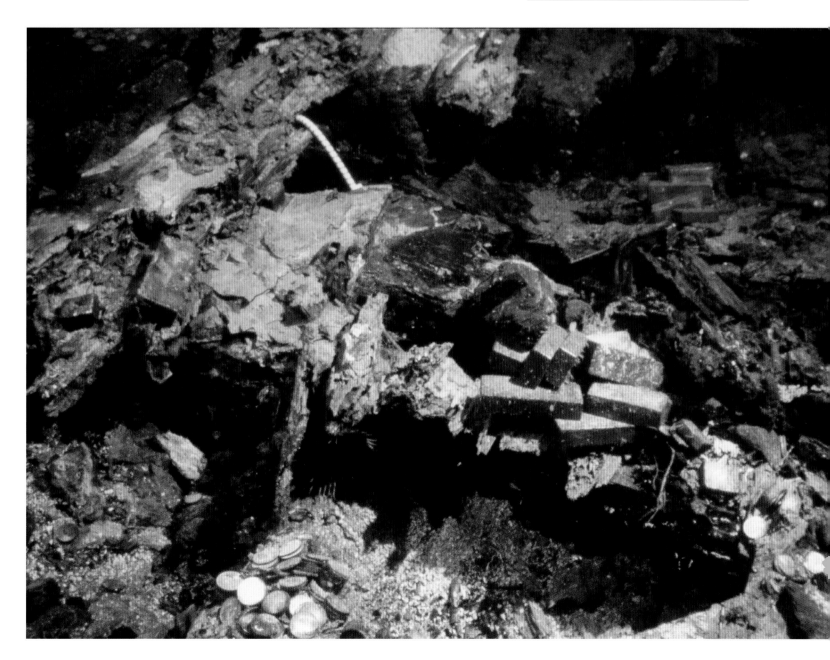

passing ships rescued around 150 people, including all the women and children, but 423 people were lost. Only floating debris remained from the wreck, far out at sea.

SALVAGE DISPUTES

Until recent decades it was impossible to locate and recover such deep-sea wrecks. As the technology developed, however, several attempts were made to find and salvage the *Central America*. In 1987 the Columbus America Discovery Group (CADG) located the wreck 320 kilometres (220 miles) off South Carolina at a depth of 2,500 metres (8,200 feet). The vessel's contents were remarkably well preserved and the salvage company even recovered newspapers from a leather trunk. Using a remotely operated vehicle (ROV), they removed some of the ship's cargo of gold as well as luggage, the ship's bell and even cigars. They made a television film of their work and published

a book and school material on the wreck. The responsible and sensitive attitude they adopted in their recovery operations stood them in good stead later.

The CADG reported its finds to the relevant authorities and in the summer of 1989 all the interested parties came to court to determine the ownership of the gold and other salvaged material. The main question was whether the original owners – or rather the insurers who had paid out after the disaster – still had a legitimate claim to the gold. After more than a century the insurers no longer had the relevant documents and the lower court, where the case was first heard, decided that they had effectively abandoned ownership. This decision was overturned by the United States Courts of Appeal in 1992: the insured portion of the cargo was still the property of the insurers, although the uninsured cargo and the ship itself were now the property of the salvors,

and the insurers owed the CADG something substantial for its salvage efforts. The case returned to the lower court for amounts to be determined. In view of the considerable expense and difficulty of the salvage, and of the salvors' responsible approach to the operation, it was decided that their share should be 90 per cent of the value of the recovered gold: a vast fortune.

THE *BROTHER JONATHAN*

The paddle steamer *Brother Jonathan* was built in 1850 in New York, originally to carry gold prospectors down the east coast to the Isthmus of Panama, but from 1852 it was

---

Below: *Gold coins recovered from the wreck of the* Central America, *which sank off South Carolina in 1857, lie on the insurance register recording the ship's original loss.*

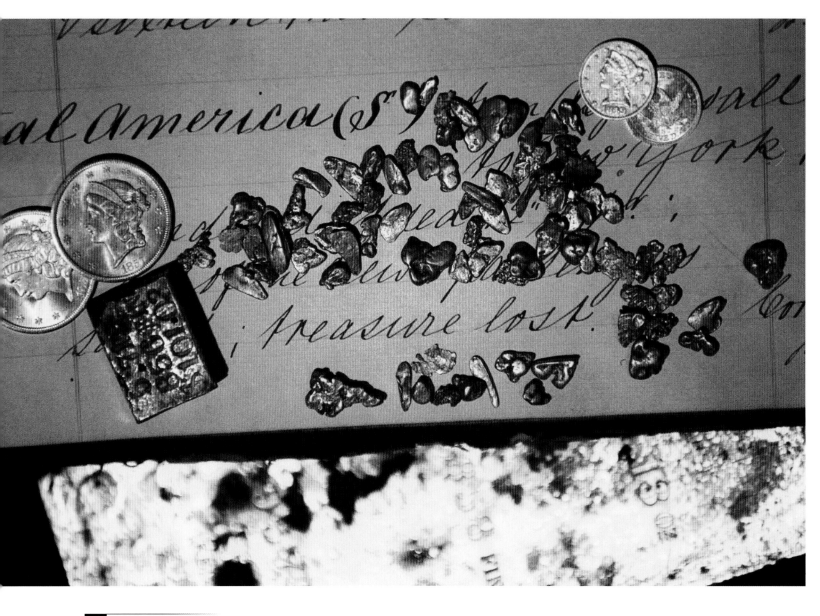

transferred to the western seaboard where it plied various routes out of San Francisco. By 1861 it was in bad shape and nearly sank, and its owner sold it. Under its new owner, the Californian Steam Navigation Company, it benefited from an overhaul and refit.

In July 1865, a temporary agent was in charge of the bookings for berths and freight and insisted on overloading the ship. Mining equipment and other machinery was packed in as well as 130 passengers, 84 crew members and a strongbox containing more than $200,000, probably in notes, which was pay for soldiers further north. The captain, DeWolf, was deeply concerned and remonstrated with the agent, but was told to take the ship as it was or lose his job. Unfortunately, he gave in – and instead lost his life.

The ship sailed for Canada on July 28, almost too overladen to move – it had to be towed out of the dock. On its second day, it encountered strong gales so Captain DeWolf decided to turn back to Crescent City. In heavy seas and fog the ship struck an uncharted rock, which thereafter was charted with the ship's name. Picked up by the heavy seas and smashed repeatedly on the rock, it was immediately clear the ship was doomed.

Two of its lifeboats were launched, only to be dashed to pieces against the ship. A third attempt was made by Mr Patterson, the third mate, with 10 members of the crew, three children, their mothers and two other women in a surf boat. There were a few anxious minutes but they made their escape, only just in time as the ship went down before their eyes. They were the only survivors.

Many attempts have been made since then to salvage the ship but for a long time its precise location was uncertain. One attempt in 1930 succeeded in locating *Brother Jonathan*'s paddle wheel but nothing else, suggesting that the ship had broken up. But in 1993 the wreck was located, largely intact. It was partially salvaged by its discoverers, Deep Sea Research Inc., who recovered a substantial number of gold coins as well as intact glass bottles and pottery. One find of particular interest was a large wooden crate, which was taken to the conservation laboratory of the Institute for Western Maritime Archaeology. Keeping it wet so that the timber would not be damaged by drying out, the crate has been lovingly excavated by the Institute's specialist team. It turned out to be a consignment of goods bound for a Canadian shop. These were still wrapped in paper and labelled, though few traces of the labels survive. They included sets of axes, scythes and other tools, along with spare wooden handles; cast-iron meat grinders; brass plumb-bobs; cast-iron pulleys and hooks; traps for catching small animals; door knobs and locks; and various other items of hardware.

TODAY'S UNFOUND TREASURES

COLUMBUS'S SHIPS

In 1492 Columbus sailed across the Atlantic Ocean from southern Spain via the Canary Islands and "discovered" America. Three tiny ships made up his fleet, the *Santa Maria*, the *Pinta* and the *Niña*. On reaching Cuba, the *Pinta* parted company from the others. On Christmas Eve the *Santa Maria* ran aground off Hispaniola. Attempts to refloat it failed and eventually Columbus sailed back to Spain in the *Niña*, leaving 40 of his men behind. They built a tiny settlement, called Navidad, from timbers salvaged from the wreck. It was two years before Columbus could return – to find that the inhabitants of Navidad had been massacred by hostile natives.

In recent years work has begun to find and excavate Navidad and to locate the wreck of the *Santa Maria*. In 1976 a sixteenth-century ship was discovered on the Molasses Reef off the Turks and Caicos Islands in the Caribbean. Could this be the *Pinta*? The salvage company that was formed thought so. The governor of the islands was unconvinced and called in archaeologists to investigate – unfortunately, not before much damage had been done by treasure-seekers who had dynamited the wreck. The wreck turned out to be an unknown ship, providing a fascinating glimpse of sixteenth-century life at sea, but the *Pinta* still remains to be found.

Since 2001 another wreck possibly associated with Columbus has been under investigation near Nombre de Dios in Panama

– this may be the *Vizcaina*, one of the ships from Columbus's fourth (and last) voyage. It is of the right period and will provide fascinating information on sixteenth-century ships, even if it cannot be identified for certain as the *Vizcaina*.

Above: *This watercolour depicts the ships of Columbus's first expedition, his flagship the* Santa Maria *and the smaller* Pinta *and* Niña.

THE *SS REPUBLIC*

Above: *A postcard showing the ocean liner, the* SS Republic. *The legally authorized salvors of the wreck are reportedly planning to raise the ship in sections in the summer of 2010.*

Below: *The magnificent, First Class Entranceway of the* SS Republic.

COLLISION IN FOG

On January 22, 1909 the White Star Line luxury liner *SS Republic* left New York with many wealthy passengers, bound for Alexandria in Egypt. It was to call at Genoa, as it was carrying relief supplies for the victims of a terrible earthquake in Italy, in which more than 85,000 people had died. On the same day the Italian steamship *Florida* was approaching New York with more than 800 Italian emigrants aboard, many of them fleeing homes ruined by the earthquake. As both ships approached Nantucket Island, a thick fog descended, blanketing out all visibility and nearly all sound. Both ships proceeded with caution, regularly sounding their foghorns, but neither knew of the other's presence until the *Florida* ran straight into the *Republic*, crushing its own bows and tearing a great hole in the *Republic*'s side.

The *Republic*'s heroic young wireless operator, John Binns, began sending out distress signals – almost the first time that the wireless had been used in sea rescue. He stayed at his post for 14 long, cold hours. The *Florida*, though damaged, was in no immediate danger and the crew of the *Republic* managed to seal off the holed section from the rest of the ship. The *Republic*'s passengers were transferred to the *Florida* and both ships awaited the arrival of the *Baltic*, which had answered the distress call. The fog was still thick and it was with great difficulty that the *Baltic* located the *Republic*. After doing so it took off the crew, the passengers of both ships, the mail and probably some of the cargo. The *Baltic* and the *Florida* now headed for port. An attempt was made to tow in the *Republic*, but it proved too badly damaged and eventually sank.

MYSTERY OF THE CARGO

The *Republic* lies in difficult and dangerous waters and it was not until 1981 that it was relocated by diver Martin Bayerle. It took him and his company, Sub Ocean Salvors

Inc., until 1987 to raise the $1.5 million needed to attempt a salvage. Although there were likely to be many valuables aboard, the property of the passengers, the salvors were pinning their hopes on a rumour. In 1909 Tsar Nicholas of Russia had been struggling against revolution and it was said that the *Republic* was secretly carrying $3 million in American gold to aid him. Another rumour made the sum $250,000 and its destination the United States Battle Fleet.

The wreck proved to be in very bad shape and the task extremely difficult. The salvors recovered little apart from china and wine bottles, and after three months they abandoned this attempt. But they still believe the gold is there and plan to try again.

Below: *The opulence of the* SS Republic *is clear from the extraordinary stained glass ceiling of the First Class Dining Saloon and the wooden statues, paintings and carved decoration around the dome.*

THE *TITANIC*

THE UNSINKABLE *TITANIC*

At the beginning of the twentieth century two great shipping lines, White Star and Cunard, were battling for dominance of transatlantic passenger traffic, each building bigger and better ships to attract potential travellers. In 1907 Cunard launched the *Lusitania*, the first ship to make the Atlantic crossing between Britain and America in just five days. White Star decided to commission the shipbuilders Harland and Wolff to construct three huge vessels that were to be the very last word in comfort, while completing the journey in very little more time than the *Lusitania*. The first of these, the huge *Olympic*, was completed in 1910, and the following year the even more vast *Titanic* was finished.

Immense excitement grew as the *Titanic* was readied for her maiden voyage. Her creators' optimistic words that she was "virtually unsinkable" had soon been popularly translated into "unsinkable" without qualification. The passengers who boarded the ship at Southampton on Wednesday April 10, 1912 included people from many walks of life: from millionaires, like John Jacob Astor and his new second wife Madeleine, accompanied by servants, to third-class passengers such as Minnie Coutts and her two sons. Also on board were Bruce Ismay, managing director of the White Star Line and Thomas Andrews, managing director of Harland and Wolff, both intensely interested in how the ship would perform on her maiden voyage.

STEAMING AHEAD

As the monstrous *Titanic* began to pull out of Southampton harbour, the *New York*, a smaller ship moored at a berth along *Titanic's* route down the River Test, was sucked out into its path. Quick thinking by the *Titanic's* captain, Edward Smith, averted disaster as he reversed his ship's engines, and the *New York* was towed to safety.

That evening the *Titanic* arrived in Cherbourg in France, where more passengers joined, and the following day, April 11, it reached Queenstown (now Cóbh) in Ireland, the last port of call before the final destination, New York. Here some passengers disembarked, having briefly tasted the luxuries of the magnificent ship, and the final travellers boarded. The historic voyage had begun.

The first-class passengers found themselves in the lap of luxury. Sportsmen like the tennis star Norris Williams could work out in the gymnasium or take a swim in the pool or a Turkish bath. A smoking room for the gentlemen was matched by a comfortable reading and writing room for the ladies. Elegant cafés and a luxurious dining saloon allowed them to eat in splendour, while a magnificent staircase under a glass and wrought-iron dome gave them access to the boat deck and an enclosed promenade deck. Luxuriously furnished staterooms were available for the most wealthy passengers, and even the third-class accommodation on the lower decks was comfortable though not spacious. Third class too had its dining room, lounge and smoking room, while those in second class could also enjoy a walk on their own promenade.

The voyage was scheduled to take a week, but progress was so good that Ismay and Captain Smith felt it should be possible to knock a day off the journey time by increasing the speed at which the ship was steaming along. So far the engines had been performing wonderfully.

HAZARD WARNINGS

The normal route across the Atlantic went into cold northerly waters where there was generally much ice in the spring. To avoid the risk of icebergs, which were reported unusually far south that year, Captain Smith laid a course farther south than was customary. Nevertheless, his wireless operators received a number of messages from other shipping in the area, warning of many icebergs and fields of ice in the vicinity. Although the general message was widely circulated, not all the specific warnings were relayed to the bridge – a fatal mistake.

The sailors on lookout duty were told to keep a careful eye open for ice. The pair

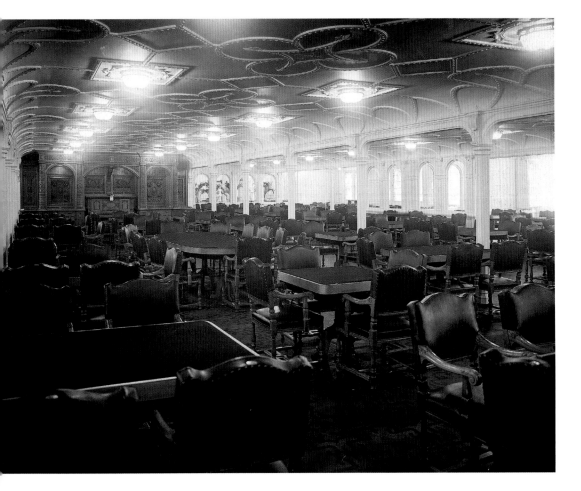

Left: *Passengers on the* Titanic *dined in style. Those in second class enjoyed food cooked in the same kitchens as the food served in the first-class dining room.*

who were on duty on the night of Sunday April 14 were having a hard time with this. A slight haze had developed and the sea was quite calm, so no telltale line of foam betrayed the presence of the iceberg that was directly ahead of the ship in the darkness. Suddenly, around 11.30 p.m., Frederick Fleet spotted the dark mass immediately before them. An iceberg! He rang the bell furiously to sound the warning, which he confirmed on the telephone to the wheelhouse. The officer in charge there, William Murdoch, ordered the ship's head to be swung round, but also set the engines in reverse, fatally reducing the speed at which it could turn. With a horrible sound the iceberg scraped the ship's side.

ABANDON SHIP!

Although the iceberg did not penetrate the ship's hull, the pressure it exerted caused some of the plates to open up and the rivets, weakened by the cold, to shear. Gaps opened between the plates and the icy water began to rush in. Although separate sections of the ship were sealed off, initially preventing the water from flooding throughout the hold, a dangerous amount of water had entered the ship and it soon began to list. Inexorably, the water filled the lower decks and the situation became increasingly serious.

But few people initially understood that the *Titanic* was doomed. Many wandered on to the boat deck for a good view, a lot of them clad in their dressing gowns. Within half an hour, however, Captain Smith had realized that the ship would sink. He ordered the wireless operators to put out a distress call; it was answered by several ships but none that could arrive in less than a few hours. However, flickering lights in the distance suggested that a ship that was not responding was much closer, within 16 kilometres (10 miles).

Several of the lifeboats were launched. Uncertain of the reliability of the mechanism for lowering them into the sea, the officers at first dispatched them with only a handful of passengers, instead of the full complement of 65. The lifeboat crews were told to make for the unknown ship, unload their passengers and return.

Right: *The massive bulk of the* Titanic *dominated the harbour where she awaited her first – and last – voyage. Although she was not the fastest vessel of her time, she and her sister ships were intended to be the most luxurious.*

But time was running out fast. The remaining lifeboats were launched, now fully loaded. Despite the desperate situation most people stayed calm. Women and children were helped aboard the lifeboats and any man who attempted to join them was turned back, although some men were included to crew them. Many of the third-class passengers were trapped below, confused by the maze of corridors and stairs that led tortuously toward the boat deck. And eventually there were no more lifeboats.

Reliance on the ship's theoretical strength and safety had led to its being equipped with far too few, enough for less than half the people aboard, even if each boat had been fully loaded.

Just after 2 a.m. the end came. The *Titanic*, already half-submerged, broke in two and sank beneath the surface. Miraculously some of those still aboard were able to climb on to floating wreckage or to survive in the icy waters long enough to be pulled aboard some of the less crowded lifeboats – although many of their passengers were reluctant to help others less fortunate in case their vessel became swamped and everyone went down.

RESCUE

The crew of the *Carpathia* had received the *Titanic*'s distress call and immediately altered course toward it. But they were many kilometres away and it was not until around 2.30 a.m. that they reached the scene of the disaster. They helped the cold, wet and desperate survivors aboard, wrapped them up and gave them hot drinks, and the ship's doctors attended to those who were injured. But, of the 2,222 people who had been aboard the *Titanic*, only 705 had survived.

Among them was Bruce Ismay, who had entered a lifeboat at a late stage in the disaster. He and many other male survivors suffered for the rest of their lives from the public opinion that they ought not to have lived when so many women and children had gone down with the ship. Ismay was also one of those who had had responsibility for the ship and he was subjected to the ordeal of two legal investigations of the causes of the disaster, one in America and one in England, to establish whether there had been negligence. The conclusion was that there had not.

Nevertheless, the disaster had far-reaching consequences. Regulations were tightened so that it would never again be possible for a ship to go to sea inadequately supplied with lifeboats. Improvements were also made in ship design. Ships were required to man their

Top left: *These decanters and other First Class glassware recovered from the* Titanic *were made of hand-cut lead crystal. They have suffered remarkably little from lying for almost a century beneath icy seas.*

Left: *The* Titanic's *First Class tableware was stylishly decorated. The only decoration on Third Class crockery was the White Star Line logo.*

wirelesses 24 hours a day. And a regular ice patrol was instituted, to monitor the movement of icebergs and issue warnings.

REDISCOVERING THE WRECK

Although there is no firm evidence of treasure carried aboard the *Titanic*, many of the passengers were wealthy. And the scale of the disaster has gripped the popular imagination ever since the ship went down. So there were always hopes that the *Titanic* would be raised again. As it lay at such a depth in icy waters, however, it was impossible for many years for anything to be done about tracing and investigating the wreck.

By the 1980s the technology to investigate the depths was beginning to be developed. Several attempts to locate the *Titanic* failed, but in 1985 Dr Robert Ballard, a geologist from the Woods Hole Oceanographic Institute in Massachusetts, began to search the area with a submersible and an underwater robot that he had devised. Initially he worked with a French team using side-scan radar to search for the wreck, but his efforts went unrewarded. Eventually he started using an underwater camera and in 1986 he spotted one of the ship's boilers.

Elated, he began a programme of filming the ship's remarkable remains. It had broken up further when it hit the seabed, its bows coming to rest nearly 610 metres (2,000 feet) from the stern. Rust had attacked much of the ship's metalwork, creating great pendant pieces like yellow icicles. Some parts of it, such as the grand staircase, still gave a glimpse of its former glory while others lay scattered in a thousand fragments. Pieces of furniture also survived, as did many of the objects on the ship.

In 1987 salvors descended on the wreck and began to remove material from it. This gave rise to many legal battles between rival salvage companies and other interested parties, such as the insurers who had paid out on the original losses in the disaster – a can of worms that once opened has been writhing ever since.

Recently, Dr Ballard has resurveyed the wreck to assess not only the effects of two more decades of natural deterioration but also the impact of tourism. He was disheartened by what he found. The *Titanic* has become a popular destination for seriously wealthy tourists and a wedding has even taken place in a submersible perched on its bows. Not only does this show contempt for what is in effect the graveyard of hundreds of people, it is also damaging the ship. The landing of heavy submersibles on the structure has weakened or destroyed some parts of the ship and Ballard was saddened to see that several important elements, such as the crow's nest from which the iceberg was spotted, have now disappeared. A treaty recently signed by Britain and the US may provide some protection but probably not enough. Some people argue that the only way to protect the heritage of the *Titanic* is to remove all the material from the wreck to where it can be conserved and looked after. Others, including Ballard, believe there should be no interference with what he regards as "hallowed ground".

Below left: *Light from a submersible filming the* Titanic *illuminates her bows, picking out the deck and its surrounding railings. Rust, clearly visible on the railings, is gradually eating away parts of the ship.*

Below right: *An ingenious robot has facilitated work on salvaging the* Titanic, *allowing small or delicate objects to be picked up using its mechanical arms with their precise grip.*

TAIRONA

VENEZUELA

COLOMBIA
MUISCA

CALIMA
1
2
TOLIMA

GUYANA

SURINAM

FRENCH
GUIANA

Gulf of Panama

Gulf of Guayaquil

ECUADOR

BRAZIL

3
4
5
6
7
8
9
10
11

PERU

12

13

BOLIVIA

1 LAKE GUATAVITA
2 MALAGANA
3 CHONGOYAPE
4 BATAN GRANDE
5 SIPAN
6 KUNTUR WASI
7 DOS CABEZAS
8 EL BRUJO
9 CHAN CHAN
10 MOCHE
11 CHAVIN DE HUANTAR
12 NEVADO AMPATO
13 CUZCO

PARAGUAY

CHILE

ARGENTINA

URUGUAY

PACIFIC
OCEAN

Gulf of San Jorge

Falkland Islands

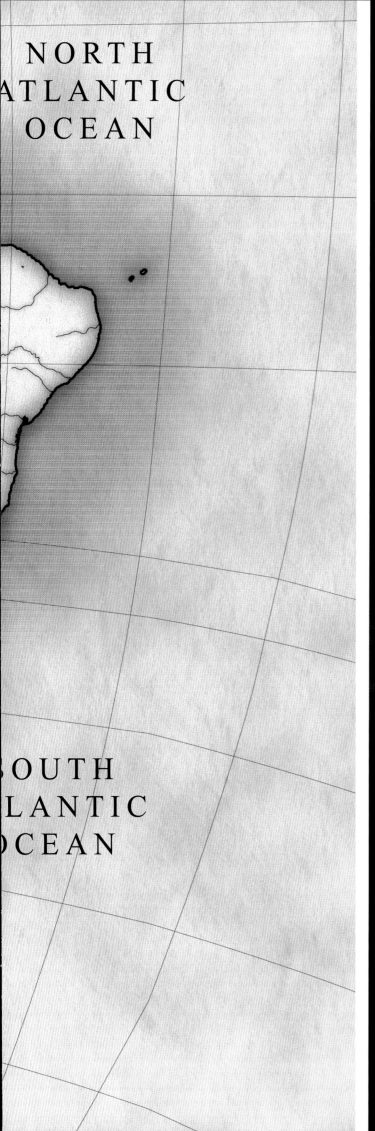

SOUTH
ATLANTIC
OCEAN

SOUTH AMERICA

Above: *Andean pottery, like this, was often made in the shape of animals.*

SOUTH AMERICAN TREASURES

The Spaniards went to the Americas dreaming of untold riches. When they reached South America they found their dreams fulfilled. For centuries afterward Spain was to import vast quantities of gold and silver from this region, altering the world's economy. Much of the gold came from the alluvium of rivers flowing down from the Andes, while some was extracted from quartz veins. After the conquest the mines at Potosí became the main source of silver.

LANDS OF GOLD

To the native peoples of South America, precious metals and stones had a deep religious significance. The Incas regarded gold as the sweat of the sun and silver as the tears of the moon. A Chimu legend recounts that, at the beginning of the world, the sun created three eggs from which humanity was born, lords from the golden

---

Below: *A gold pendant made by the Tolima.*

---

egg, ladies from the silver egg and common people from one of copper.

Metalworking began in South America as early as 2100 BC, and from early times metal objects were placed in the burials of important individuals and served as signs of rank associated with supernatural power. Gold's life-giving association with the sun was often emphasized by alloying it with copper to produce a metal, called tumbaga, of a richer colour. The civilizations of Peru and adjacent regions developed sophisticated metallurgical techniques, including the beaded effect known as granulation. The goldwork of the Moche was particularly fine: they developed several ways of gilding metal, including one technique that used chemicals to electroplate gold on to copper. To the north in Ecuador and Colombia, smaller chiefdoms flourished, each developing its own style of goldworking. For example, the Muisca produced flat figures with details added in thin wire, the Tolima specialized in a strange half-human figure with a tail like an anchor, while the Tairona cast larger figures using the lost-wax technique and added elaborate details afterward. The Chimu brought skills in sheet-metalworking to a remarkable peak.

CITY OF PALACES

The great city of Chan Chan (ancient Chimor) on the north coast was the origin and focus of the Chimor (Chimu) Empire, at its height in the fourteenth and early fifteenth centuries. A vast residential sprawl accommodated tens of thousands of people, mainly artisans manufacturing pottery, wooden objects, textiles and metalwork, as well as servants and other service personnel, in small clusters of workshops and houses with kitchens and sleeping quarters, set around the compounds where the elite lived. Much of the city is taken up by 10 spacious enclosures (*ciudadelas*) with impressive adobe walls, decorated with

animals and geometric patterns in relief. Entry to each *ciudadela* was channelled and restricted; within it the royal residential quarters were accessible only to a chosen few. The *ciudadela* also contained numerous administrative buildings, storerooms to house all the treasures accumulated by the ruler, walk-in wells and courtyards. Many courtyards contained a U-shaped structure, often roofed, known as an *audiencia* – these probably served many purposes, among them as places where the ruler sat to give audiences or from which administrators could supervise activities or guards monitor access to restricted zones. Behind the royal quarters lay the royal burial platform, a great chamber surrounded by small cells in which were placed sacrificed women and lavish funerary offerings. As there are 10 compounds and there were also 10 recorded Chimu kings, some scholars believe that each was occupied during the reign of a different king and abandoned on his death, each new ruler building his own compound and accumulating his own treasury of valuables.

These treasures were mainly the regalia and other items worn by the ruler and nobility on a host of ceremonial and ritual occasions, made from expensive materials often imported from distant lands: gold, silver, gems and the feathers of exotic birds.

During the later period of the empire Lambayeque goldworkers were forcibly resettled in Chan Chan so that they were on hand to serve the needs of the elite. Working almost exclusively with sheet gold and silver, they constructed extraordinary and elaborate objects such as ear and chest ornaments, often made of more than 100 individual pieces. These were fastened together with rings, wires, hinges and rods. Some pieces dangled, others were built up in layers, so that they constantly shimmered and vibrated, catching and reflecting the light as the wearer moved. Birds and serpents often formed part of the ensemble, while the superimposed layers created elements resembling stepped pyramids or geometric floral designs. There were also more solid-seeming objects, such as ear spools in the form of a disc mounted on a rod, decorated with a scene from Chimu life: a noble being borne in his palanquin, for example, or a group of divers gathering spiny oyster shells from the ocean floor.

When the Inca gained control of Chan Chan around AD 1470, they emptied many of the storerooms and tombs of their valuables, beginning a process of looting Chimu settlements and burials that has continued into the present day.

Right: *The Incas made many figurines of gold and silver. Elongated earlobes indicate the figure (far right) represents a member of the elite.*

Below: *The people of the Cordilleras (in modern Ecuador and Colombia) made a variety of fantastic gold figures and faces of humans and gods.*

INCA REALMS

Around AD 1410 the small southerly highland state of the Incas began to expand, conquering its neighbours. Under Pachacutec and his son Tupac Yupanqui the Inca Empire reached to the borders of Ecuador in the north and a considerable distance through previously unconquered lands to the south, controlling both highland and coastal regions. Magnificent roads linked all quarters of the empire and along these were frequent waystations and government outposts to collect taxes and administer conquered lands. Some taxes took the form of compulsory labour on government projects while others were collected as goods. Pre-eminent among these were textiles made from cotton and alpaca wool. The Incas had hierarchical sumptuary laws governing the grades and decoration of cloth to be worn by people in different levels of society. The emperor himself wore cloth of the finest vicuña wool woven by specially chosen beautiful virgins who were housed in a nunnery in the capital, Cuzco.

Goldworkers also resided in the capital; many of them were Chimu from the northern coast, whose metalworking skills were highly prized. Gold and silver were used in circumstances of particular sanctity. The great temple of the Sun at Cuzco, the chief Inca shrine, had doors and walls coated with sheet silver and gold. Small figurines made of gold, silver or spiny oyster shell (another highly valued material, symbolizing water) and representing people or llamas were used as offerings, placed in stone boxes in the holy lake of Titicaca or with sacrificed children among the mountain peaks.

Below: *The Incas made beautiful naturalistic objects like this llama.*

MOUNTAIN SHRINES

The Incas venerated mountains as the place where they could get closest to the gods and constructed high mountain platforms as shrines where offerings were regularly made. In times of crisis, such as drought, earthquake or volcanic eruption, unblemished children or youths were selected as offerings, bringing honour to their families and sending them to eternal paradise. In recent years a number of these children have been rediscovered, their bodies often perfectly preserved by the freezing conditions. They had been finely dressed in beautiful robes and were probably drugged before being killed, in some cases by a blow to the head or strangulation, in others perhaps by exposure. With them were placed offerings such as fine pottery and small figurines of their own gender dressed in miniature textiles. These figurines were generally made of shell, silver or

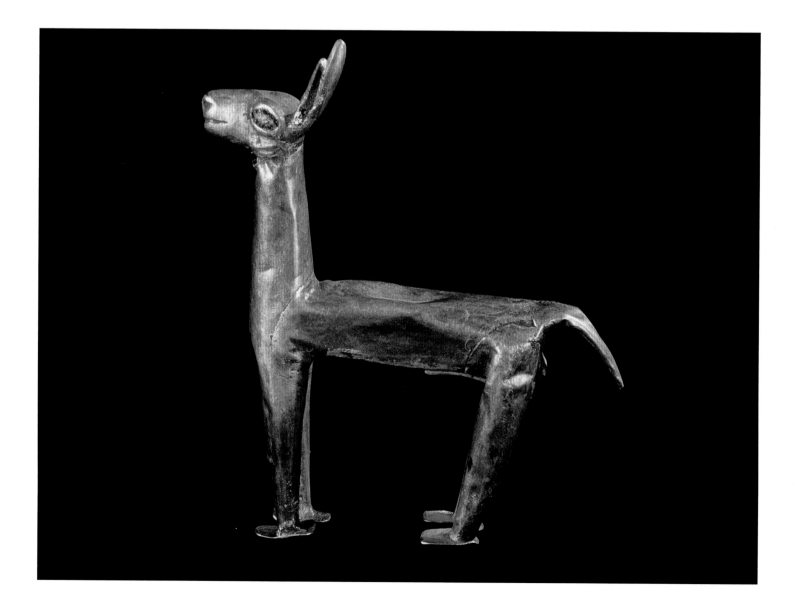

gold: female figurines wear a rectangle of cloth fastened with silver pins, a tasselled belt and a shawl fastened with a silver pin, while male figurines wear a tunic and a shawl knotted under the chin; both wear a cap, often with feathers. Figurines were also placed as separate offerings in these mountain-top shrines. Where several figurines were placed together, they were always of the same gender.

One sacrifice discovered in 1995 aroused particular excitement among archaeologists. This was a girl in her teens who was exceptionally well preserved. An avalanche on Nevado Ampato had disturbed an Inca platform in which she had been buried. Part of the platform and the frozen body of the girl had tumbled down the mountainside, where they were discovered by chance by Johan Reinhard. He has spent many years

Below left: *Clad in a perfect miniature set of women's clothing, this silver figure of an Inca goddess was buried as a votive offering on the peak of Cerro Copiapó in the Andes.*

Below right: *Calmly seated as if asleep, this Inca boy was offered as a sacrifice to the gods of the Andes mountains. Victims were drugged and often died of exposure without ever regaining consciousness.*

investigating these mountain shrines, but he happened on that occasion to be out on the mountain to admire an active volcano. In order to ensure that the "ice maiden", as they called her, did not thaw in the sun, he and his companion had to carry her down from the mountain: a daunting task. But eventually they got her to safety and refrigeration. Since her discovery and rescue, she has been subjected to a battery of tests, including a CAT scan, which revealed the blow on her forehead that had killed her, and analyses establishing what she last ate.

Below: *Conquistadors, including Pizarro, on an Inca wooden beaker.*

DESTRUCTIVE PLUNDERERS

In 1525 the Europeans indirectly began the destruction of the Incas. Smallpox brought from Europe swept through South America, decimating the Incas and their subjects and killing both the emperor, Huayna Capac, and his heir. Civil war between two of his sons ensued, from which Atahualpa emerged as victor.

But he had no time to consolidate his rule. In 1532 Francisco Pizarro, drawn by rumours of the golden riches of this region, landed with a small force of around 200 men on the northern coast at Tumbes. There he was met by friendly envoys and marched inland, climbing the gruelling mountain paths into and over the Andes. At Cajamarca Atahualpa was waiting for him with a

vast army; to demonstrate his good faith, he accepted an invitation to meet Pizarro unarmed in the centre of the town. Pizarro, however, had no compunction about using treachery and, when the unarmed Inca forces were in place, the Spanish soldiers attacked them, massacring perhaps as many as 10,000 of them and capturing the emperor.

Atahualpa offered to buy his freedom with a vast quantity of treasure: enough gold to fill a room. Pizarro accepted this easy way of collecting the Inca gold and messengers were sent throughout the Inca realms to gather the ransom. Huge quantities of gold were brought, but again Pizarro failed to keep his side of the bargain: he executed Atahualpa for "idolatry" – his failure to embrace Christianity – and set up a puppet ruler.

ELDORADO

THE GILDED MAN

Pizarro's rapacious expedition was followed by others as Spaniards' appetites were whetted by what had already been found. Many Indians were tortured to reveal where further gold – and silver and jewels – might be hidden. A curious story began to gain wide circulation: the legend of the gilded man.

Among the goldworking chiefdoms in the north were the Muisca. Although they themselves had no local gold source, they were able to gain substantial quantities of gold dust by trade. Some they made into golden figures, but some they reserved for the investiture of their kings. The new king would be stripped naked, coated with sticky mud and then covered from head to foot with gold dust. Seating himself on a raft and accompanied by his principal lords, he would be taken out to the centre of a lake, where he would bathe, washing off the gold, which became an offering to the gods. Large quantities of gold and emeralds would be offered at the same time.

The story grew in the telling: instead of an investiture once in a ruler's lifetime it became an annual event and then a daily ritual. Expeditions were mounted to seek the location of this gold-filled lake, which indeed turned out to exist: it was identified as Lake Guatavita. (One theory suggests that, as the lake was formed by a meteor, the golden offerings of the Muisca were to imitate the fiery appearance of its creation.) Now the problem for the Spaniards was how to retrieve the gold. The lake, which is situated in the mountains near Bogotá, is 4 kilometres (6½ miles) around and 37 metres (120 feet) deep. Could the lake, large as it was, perhaps be drained?

An expedition led by Jiménez de Quesada made a first attempt. In the dry season of 1545 one of his captains organized a team of Indians furnished with gourds and got them bailing. He succeeded in lowering the water level by about 4 metres (13 feet) and in the exposed mud he recovered a small amount of gold.

Some years later an assault was mounted on a much larger scale. Antonia de Sepúlveda, a rich merchant, obtained a royal licence to drain the lake and began work with a labour force of 8,000. They excavated a notch in the edge of the lake and the water began to drain out, reputedly lowering the lake's level by 20 metres (66 feet). But again the finds were meagre: a mere 232 pesos of gold and one large emerald.

UNDEFEATED

Perhaps discouraged by the lack of success or perhaps infected by persistent rumours of golden treasures in unlikely corners of the continent, the Eldorado legend changed. The gilded man faded from popular memory, to be replaced by the notion that Eldorado was a city of gold. Nevertheless, Lake Guatavita never lost its association with gold and attempts continued to be made to recover its treasures.

In 1823 a consortium was formed to attempt to drain the lake completely. They made another cutting in its edge and

---

Below: *This votive model is made of tumbaga, a copper-gold alloy whose vivid colour looks more golden than gold. It depicts the Muisca investiture ceremony of the king.*

significantly lowered the water level, but after running way over budget they were forced to abandon the attempt without having recovered anything. An English friend of the consortium's leader suggested using a siphon to perform the drainage, but he withdrew his suggestion when he visited the lake and saw the scale of the problem.

Another group decided that the wrong lake was being investigated. In 1856 they attacked Lake Siecha, somewhat to the south of Guatavita, and succeeded in lowering the water level by several metres. They were rewarded by the discovery of a fabulous object: a gold model of the raft from the ceremony of the gilded man, complete with the imposing figure of the chief and the smaller figures of 10 of his lords.

After a while attention returned to Lake Guatavita. In 1899 the most ambitious

---

Above: *Lake Guatavita, sacred place of the ancient Muisca people.*

---

scheme to drain the lake was begun, with the formation of a company, Contractors Limited. The plan was to drain the lake's waters out through a tunnel. Armed with quantities of equipment, including a steam pump, the company began work. In 1910 it was still hard at work, but the task was nearing completion. Indians employed by the company searched the mud at the lake's edge and occasionally turned up objects, but it was virtually impossible to explore the lake bed thoroughly. When first exposed, the mud was soft to a considerable depth and would not bear a person's weight, while it turned as hard as concrete after it had

been in the sun for a day or so. The residual waters accumulated in the centre, creating a hollow, and the company suspected that this was where the bulk of the treasure must lie. It recovered enough material to mount a public auction, but nothing like the amount it had hoped to find. The lake was abandoned and allowed to refill.

Other attempts were later made, but eventually the Colombian government stepped in to ban treasure-hunting in the lake. Although many still believe that great treasures lie in its bed, this is unlikely.

GOLDEN TOMBS
Despite the disappointments of the lake, over the last century Columbia has shown itself to be a region rich in Pre-Columbian goldwork of great sophistication. One particularly rich area is Calima, in the

western mountains, where ancient communities flourished around 1000 BC to AD 700. Farmers who settled here in the early twentieth century found, as they cleared the forest, many remains of ancient fields and houses and thousands of graves, some containing objects of gold which they were able to sell to the National Bank. At first these objects were melted down for bullion but as their superb craftsmanship and artistry came to be appreciated, many were kept intact and a museum was built in Bogotá to house them.

The ancient people of the Calima region were extremely skilled goldworkers, producing complex objects from beaten gold sheet or by lost-wax casting. Gold masks, breastplates and jewellery were made to be worn by the elite. Gold and pottery figurines give a vivid impression of how the people of Calima saw themselves. Other gold objects may have belonged to shamans: bowls, spoons and containers for lime, along with pottery pipes, all associated with ingesting a

hallucinogenic mixture of coca and lime to induce a trance.

The ransacking of casually discovered tombs reached a peak in 1991 with the discovery at Hacienda Malagana of a 20-hectare (8-acre) site containing two cemeteries with numerous rich graves. A

Below left: *Locals sell their finds to the Colombian National Bank, which now has an unparalleled collection of Precolumbian art that is on public display in the Museo del Oro in Bogota. This funerary mask was made by the Calima people 2,500 years ago.*

Below centre: *This pectoral of beaten gold in the form of a grotesque horned head was also made by the Calima people.*

Below right: *This naturalistic gold mask reflects the range of different styles adopted by the Calima people through the ages.*

---

large part of the ancient site was rapidly plundered and destroyed, obliterating all the information that it held about the site's inhabitants. Fortunately, in 1994 archaeologists were able to begin investigating what was left of Malagana. They found a settlement surrounded by a ditched enclosure set on an island of dry land within a swamp, which would have provided abundant supplies of fish and game. Elsewhere on the site they found a large number of intact burials of ordinary people; though no unlooted rich burials were discovered, the archaeologists were able to glean some information by interviewing the tombs' plunderers. It seems that the elite were buried in deep pits lined with stone querns. Often more than 3 metres (10 feet) deep, the base of these pits, where the burials were placed, now lie below the water table, so they are waterlogged. This had made their looting a difficult and unpleasant business. How they were originally dug, and the burials made, remains a puzzle.

GOLD FOR THE LORDS OF SACRIFICE

TOMB ROBBERS

Ever since the Spaniards discovered the Inca civilization, Peru has drawn treasure-hunters mad for gold. Huge mounds of sun-dried brick, constructed by the Moche people in the early centuries AD, particularly attracted their attention; when these were excavated, tombs were found, rich in gold and silver. Looters in the seventeenth century even diverted the River Moche to undermine one of the largest of the mounds, known locally as *huacas*. Among the people of the region an illegal industry has grown up, plundering these tombs. The *huaqueros* (*huaca* robbers) dig deep into the mounds, destroying everything in them except for the valuable objects that they can sell. They themselves receive relatively small sums for these treasures but the middlemen who resell them on to international collectors can make vast fortunes.

Working precariously at night to avoid the eyes of the law, in 1987 a group of *huaqueros* dug a pit 7 metres (23 feet) deep in one such mound at Sipán, in the Lambayeque Valley in northern Peru. On the night of February 16 they struck lucky, breaking into an intact royal tomb filled with unimaginable riches. However, a tip-off soon sent the police to the house of one of the looters, where they found discarded fragments of gilded copper: unsaleable rejects from the plunderers' haul. They set an ambush and in the ensuing confrontation one of the robbers was shot dead.

The police began surprise raids on the mound to discourage further looting as it was now being besieged by gold-fevered villagers. They called in Walter Alva, director of Peru's Brüning Archaeological Museum, to inspect the objects they had seized. Realizing that the looted grave had been exceptionally rich, Alva organized a rescue excavation, beginning in April, to investigate what remained of the grave. He hoped to find out a little about the person buried there and, with luck, to recover any objects that the looters had missed or discarded, such as pots. The Moche made elaborate pottery, some painted with scenes from their lives, other pieces moulded into portraits, models and scenes. Usually ignored by tomb robbers, these pots provide a valuable picture of how the Moche lived, and in particular of their violent wars and human sacrifices.

Below: *The Lord of Sipán was richly provided with fine pottery and servants to tend to his needs who were placed in wooden coffins around his central burial.*

Opposite: *This astonishing miniature figurine of gold and turquoise is a nose ornament which would have been worn by the Old Lord of Sipan.*

Once Alva started work the site had to be guarded night and day. Not only were the local villagers angry at being prevented from continuing to plunder this and other local *huacas*, they were also extremely resentful about the death of the *huaquero*. Several times Alva was startled to hear shots, as the police fired over the heads of prowling looters.

Although the grave had been thoroughly plundered, Alva did find a few objects left in it, such as a copper sceptre. He also found traces of the wooden beams of the burial chamber. Their arrangement told him that this chamber had been added during one phase of the mound's construction. Perhaps other royal tombs had also been cut into the mound? A close examination of the mound's surface revealed several disturbances where bricks had been removed to form a pit that had been backfilled with sand and stones in Moche times. Could either be the entrance to an intact tomb? The excavators hardly dared hope so.

The first was not, but it nevertheless produced exciting results. The pit contained a small chamber roofed with wooden beams, now decomposed but still visible. Within this they found a mass of pottery, including figurines arranged in scenes, and among them the contorted body of a man who had probably been sacrificed.

A ROYAL GRAVE

Digging down into the second pit, the archaeologists came upon the wooden beams of a much larger chamber – the intact royal tomb that they had hoped for, but of a magnificence they had never dreamed possible. On the ground above the beams they found the body of a man, wrapped in a cotton shroud and armed with a club and shield: the guardian of the tomb, whose feet had been removed, perhaps to stop his spirit leaving its post. Within the wooden chamber were five cane coffins surrounding a larger main one of wooden planks bound together with copper straps: two cane coffins were superimposed at the head end and one placed on each of the other sides. These contained five more people: three young women, another warrior and a servant with the royal dog. One woman and the warrior, like the guardian, had had a foot removed. A sacrificed child was seated between two of the coffins by the head of the main coffin. Above the chamber a niche held another seated man. Two llamas were also sacrificed and lay beneath the cane coffins on two sides. The men were probably sacrificed but the women had died earlier and had been stored elsewhere as mummy bundles within coffins: their bodies were reduced to bones by the time they were buried here.

In the main coffin lay the Lord of Sipán, a warrior priest like those who were so often shown on pottery vessels. He had been buried clad in astounding wealth. Beside him lay a golden crescent-shaped headdress while the lower part of his face was wrapped in a gold mask. From his nose hung another ornament in gold and by his ears were three pairs of magnificent ear ornaments of gold and turquoise. One pair was decorated with a tiny figure, about the size of a thumb, lavishly attired in gold like the ruler and clutching a shield and war club. More representations of this warlike figure appeared on two banners of gilded copper mounted on cloth and on another headdress.

Left: *This elaborate necklace was worn by the Old Lord of Sipán. Each bead is a rattle containing gold balls, capped by a gold-wire spider's web, on which crouches a spider with a human face on its back.*

The rest of the lord's body was just as sumptuously dressed. Round his neck were two necklaces of peanuts fashioned in gold and silver, a massive necklace of gold discs and others of gilded copper and silver beads in the form of human heads. Bracelets of tiny gold and turquoise beads adorned his arms, while 11 chest ornaments of white coral and red shell beads had been placed in various parts of the coffin. On his feet were ornamental silver sandals – he could never have walked in them.

Like the warriors so often seen fighting on the Moche pots, the lord wore a backflap to protect his abdomen; it was of solid gold and weighed 0.9 kilograms (2 pounds). A matching one was made of silver. They were decorated with the figure of a sinister deity that archaeologists call "the decapitator", a ferocious figure who in one hand holds a *tumi* (sacrificial knife) and in the other a severed head. A small symbolic war club lay at the bottom of the coffin, along with many darts for use with an *atlatl* (spear-thrower). In his hand the lord held a gold sceptre with a silver handle – very similar to one recovered from the looted chamber, which seems likely to have held an equally lavish burial. Both were decorated with a scene in which a warrior is holding a victim by his hair and brandishing a war club in

Above: *Three of the beautiful gold and turquoise ear ornaments worn by the Lord of Sipán. Two depict animals, a deer and a duck, while the third bears a tiny figurine of a warrior armed with a club.*

his face. The Moche fought battles not to kill their enemies but to capture them for later sacrifice.

...AND TWO MORE

Alva continued to work at Sipán, uncovering a second burial of much the same period, accompanied by five retainers and a sixth lying above the chamber, matching the guardian of the first burial. A dog and a snake were placed in the coffin of a child and a headless llama at the feet of one of two young women, who was buried without a coffin: the llama's head was placed in the upper grave fill. The main burial was also richly furnished, though less so than the lord, with fewer objects and some in less precious materials: copper instead of silver slippers, for example, though there were also objects of gold and silver. Many of the objects were similar to those worn by the lord, including gold and turquoise ear spools, nose ornaments, necklaces of human-head beads, a gold and silver backflap and beaded pectorals. Others matched those shown with the Bird Priest in Moche sacrificial scenes on pottery. The most spectacular of these was a gilded copper headdress in the form of an owl. Its outstretched wings were fashioned as three pairs of rigid curving bands from which dangled plaques representing feathers, which would have shimmered as the priest moved.

In the lowest levels of the mound was the grave of another royal individual, accompanied by a young woman and a llama. Dubbed the "Old Lord", the man buried here died around AD 100,

about 200 years earlier than the Lord of Sipán. He had been wrapped in a mat and shrouds but had no coffin. On his face was placed a funerary mask of gilded copper and beneath this he wore nose and ear ornaments. Others lay nearby. One nose ornament was an astounding work of craftsmanship: mounted on a rectangular silver plaque was a tiny gold figure armed with shield and club and itself wearing a moveable gold nose ornament, a turquoise tunic and a golden skirt. On its head was a magnificent gold owl headdress similar to that worn by the priest.

Like the later lord, this ruler was buried with a mass of jewellery, including thousands of beads that had spilled over everything. There were magnificent shell ornaments and one of metal pieces in the form of an octopus. Six necklaces of gold and silver hung round his neck. Some were made up of snarling feline heads but the finest was assembled from intricate gold beads in the shape of spiders poised above their webs. These held three tiny gold beads that would have rattled when the lord moved. On the back of each spider was a human face.

Two extraordinary figures of gilded copper may have originally been mounted on textiles. One was a huge figure of a crab with a human face and legs; the other had a snarling feline face and headdress inlaid with shell and coloured stone and an infant human body with claws on hands and feet. Three banners covered with metal plates were each decorated with a large human figure and embossed with ulluchi fruit; one contained actual examples of this fruit, believed to have produced an anticoagulant substance. The Moche may have added this to the goblets of blood they collected from their sacrificed prisoners so that it would stay fluid long enough for the ruler to drink it.

Other objects from this grave included sceptres and backflaps like those buried with the Lord of Sipán. Aspects of the Old Lord's grave furnishings suggest that he fulfilled the roles of both ruler and priest, which in later times had separated, as exemplified by the burials of the priest and the Lord of Sipán. In addition, within the mound nine other far less spectacular tombs were found, some containing two principal burials, in some cases with sacrificed retainers and llamas. These individuals seem from their grave furnishings to have been elite warriors, priestesses and assistant priests.

MOCHE MOUNDS

Sipán is not the only Moche site to be investigated recently. In the Moche valley, the site of Moche itself has long been known for its two huge mounds, Huaca del Sol, largely destroyed but originally vast, built from around 140 million bricks, and the smaller Huaca de la Luna. Between and around these mounds are the remains of a large settlement.

The Huaca de la Luna is a complex structure, composed of at least three platforms and four plazas, one subdivided into three. Platform I is a stepped pyramid accessed by a ramp from the large adjoining plaza. Portions of sculptured reliefs and painted murals still survive along the sides of the ramp, some depicting warriors armed with knobbed staffs, others geometric patterns and stylized designs with iconographic significance, including versions of the Decapitator familiar from Sipán. The top of the platform is divided into courtyards and rooms. Excavation has revealed that the mound was built in at least five stages: traces of decorations associated with earlier stages still survive. The mound is riddled with tunnels made by looters from the nineteenth century onward, so little remains of the burials once present in the mound: just denuded tombs, a few pots and one reed coffin.

In one of the smaller plazas of Huaca de la Luna (plaza 3) dozens of male skeletons were found, all of whom had bones that had been broken before their death: the victims of torture and sacrifice. Marks on the neck bones showed that their throats had been cut. Some had been dismembered. The plaza also yielded baked clay figurines of naked men, deliberately broken, probably also representing sacrificial victims. More skeletons were buried in the adjacent subdivision of the plaza: these included some that had been decapitated and their flesh removed. Around 70 men had been sacrificed here.

Forty miles (64 miles) south of Sipán, another *huaca* has recently also revealed its treasures. The great mound at Dos Cabezas in the Jequetepeque valley had been plundered first by the conquistadores and their successors, and more recently by modern *huaqueros*, all of whom had nevertheless missed a series of burials on the side nearest the sea. Each grave had an associated miniature chamber containing a copper statuette of the deceased, wrapped in textiles, and miniature grave goods matching those placed with the burial. The principal burial in each tomb was a young man – all were giants, 15 centimetres (6 inches) or more taller than the average Moche man. It

Above: *With infinite care, using a puffer to blow away the dust, an archaeologist exposes the fragile skull of the occupant of tomb 3 at Dos Cabezas. A llama's head was buried with him.*

Opposite: *A magnificent example of Moche ceramic craftsmanship, this bottle portrays a a strange beast with fangs and a crest. It was found in the richly furnished tomb 2 at Dos Cabezas.*

is thought possible that they were sufferers of Marfan's syndrome, a congenital condition producing elongated limbs and heart problems that often lead to early death.

Traces remain of the layers of textiles in which each body was wrapped, along with a rich array of grave goods, including gilded weapons, gold and silver jewellery, beaded chest ornaments and pottery. Several sacrificed people accompanied these burials, as well as llamas. The most richly bedecked burial was wearing a gold and copper mask with inlaid eyes, covered by a copper bowl. On his head was a cylindrical gold crown decorated with bats; an exquisite gold nose ornament also took the form of a bat. Many

other gold objects were found with him, along with pottery including a ceramic vampire bat, and many weapons – these were unused, perhaps suggesting that he was not a warrior. This burial was even richer than those of the two lords at Sipán.

EL BRUJO

Near the mouth of the Chicama valley, which is situated between the Moche and Jequetepeque valleys, lies an impressive complex known as El Brujo, dominated by two great mounds, Huaca Cortada and Huaca Cao Viejo. Between these is a substantial spread of houses, workshops and cemeteries. Huaca Cortada is badly damaged

but recent work has revealed that much of the original lower face of Huaca Cao Veijo survives, decorated with moulded or carved and painted reliefs. Smaller fragments of other decorative panels survive on the walls of the three ramps that gave access to the mound's summit and on those of the associated plaza. The mound had been built and rebuilt over a long period, from first to seventh centuries AD. Murals painted on the walls of the mound's earlier phases are also partially preserved.

These panels vividly depict aspects of Moche ritual and iconography, including vultures, snakes and fish. Along the mound's wall fronting the plaza march a line of naked prisoners, bound by a rope around their necks, led by a warrior. Behind them walk other warriors carrying the spoils: the clothing, armour and weapons of the vanquished. What remains of the plaza reliefs suggests that these themes were repeated right around the plaza's walls. Wounds on the prisoners' bodies indicate that they had been subjected to ritual bloodletting. Elsewhere on the mound and plaza are reliefs showing pairs of figures, one brandishing a *tumi* grasping the other by the hair; warriors armed with warclubs fighting in pairs; a half-human, half-spider figure carrying a *tumi*; and a possibly mythological scene representing different regions of the Moche lands.

In 2005, an extraordinary burial was uncovered in the Huaca Cao Viejo, dating to AD 450, containing the perfectly preserved

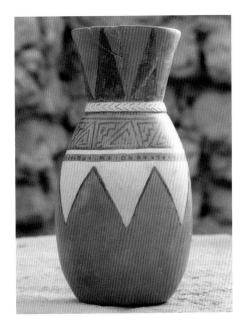

Opposite: *Like other Moche mounds, the great Huaca Cao Viejo at El Brujo is constructed of thousands of mud bricks. The roofed shelters on the mound's side have been put up to protect the extraordinary murals discovered here.*

Left: *Not all Moche pottery was made in the shape of animals or people, and not all was painted with gruesome scenes; some had purely geometric decoration, like this fine water vessel from El Brujo.*

Below: *This elaborate, stirrup-spouted jar, also from El Brujo, is decorated with the figure of a man sheltering beneath a roof. In the background is the skull of a sacrificed woman.*

mummy of the woman who had died in her late twenties. She was covered with cinnabar, which had helped preserve her body, and wrapped in layers of white cotton cloth. Tattoos covered her arms and legs, probably executed with a cactus spine or needle and charcoal: the tattooed designs included spiders and snakes. Like the elite individuals at Sipán, she was buried with a wealth of gold, silver and gilded copper jewellery, including elaborate headdresses, nose ornaments, ear ornaments and necklaces, while a gold bowl was placed over her face. Gold sewing needles and weaving equipment reflected female occuptions, but surprisingly, she was also furnished with weapons sheathed in gold: two warclubs and atlatls (spearthrowers). A teenage girl had been sacrificed to accompany her, strangled with a hemp rope. Although this burial is still something of a mystery, it is possible that the woman was the priestess depicted with the priest and the warrior priest in the Moche sacrifice scene.

SACRIFICES TO THE GODS

These Moche elite burials contain regalia, clothing and other objects familiar from a sacrificial scene frequently shown on Moche pottery and in the reliefs now being revealed on the best preserved *huacas*. They show warriors wearing tunics, backflaps and elaborate helmets, armed with darts, spears, clubs and small round shields, fighting in pairs or seizing enemies by their hair. Defeated enemies walk naked before their captors with ropes round their neck and their arms sometimes bound, while behind them other warriors bear their weapons and armour as trophies. Naked, bound prisoners are being sacrificed, their throats cut by a priest and their blood collected in a cup by a priestess, to be offered to an elaborately attired warrior priest, standing or seated on a canopied throne. Sacrificed victims are dismembered and strings attached to the heads and limbs to make trophies. As well as priests, sinister bird-headed figures and menacing priestesses take part in these ceremonies.

The numerous bones found at Moche's Huaca de la Luna suggest sacrifices on a larger scale. Environmental evidence indicates that some of the mass sacrifices took place when the region was suffering torrential rainfall from El Niño events. Steve Bourget,

one of the archaeologists investigating the Huaca de la Luna, points out that the iconography of Moche relief decorations and elite jewellery feature creatures appearing with the El Niño, such as the Peruvian eagle ray, or affected by the conditions it brought, such as local spiders and seabirds, and argues that this may show that the Moche rulers embraced El Niño events as a symbol of their own awe-inspiring power.

MAGNIFICENT MASKS

The successors to the Moche, the Sicán, who flourished in the Lambayeque region until conquered by the Chimu, also constructed mounds containing elite tombs. Though most have been plundered, two intact tombs were discovered in the Sicán Precinct at Batan Grande when the Huaca Loro was investigated in the 1990s. These were apparently the principal tombs in an elite cemetery laid out along the North Platform, a low tiered mound extending north from the Huaca Loro. Each tomb was a shaft, 11–12 metres (36–39 feet) deep, and in each the principal burial was furnished with gold, silver, tumbaga, textile and feather

TODAY'S UNFOUND TREASURES

PIRATE TREASURES OF COCOS ISLAND

Four hundred and eighty kilometres (300 miles) south-west of Costa Rica lies Cocos Island, a place inextricably linked with pirates. Captain Edward Davis, an English privateer, used the island as his base and may have buried treasure here before he vanished in 1702. The pirate Benito Bonito certainly did so in 1819: it was found in 1932. But the most intriguing cache has still to be rediscovered. In 1821 revolution threatened Lima. The treasures of the cathedral seemed particularly at risk, so they were taken to Callao, to be transported to Panama. Only one ship was available but its captain willingly accepted the commission. Once at sea he knocked the treasure's guards on the head and sailed for Cocos Island. Here he shared some of the treasure with the crew and hid the rest. Many desperate adventures followed but he was never able to return. On his deathbed he handed a map locating the treasure to his friend, John Keating. It seems Keating recovered part of the hoard, but much remained. However, Keating seems to have moved it, and although he in turn passed on a treasure map, no one has yet located the missing treasures, which are said to include a 2-metre (7-feet) jewelled gold statue of the Virgin Mary.

Above: *A modern sailing ship lies peacefully near Cocos Island, once haunted by pirates and perhaps still concealing their treasures.*

regalia including elaborate masks, crowns and headdresses, ear spools, arms or gloves and textiles attached to sheets of tumbaga, as well as weapons and other valuables and was accompanied by other bodies – but they were very different in form.

In the burial chamber at the base of the East Tomb shaft, the mummified body of the principal occupant, an old man, wearing a gold mask painted with cinnabar and decorated with gold pectorals, ear spools and a backflap, was arranged in a seated position and placed upside down, with his head detached and placed right-way up beside the body. On either side of him were a pair of gloves covered with gold foil and other objects, laid on the textiles covering the tomb's floor. Beside him were a pair of women, one seated before the open legs of the other who was lying on her back: the excavator, Izumi Shimada, suggests that the three were thus arranged to symbolize the lord's rebirth. Two children were placed higher in the tomb. Above and to the lord's side were arranged numerous grave goods, including heaps of shells and of tumbaga scraps, wrapped in mats backed by tumbaga sheets; bundles of copper rods; several sceptres or staffs; pots wrapped in tumbaga and a cane basket filled with objects of gold, silver and tumbaga, including splendid headdresses.

The principal occupant of the West Tomb, a middle-aged man who had suffered a serious wound to his pelvis, was probably quite closely related to the nobleman in the East Tomb, perhaps his nephew. Wearing his regalia he was seated in a central chamber in the floor of the large grave shaft, with a woman in a niche on either side. A large antechamber lay above the central chamber, with niches along the sides and pits in the floor: these held the bodies of 18 young women, nine in the south who belonged biologically to the same community as the man and nine in the north who were unrelated either to the first group or to each other, perhaps representatives of peoples subject to the Sicán. A cloth painted with a design of armed warriors carrying trophy heads was placed along the north side of the chamber, perhaps hinting that these women were captives. One of the niches held the body of a young teenage boy. The tomb also contained the heads and feet from at least 25 llamas: the meat from these animals may have been consumed by the mourners in a funerary feast. Despite the larger number of accompanying burials and the much greater dimensions of the grave shaft, the grave goods here were fewer and less splendid than in the East Tomb. The women may not have been sacrificed: small missing bones and other clues suggest that some at least

had died earlier and had been reburied here, either with the nobleman when he died or later.

The most magnificent objects in both tombs were the sets of gold headgear. These were composed of a number of elements, perhaps worn interchangeably depending on circumstances: a mask depicting the Sicán Deity, a pair of ear ornaments, a crown mounted on a cloth cap for comfort, a huge inverted U-shaped headdress and a forehead ornament with matching decoration. Of the several sets within the East Tomb, the most impressive had a forehead ornament decorated with rings and a central three-dimensional head of a vampire bat, complete with fangs and a moveable tongue. The accompanying headdress was ringed with feathers made of gold. The mask had eyes of emerald and amber, a nose ornament and four nose

---

Below left: *A brightly painted funerary mask, the distinctive product of Sicán metalworkers. Discoveries at Batán Grande show that such masks formed part of elaborate headdresses.*

Below right: *Crafted from beaten metal, this typical Sicán mask has comma-shaped eyes, wears earspools and a nose ornament, and is decorated with small metal plaques attached with wire.*

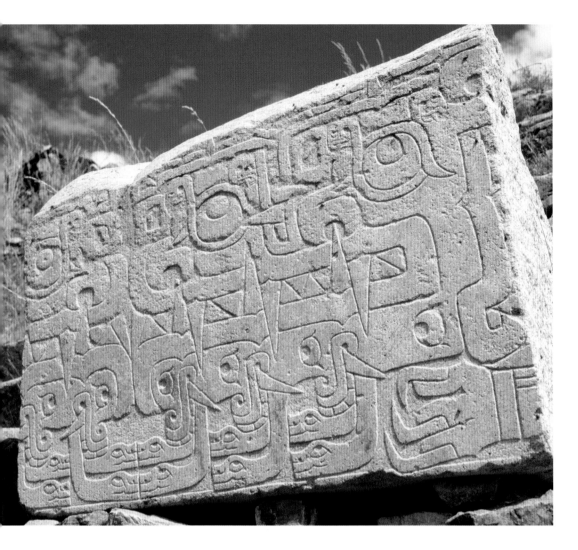

pendants. Goldwork such as this was reserved for the chief men in Sicán society: lesser members of the elite had ornaments in gilded copper or tumbaga, while commoners had only simple copper ornaments.

SUPREME LORD OF THE CHAVÍN

The pyramids of the Moche and Sicán were part of a long, developing tradition. As early as the third millennium BC, the people of the Andean coast were building U-shaped ritual centres with stepped pyramids stretching skyward, perhaps as artificial mountains, and sunken plazas that were probably the place where people congregated to take part in religious ceremonies and festivals. Gruesome carvings at Cerro Sechín suggest that some of these ceremonies involved human sacrifice, foreshadowing the practices that were a regular part of religious activity in Moche times.

In the early first millennium one such complex was founded in a high mountain valley at Chavín de Huántar and developed into a great religious centre and place of pilgrimage: here stepped platforms enclosed plazas with sunken courtyards in their centres. A series of carved heads protruded from the exterior walls of the complex, gradually progressing from benevolent human to grim monster. Within the platforms were temples, entered through a stone doorway. Inside was a maze of corridors leading past rooms filled with offerings, twisting and turning to confuse and awe those who entered, an effect heightened by the strange and frightening noises deliberately produced by a system of underground water channels. At the heart of the maze was a small chamber containing a great stone, the Lanzón, carved in the form of a deity with a half-snarling, half-smiling face and massive fangs. The worshipper probably also inhaled some type of hallucinogen, which further heightened the supernatural quality of the experience. An extraordinary gold spoon, probably for inhaling hallucinogenic snuff, was found in the complex. The handle is in the form of a three-dimensional figure squatting on a decorated post blowing a conch shell trumpet. It was built up from 22 separate gold and silver pieces and is a work of remarkable craftsmanship.

The deity of the Lanzón appears again and again in Chavín art and iconography, usually brandishing a staff in each hand and wearing a headdress in the form of an inverted monster head. There are several representations of this Staff god in stone in the Chavín de Huántar complex. He reappears on plaques of thin hammered gold, probably originally attached to clothing. Two of these

plaques were found in one of the rich Chavín-period tombs at Chongoyape in the Lambayeque valley. One woman buried here wore a gold headband, pins of gold and silver, gold rings, necklaces of gold beads and gold throat ornaments, and was accompanied by vessels containing food, a mirror of polished anthracite and a stone spoon probably for inhaling halluginogenic snuff; two other individuals were buried with her. Nearby was the rich burial of a man, his grave goods including gold tweezers for plucking his facial hair. He also had several gold crowns and beautiful gold earspools with sinuous decoration.

A number of other well-furnished tombs were found within a platform of a temple high in the Jequetepeque valley at Kuntur Wasi. In one was buried an elderly man with a gold crown decorated with cut-out hexagons within which were suspended small human faces, as well as other precious objects including three trumpets made of *Strombus* shells imported from Ecuador. Carvings at Chavín de Huántar show such trumpets being blown, presumably during religious ceremonies. In another of the burials, that of a woman, were around 7,000 beads of shell and stone that had probably been sewn to a robe she was wearing.

Opposite top: *This frieze of jaguars at Chavín de Huántar is typical of Chavín art. Highly stylized, the figures seem to be both in profile and full-frontal, and have snakes as feet and fanged jaws as kneecaps.*

Opposite below: *These grim faces originally decorated the exterior wall of the sacred complex at Chavín de Huántar. They may depict priests in a drug-induced trance; others show priests transforming into animals.*

Right top: *This fine Chavín gold figurine of a cat, from Pampa Grande in the Lambayeque valley, is unusually naturalistic.*

Right below: *This unusual late Chavín gold object from Peru's north coast may be a funerary mask. Its apparent overall simplicity contrasts with the extremely elaborate decoration around the edges.*

INDEX

Figures in italics refer to captions

BIBLIOGRAPHY

Allen, G. and D. *Clive's Lost Treasure*, Robin Garton, 1978

Allen, J. *Glittering Prospects*, Hamish Hamilton, 1975

Alva, W. "Discovering the World's Richest Unlooted Tomb" *National Geographic*, October 1988

Alva, W. "New Royal Tomb Unearthed" *National Geographic*, June 1990

Andronicos, M. "Regal Treasures from a Macedonian Tomb" *National Geographic*, July 1978

Andronikos, M. *The Royal Graves at Vergina*, Athens, 1980

Anon "Mystery Statue Surfaces on a Bronze Age Wreck" *National Geographic*, May 1993

Antonova, I., Tolstikov V. and Treister, M. *The Gold of Troy*, Thames and Hudson, 1996

Artamonov, M. *Treasures from Scythian Tombs*, Thames and Hudson, 1969

Bacon, E. (ed) *The Great Archaeologists*, Martin Secker and Warburg, 1976

Bahn, P. (ed) *The Story of Archaeology*, Weidenfeld and Nicolson, 1996

Bahn, P. (ed) *Wonderful Things*, Weidenfeld and Nicolson, 1999

Baines, J. and Málek, J. *Atlas of Ancient Egypt*, Andromeda, 1996

Ballard, R. and Michel, J.L. "How We Found Titanic" *National Geographic*, December 1985

Ballard, R. and Tarpy, C. "A Long Last Look at Titanic" *National Geographic*, December 1986

Ballard, R. "Epilogue for Titanic" *National Geographic*, October 1987

Barnes, G.L. *The Rise of Civilization in East Asia*, Thames and Hudson, 1999 (1993)

Bass, G.F. "Oldest Known Shipwreck Reveals Splendours of the Bronze Age", *National Geographic*, December 1987

Bass, G.F. "From Bronze Age Wreck, More of Everything" *National Geographic*, May 1992

Bedoyere, Guy de la. T*he Golden Age of Roman Britain*, Batsford, 1999

Beresford Ellis, P. *The Ancient World of the Celts*, Constable, 1998

Bland, R. and Johns, C. *The Hoxne Treasure*, British Museum, 1993

Blunden, C. and Elvin, M. *Cultural Atlas of China*, Phaidon, 1983

Branigan, K. *The Atlas of Archaeology*, Macdonald, 1982

Bray, W., E.H. Swanson and I.S. Farrington *The Ancient Americas*, Phaidon, 1989

Brothwell, D. *The Bogman and the Archaeology of People*, British Museum, 1986

Bruhns, K.O. *Ancient South America*, CUP, 1994

Carter, H. *The Tomb of Tutankhamen*, Sphere, 1972

Carver, M. *Sutton Hoo: Burial Ground of Kings?*, British Museum, 1998

Caso, A. "Monte Alban, Richest Archeological Find in America" *National Geographic*, October 1932

Ceram, C.W. *Gods, Graves and Scholars*, Alfred A. Knopf, 1967

Champion, T., Gamble, C. Shennan, S. and Whittle, A. *Prehistoric Europe*, Academic Press, 1984

Coe, M. *Mexico*, Thames and Hudson, 1994

Coe, M., Snow, D. and Benson, E. *Atlas of Ancient America*, Facts on File, 1986

Collis, J. *The European Iron Age*, Batsford, 1984

Cunliffe, B. (ed) T*he Oxford Illustrated Prehistory of Europe*, OUP, 1994

Cunliffe, B. *Iron Age Britain*, Batsford, 1995

Cunliffe, B. *The Ancient Celts*, OUP, 1997

Dahl, Roald *The Mildenhall Treasure*, Jonathan Cape, 1999

Daniel, G. *A Short History of Archaeology*, Thames and Hudson, 1981

Darville, T. *Prehistoric Britain*, Batsford, 1987

Davalos Hurtado, E. "Return to the Sacred Cenote" *National Geographic*, October 1961

Davidson, B. *The Story of Africa*, Mitchell Beazley, 1984

Delgado, J. (ed) *British Museum Encyclopedia of Underwater and Maritime Archaeology*, British Museum Press, 1997

Desroches-Noblecourt, C. *Tutankhamen*, Penguin, 1965

Deuel, L. *Testaments of Time*, Secker and Warburg, 1966

Dixon, P. *Barbarian Europe*, Phaidon, 1976

Donnan, C.B. "Iconography of the Moche: Unravelling the Mystery of the Warrior-Priest" *National Geographic*, October 1988

Donnan, C.B. "Masterworks Reveal a Pre-Inca World" *National Geographic*, June 1990

Evans, A.C. *Sutton Hoo Ship Burial*, British Museum, 1986

Feather, R. *The Copper Scroll Decoded*, Thorsons, 1999

Fenwick, V. and Gale, A. *Historic Shipwrecks*, Tempus, 1998

Forte, M. and Siliotti, A. (eds) *Virtual Archaeology*, Thames and Hudson, 1997

Foster, S. *Picts, Gaels and Scots*, Batsford, 1996

Franzen, A. "Kronan: Remnants of a Warship's Past" *National Geographic*, April 1989

Furneaux, R. *On Buried and Sunken Treasure*, Puffin, 1973

Godard, P. *The First and Last Voyage of the Batavia*, Abrolhos Publishing, 1993

Graham-Campbell, J. (ed) *Cultural Atlas of the Viking World*, Facts on File, 1994

Groushko, M. *Treasure*, Apple Press, 1990

Gryaznov, M. *Southern Siberia*, Nagel, 1969

Hall, Alice J. "A Lady from China's Past" *National Geographic*, May 1974

Harding, D. *Prehistoric Europe*, Elsevier Phaidon, 1978

Harris, N. *Hamlyn History of Imperial China*, Hamlyn, 1999

Harris, R. *The World of the Bible*, Thames and Hudson, 1995

Hemming, J. *Philip's Atlas of Exploration*, Philip's, 1996

Hemming, J. *The Search for Eldorado*, Michael Joseph, 1978

Hills, C.A.R. *The Destruction of Pompeii and Herculaneum*, Dryad Press, 1987

Hunter, J and Ralston, I. (ed) *The Archaeology of Britain*, Routledge, 1999

Huntington, S. *The Art of Ancient India*, Weatherhill, 1985

James, S. *Exploring the World of the Celts*, Thames and Hudson, 1993

James, P. and Thorpe, N. *Ancient Inventions*, Michael O'Mara Books, 1995

Jettmar, K. *Art of the Steppes*, Methuen, 1964

Johnson, S. *Hadrian's Wall*, Batsford, 1989

Kenoyer, J.M. *Ancient Cities of the Indus Valley Civilization*, OUP, 1998

Lerici, C. "Periscope on the Etruscan Past" *National Geographic*, September 1959

Littlehales, B. "Treasure Hunt in the Deep Past" *National Geographic*, October 1961

Lyon, E. "Atocha, Tragic Galleon of the Florida Keys" *National Geographic*, June 1976

Lyon. E. "Treasure from the Ghost Galleon: Santa Margarita" *National Geographic*, February 1982

Lynch, D. *Titanic. An Illustrated History*, Hodder and Stoughton, 1992

Maiuri, A. "Last Moments of the Pompeians" *National Geographic*, November 1961

Martin, C. *Scotland's Historic Shipwrecks*, Batsford, 1998

McCormick, F. "China's Treasures" *National Geographic*, October 1912

MacInnis, J.B. "Titanic: Tragedy in Three Dimensions" *National Geographic*, August 1998

McQueen, E.I. *Diodorus Siculus: The Reign of Philip II*, translated, Duckworth, 1995

Madden, R. "China Unveils her Newest Treasures" *National Geographic*, December 1974

Mazzatenta, O.L. "A Chinese Emperor's Army for an Eternity" *National Geographic*, August 1992

Mazzatenta, O.L. "China's Warriors rise from the Earth" *National Geographic*, October 1996

Millett, M. *Roman Britain*, Batsford, 1995

Moorehead, C. *The Lost Treasures of Troy*, Weidenfeld and Nicolson, 1994

Montet, P. *Lives of the Pharaohs*, Weidenfeld and Nicolson, 1968

Moseley, M. *The Incas and their Ancestors*, Thames and Hudson, 1992

Nelson, S.M. *The Archaeology of Korea*, CUP, 1993

Norvill, R. *The Treasure Seeker's Treasury*, Hutchinson, 1978

O'Brien, P. *Philip's Atlas of World History*, Philip's, 1999

O'Kelly, M.J. *Early Ireland*, CUP, 1989

Parker Pearson, M. *Bronze Age Britain*, Batsford, 1993

Parker Pearson, M. *The Archaeology of Death and Burial*, Sutton, 1999

Peterson, M. "Graveyard of the Quicksilver Galleons" *National Geographic*, December 1979

Petrie, A. *An Introduction to Greek History, Antiquities and Literature*, 2nd edition, OUP, 1962

Phillips, E. *The Royal Hordes*, Thames and Hudson, 1965

Phillipson, D. *African Archaeology*, 2nd edition, CUP, 1993

Platt, C. and Wright, J. *Treasure Islands*, Michael O'Mara, 1992

Pickford, N. *The Atlas of Shipwrecks and Treasure*, Dorling Kindersley, 1994

Piggott, S. *Early Celtic Art*, The Arts Council, 1970

Postgate, N. *Early Mesopotamia*, Routledge, 1992

Potter, T. *Roman Britain*, British Museum, 1983

Prag, J. and Neave, R. *Making Faces*, British Museum, 1997

Pritchard, J. (ed) *The Times Atlas of the Bible*, Times Books, 1989

Quirke, S. and Spencer, J. *The British Museum Book of Ancient Egypt*, British Museum, 1992

Rawson, J. (ed) *Mysteries of Ancient China*, British Museum, 1996

Rawson, P. *Indian Asia*, Phaidon, 1977

Reinhard, J. "Sacred Peaks of the Andes" *National Geographic*, March 1992

Reinhard, J. "Peru's Icemaiden: Unwrapping the Secrets" *National Geographic*, June 1996

Reinhard, J. "Sharp Eyes of Science Probe the Mummies of Peru" *National Geographic*, January 1997

Reinhard, J. "Research Update: New Inca Mummies" *National Geographic*, July 1998

Renfrew, C. "Ancient Bulgaria's Golden Treasures" *National Geographic*, July 1980

Renfrew, C. and Bahn, P. *Archaeology*, Thames and Hudson, 1996

Richards, J. *Stonehenge*, Batsford, 1991

Roaf, M. *Cultural Atlas of Mesopotamia*, Facts on File, 1990

Robertshaw, P. A. *History of African Archaeology*, Heinemann, 1990

Rolle, R. *World of the Scythians*, Batsford, 1989

Roux, G. *Ancient Iraq*, 2nd edition, Penguin, 1980

Rudenko, S. *Frozen Tombs of Siberia*, Dent, 1970

Sacks, D. *Encyclopedia of the Ancient Greek World*, Constable, 1995

Sayer, I. and Botting, D. *Nazi Gold*, Granada, 1984

Scarre, C. *Past Worlds. The Times Atlas of Archaeology*, Times Books, 1988

Scarre, C. *Exploring Prehistoric Europe*, OUP, 1998

Shaw, I. and Nicholson, P. *British Museum Dictionary of Ancient Egypt*, British Museum, 1995

Smith, M. *The Aztecs*, Blackwell, 1996

Stein, M.A. *On Ancient Central Asian Tracks*, University of Chicago Press, 1964

Stenuit, R. "Priceless Relics of the Spanish Armada" *National Geographic*, June 1969

Stenuit, R. "The Sunken Treasure of St. Helena" *National Geographic*, October 1978

Topping, A. "China's Incredible Find" *National Geographic*, April 1978

Villiers, A. "Sir Francis Drake" *National Geographic*, February 1975

Wagner, K. "Drowned Galleons Yield Spanish Gold" *National Geographic*, January 1965

Townsend, R. *The Aztecs*, Thames and Hudson, 1992

Wagner, K. and Taylor, L.B. *Pieces of Eight*, Longmans, 1966

Watson, W. *The Genius of China*, Times Newspapers, 1973

Whittle, A. *Europe in the Neolithic*, CUP, 1996

Williams, M.O. "At the Tomb of Tutankhamen" *National Geographic*, May 1923

Wilson, D. *The World Atlas of Treasure*, Collins, 1981

Wilson, I. *Undiscovered*, Chancellor Press, 1987

Woolley, L. "Archeology, the Mirror of the Ages" *National Geographic*, August 1928

Woolley, L. "New Light on Ancient Ur" *National Geographic*, January 1930

Woolley, L. *Ur 'of the Chaldees'*, revised edition by Moorey, P.R.S., Herbert Press, 1982

Wright, J. *Encyclopedia of Sunken Treasure*, Michael O'Mara, 1995

PICTURE CREDITS